THE NEW GUIDE TO

ILLUSTRATION

···················· AND ····················

DESIGN

THE NEW GUIDE TO

ILLUSTRATION

············· AND ·············

DESIGN

CONSULTANT EDITOR
SIMON JENNINGS

HEADLINE

THE CONTRIBUTORS

Elizabeth Burney-Jones worked with Kenneth Grange before joining Pentagram, where she was appointed corporate identity co-ordinator and later assisted in developing sign projects for the company's New York office. She is now programmes manager with Wood & Wood International Signs.

Colin Cheesman attended art college and then worked as a graphic designer for television. In 1974 he was appointed Head of Graphic Design at BBC Television. He is now an independent consultant/producer of computer graphics and animation for television, commercials and corporate productions.

Bob Cotton is an artist who runs a computer graphics workshop and lectures in the subject at the School of Communication Arts and the Polytechnic of Central London. He is a director of Synergy: Applied Interaction, which develops programmes for interaction laser and compact disc.

Clive Crook was art editor of *The Sunday Times Magazine* and art director of *The Observer Magazine* before joining the staff of *Elle* as art director. He is also a visiting lecturer at the Royal College of Art and other art schools.

Peter Cull trained as a commercial artist and served in the Royal Army Medical Corps in World War II. After various appointments in medical illustration, he joined St Bartholomew's Hospital, London, to direct their Educational and Medical Illustration Service. He has also chaired the Medical Artists' Association and the Institute of Medical and Biological Illustration.

Nick Dawe worked in advertising, then acted as an illustrator's agent before setting up his own agency, Folio, which represents artists in advertising and editorial media.

Leo de Freitas studied illustrative processes of the eighteenth and nineteenth centuries, after which he took diverse jobs — among them farm worker, apprentice garage mechanic and librarian — before becoming a freelance illustrator. He has written a number of books and many articles.

Naomi Gornick is a consultant in design management and lectures on the subject in colleges of art and design in Britain and the United States. She trained as a designer and worked at the Royal Shakespeare Theatre, Stratford, and the Design Council, London. She is founder-chairman of the Chartered Society of Designers' Design Management Group and is responsible for seminars, conferences and publications funded by the Department of Trade and Industry to promote greater understanding between design and industry.

George Hardie trained as a graphic designer and then worked in conjunction with the company, Hignosis, designing record covers. He now works freelance solving graphic problems with illustration.

F. H. K. Henrion OBE studied design in Paris in the 1930s. During World War II he worked for the British Ministry of Information and the American Office of War Information. He then became art director of the Isotype Institute and was awarded the MBE. From 1959-84 he was consulting designer on corporate identity for KLM Royal Dutch Airlines and he also worked for the British Post Office on corporate identity and product design. Author of several books, he is consultant to colleges and institutions, lectures widely and is visiting professor to a number of universities.

A QUARTO BOOK

Copyright © 1987 Quarto Publishing plc

First published in Great Britain in 1987 by Headline Book Publishing plc Headline House 79 Great Titchfield Street London WIP 7FN

First published in paperback in 1991

British Library Cataloguing in Publication Data

Simon Jennings, ed.
The new guide to professional illustration and design.
I. Commercial art
I. Title
741.6   NC997

ISBN 0-7472-7948-9

Simon Jennings studied graphic design communications at the Royal College of Art, London and then gained practical experience with leading design companies in London, New York and Chicago, before establishing his own business which now specializes in book design and packaging. He has also lectured extensively on graphic design and, in particular, book design.

Mary Lewis studied graphic design. She began her career as a printmaker and art school lecturer, then freelanced for advertising agencies before becoming creative director of a London-based packaging design company. She formed Lewis Moberly in January 1984 with her partner Robert Moberly, then a director of an advertising agency. She is a lecturer and external tutor at the School of Communication Arts. She has sat on many design juries and her own work has received several awards internationally.

Howard Milton studied art and design and worked with Michael Peters for five years before joining the New York agency, Burston Marstellar. In 1980 he returned to Britain to form Smith & Milton with Jay Smith. The consultancy are specialists in packaging, corporate identity and financial commun-ications. Milton is a member of the D & AD Executive Committee and has won several medals for packaging design.

John Norris Wood studied illustration and works as a freelance artist, writer and photographer specializing in natural history. He founded and runs the Natural History Illustration Department at the Royal College of Art, London. A conservationist, he has led expeditions to America and Africa. He has contributed to television programmes and to many books including the *Hide and Seek* series.

Tilly Northedge trained first as a graphic designer and later specialized in the analysis of information design problems. In 1980 she established Grundy Northedge, with Peter Grundy, a company which produces creative diagrams as well as work in other areas of graphic design.

Wally Olins was born in London and spent his early business years in advertising in India. He was one of the founders of Wolff Olins, the identity, design and communications company, of which he is chairman. He is the author of *The Corporate Personality*, and he frequently speaks on design, communication identity and allied subjects.

Colin Rattray worked as a trainee technical illustrator at the De Haviland Engine Company and as an editor of modelling magazines before becoming a freelance illustrator and senior lecturer at Middlesex Polytechnic.

Nick Souter studied graphic design and photography and started work as a photographer's assistant. He joined J. Walter Thompson as a junior art director and later moved to Leo Burnett Advertising, where he is a senior copywriter.

Howard Tangye studied fashion design in Britain and the United States and then worked for a number of New York stores. After running his own fashion business, he joined Zandra Rhodes as assistant designer and illustrator. He also teaches part-time.

Nicholas Verebelyi trained as a product designer before joining Packaging Innovation Group Ltd, a company whose clients include brand and packaging manufacturers and retailers.

Andrew Wakelin trained in typographic design and formed his own design practice in 1969. He has been senior partner at Thumb Design Partnership, London, since it was established in 1974.

This book was designed and produced by
Quarto Publishing plc
The Old Brewery
6 Blundell Street
London N7 9BH

Senior Editors Hazel Harrison, Judy Martin
Art Editor Hazel Edington

Editors Eleanor Van Zandt, Susan Ward

Project Coordinator Anne-Marie Ehrlich

Designers Philip Chidlow, Ralph Pitchford

Picture Researchers Lucy Bullivant, Annabel Assel

Art Director Moira Clinch
Executive Art Director Alastair Campbell
Editorial Director Carolyn King

Typeset by Comproom Ltd, London and
QV Typesetting, London
Manufactured in Hong Kong by Regent Publishing
Services Ltd
Printed by Leefung-Asco Printers Ltd, Hong Kong

CONTENTS

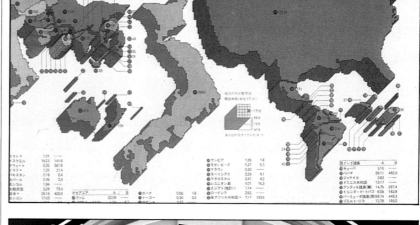

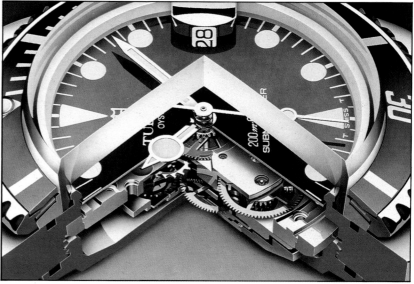

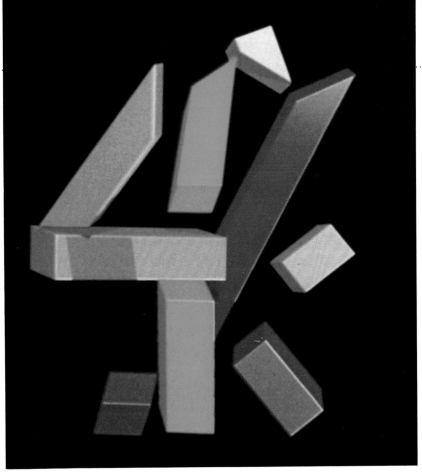

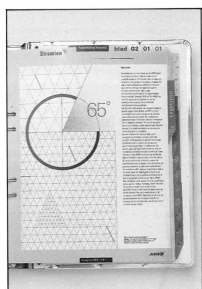

FOREWORD

The key word in the title of this unique new work of reference is 'professional'. The team of authors who have contributed to the book are all active in the world of visual communications as practising illustrators, graphic designers or administrators — in some cases all three. Their combined skills, wisdom and experience have been assembled here in a book which has been conceived as a practical guide, with a strong emphasis on information, to provide the student, professional and lay reader alike with an insight into current professional practices in the twin fields of design and illustration.

In addition to describing techniques, materials and methods, the book attempts to give a reasonable idea of what it is like to be a practising illustrator or designer. Contributors have viewed their work against an historical background or placed their particular branch of activity in context to explain its function in society and its role within the professional and business environment. Thus job activities, client relations, fees, deadlines and types of briefing are all discussed, together with essential skill requirements, and the discussions are backed up with case histories describing the specific problems confronting the designer and illustrator.

The book is divided into two main parts — illustration and design — and deals with 18 separate areas of visual communication. There are those who feel that 'pure illustration' and 'commercial graphic design' should not be mentioned in the same breath. They are sometimes seen as opposite poles, with the archetypal impoverished artist working alone on a line illustration for a tiny fee at one end and the fashionable 'trendy' smoothly articulating through a multi-screen corporate presentation at the other. Yet collectively graphic design and illustration is a broad field of activity with room for a variety of skills, personalities and attitudes, and the book discusses these various branches of the profession and examines the choices and opportunities they offer. The common ground which links all the varied disciplines, is the work itself which is always client-orientated rather than being done for its own sake, and is essentially autographic in nature, based on the disciplines of drawing, observation and visual articulation before ending up as ink on paper or as a mass-produced object.

There has always been a strong inter-relation between graphic design and illustration, since these skills are common to both, and this is even more apparent today, with the revived enthusiasm for free-drawn imagery and calligraphy. During the past 20 years the design business has blossomed — indeed, it has become a growth industry. Previously, graphic design and illustration were lumped together under the generic term 'commercial art', but the economic climate and the educational system have helped to elevate both activities to the status of high-profile professions.

However, the quest for profit should never blind the artist to the need for creativity, imagination, good craft skills and an ability to draw and observe — the fundamentals of design. Nor should design be allowed to become overly expensive or elitist — good design is for everybody, and quality should be present for its own sake whether it's a small job for a small fee or a million-pound contract. This, I feel, is the benchmark of true professionalism.

Simon Jennings

I
ILLUSTRATION

Introduction by
George Hardie

INTRODUCTION TO ILLUSTRATION

Part of art is the making of pictures and part of the making of pictures is illustration. Definitions and boundaries are vague, moveable and important to the illustrator.

Imagine the tuning scale on my imaginary 'Visuola' radio. One end is labelled (rather less than snappily) 'Complete communication of other people's information': the other end 'Complete secrecy about the artist's own information'. A range that stretches from the road sign to the artist's private sketchbook.

Tuning scales on radios are marked with wavelengths for the various stations: on the 'Visuola' dial positions have to be found for graphic design, commercial art, drawing, painting, illustration, fine art, etc. Eventually a personal position has to be marked, however temporarily, for each individual working in illustration.

The scale could perhaps be more crudely labelled 'Client-motivated' through to 'Self-motivated'. As with the tuning on real radios, the whole system is crude. Trying to define illustration is like trying to find your favourite station, through interference and overlap, late at night, and then having it gradually become untuned in the early hours. (Working as the sun comes up seems almost symbolic of illustration. Can this really be purely self-motivated?)

Part of a definition could try to separate illustration from the other stops on the tuning dial. The most useful definition (although it doesn't cover everything and it obviously includes work that is not illustration) is that illustration is the production of images which are then multiplied, up to now usually by printing. The nature of this process involves economics. The multiplying of the illustrator's image costs money and the person who supplies the money (hereinafter, and again crudely defined, 'the client') has ideas about the function of that image. This simple definition begins to separate illustration from painting or drawing; it also outlines the basic compromise the illustrator makes. In exchange for thinking about the client's problems and tackling the given subject matter, the illustrator gets paid, and has work disseminated to huge audiences (5.5 million people see each issue of *Time* magazine; some albums have sold over 10 million copies; the British Post Office prints 40 million stamps at Christmas). How much compromise can the illustrator make without wandering down the scale towards commercial art? How little compromise can she or he make and still be within the illustration wavelengths?

The next approach to a definition is to describe the functions of illustration.

THE FUNCTIONS

Illustration has three main functions. These can be loosely described as decorating, informing and commenting. All illustrations probably do a bit of each. People who use illustration to comment or inform might regard decoration as a dirty word, but any care in arrangement, composition and the choosing of colours will have decorative effects. A safety pin through the nose is an opinion and a comment, but it is also a jewel.

As these functions don't exist in isolation, it's difficult to pinpoint them.

Decoration is used to alleviate typography, act as a frame or rule, or break up an area. Of course, all illustration can do this, but decorative illustration only does this, without having any greater meaning or use. Pattern is a good example. Early Soviet textiles are a good example of how easily the categorization breaks down: taking traditional floral and geometric patterns and adding tanks and tractors, because of a recent revolution, changes decoration into political comment.

Information covers the area of explaining visually. It is at its most straightforward in maps and diagrams (how to wire a plug, how a blast furnace works, what proportion of the cost of a bottle of wine goes to the tax collector). Illustration of any kind can be informative when the illustrator makes accurate research into the subject in hand. This research often goes well beyond any text supplied or brief given, and thus adds information to the initial subject: for example, accurate period details illustrating a book in which the author's theme is confined to the personal relationships of the characters; this begins to take information over into the category of comment.

Comment or opinion are inadequate words to describe what is perhaps the most complex and interesting area of illustration: the area where illustrators start to express their own feelings. Because of the compromise already described, these feelings will be tempered with 'appropriateness'. Take portraits of Ronald Reagan as an example: 'decorative' is hard to imagine, but must be possible; 'informative' might show how his face has changed over the years, or where he was wounded in the assassination attempt. Comment could be made. The Ronald Reagan Marketing Board require an illustrator to admire him, or at least pretend to. Some Nicaraguans would require an illustrator to find fault with him. *The Economist* magazine would want an illustrator to explain Reagan's attitude to economics for their portrait.

Good clients understand this problem of appropriateness and choose illustrators carefully. When clients make a wrong choice the illustrator can either compromise or reject the commission. This doesn't only arise with political jobs. Comment can be concerned with the illustrator's feelings about how two colours work together, how two images echo each other; it's not just about 'ideas'. The best comment is based on discovering a truth and then passing it on.

APPROACH

Perhaps we should now think about changing the waveband on the 'Visuola'. Unlike a real radio this doesn't go click, click, click, but is an infinitely adjustable knob marked simply with Head, Hand, Heart and Eye.

The moment an idea, notion, dream or whatever is put down on paper in visual form it becomes a picture. All illustrations are pictures and how these pictures arrive is governed by head, hand, heart and eye. Pictures end up as visual expression, so the eye plays a large part: observation is a key word and much picture-making is observational. The head can combine with the eye to observe, and a truth noticed can be worth a lot of nature copied. The head can act alone to pluck notions out of the ether and sort out the logic of problems. The heart, given our modern understanding of anatomy, is now replaced by the head, but it is a good label for the less logical feelings and notions, which are as important for illustration as hard ideas. The hand governs the skills and techniques of illustration which in turn reach and affect the other parts.

If these anatomical gradations represent talents or abilities, these in turn cause illustrators to be employed in various ways. Some are used mainly for thinking: cartoonists can make extraordinarily apposite comments using simple drawing that owes little to visual observation. Other illustrators are used for their ability to observe: this includes a huge range from technical and natural history experts, through landscape and fashion artists, to reportage and war artists. Illustrators are used for their talent to decorate: for their logical and organized minds; some are sought for their opinions. They are also used for their skills: wood engraving, airbrushing, etc. Again these divisions never really separate; even an illustrator employed to retouch photographs of refrigerators has to observe, and have ideas about, light.

THE CAREER

Imagine opening a newspaper at the careers page. There is an advertisement for an illustrator. It begins 'The position of . . .' We hit our first snag. There are no positions for illustrators. There are no jobs except for some salaried work in technical areas of illustration; on newspapers, particularly as cartoonists; and for a few illustrators in government service. Most illustrators choose illustration (as most people choose their careers) either because it is what they do best or because it is the only thing they can do. A few choose it at art school because they think it an easy option (no sharply defined thinking needed as in graphic design). It becomes a very hard option when they leave art school because, unlike in graphic design, there are no salaries. Illustrators stand or fall on their portfolios and the ways they tackle the commissions they are given. Because all illustration is drawing-based, some courses in art schools concentrate entirely on illustration for three years. This is an admirable education but it's very 'all or nothing' in that, again unlike graphic design, there are no lowly skills to sell while the illustrator is starting out on his or her career. Basically all illustrators are self-employed and live on their ability and wits.

Returning to the advertisement, the next word is '. . . wanted . . .' At present there seems to be plenty of work for all sorts of illustrators. This is closely connected with economics and fashion (there could be a swing back to photography). To look at the negative aspect, a well-prepared illustrator should be able to cope with enforced 'leisure'.

'Men and women can apply. . .' It would of course be unnecessary to state this in a modern advertisement, but the career of illustration has genuinely equal opportunities for both sexes. In fact more women are trained as illustrators but this evens out in the profession.

'Career structure. . .' There are no ranks in illustration, as there are hierarchies in graphic design. People with experience and ability can command higher fees and, perhaps more important, choose better work.

'Remuneration.' There is an adequate living to be made in illustration. It's difficult to make huge fortunes as there is little opportunity for entrepreneurial activity. Most illustrators are commissioned to make their own images with their own hands, and this imposes limitations. 'Pension plans. . .' There are no pensions. In fact, finance for the self-employed is a bit of a quagmire and advice should be sought early.

'Hours...' are long and hard: enough said.

'Working conditions...' are up to the individual but tend to be lonely and a great contrast to the gregariousness of art school. It is possible to organize conditions so as to continue to work with other people.

'Academic qualifications...' Education is vital, particularly a knowledge of the history of art and illustration. (The names and work of artists are part of a language which is spoken by illustrators.) Academic qualifications are of no importance. It is unlikely that a client will ask what college an illustrator went to, let alone what qualifications she or he achieved. Hopes and reputations again rest entirely on the portfolio.

AREAS OF EMPLOYMENT

The areas in which an illustrator can work are similar to, and as numerous as, the badges a scout can collect: map-maker, technical illustrator, book illustrator, satirist, puppet-maker, cartoonist, portraitist, natural history artist, wood engraver, line cutter, airbrush artist, fashion artist, reportage expert, war artist. These have already been discussed or implied. Each style or skill can have its scout badge, as can each area of employment: editorial, technical, scientific, medical, architectural, publishing, design, advertising, packaging, animation, fashion, and so on.

Comics are drawn by illustrators: illustrators make models, design lettering, invent patterns, design carpets, decorate ceramics. Illustrators can exhibit their work in galleries. They can write and illustrate books for adults or children. They can publish their own books. They can pass on their experience as teachers, or they can write introductions to books on design and illustration.

FASHION AND STYLE

Illustration and graphic design are fashion businesses. Graphic designers can look smug when this is stated, but an expert can date and place the driest piece of typography. The most information-based graphics will eventually look 'old fashioned' – just like frocks. As with all fashion, there are leaders and followers. The individual illustrator needn't be concerned with fashion, but will be affected by it. Because of fashion, clients are always looking for something new. The most difficult clients are looking both for something new and

the safety of it being like something they've already seen; this can obstruct your progress at the beginning of a career. An illustrator will be employed for a fresh approach, and the client will then be shocked if the image produced is even fresher. This could be partly due to a style trap. If the images made are largely decorative, or mainly a celebration of a particular technique, and therefore involve only surface as opposed to the depth achieved by observation, research and thought, the illustrator runs the risk of being employed 'by the yard'. They will be employed to carry out other people's wildest dreams. All of this is less of a problem if the illustrator is selling not only a style but also real observation of every kind, and thinking as well as drawing.

New illustrators can be discovered, overwhelmed with totally unsuitable work and become 'successful' very quickly. They can then be passed over in favour of some newer flavour. The good illustrator's real career begins at this point. She or he will start to be employed for particular qualities and expertise, and begin to be given suitable work by better clients. The relationship with the client is vital if the illustrator wants to continue to develop: the client pushing the illustrator to stretch into new areas, the illustrator surprising the client with dreams that the client hasn't already dreamed.

TO FINISH
Pieces to introduce books about illustration often begin with an allusion to cave painting, for the graphic artist possibly a somewhat tenuous art historical connection. The parallels seem much better when we talk of the bravery of the caveman and the illustrator: the lonely illustrator working in a cave while the tribe is out hunting; the clients wanting bigger and bigger drawings of the woolly mammoths they have slaughtered.

It's a good time to be an illustrator. There are lots of cave walls to paint and enough bison to go around.

Illustration has three main functions: decoration, information and comment.

1/EDITORIAL ILLUSTRATION

The history of serious illustration of magazines and newspapers does not go back beyond the nineteenth century. Unlike printed book illustration, which can be found within a few years of the invention of printing from moveable types in the fifteenth century, the illustration of periodical publications had to await the coming of a mass reading public and publishers of nationally distributed illustrated newspapers and magazines catering for this new public.

Magazine illustration, however, enjoyed early success in western Europe and North America. In the mid-nineteenth century, illustrated magazines became household names and *Once a Week, The Cornhill Magazine,* and *Good Words* carried much of the best of British illustration, while in America *Scribner's Monthly* and *Harper's Weekly* did likewise.

Towards the end of the century, following the introduction of photomechanical methods of reproduction, illustration received a further great impetus with the appearance of many new magazines. *The Strand,* and *The English Illustrated Magazine,* in Britain, for example, were among the many new magazines that used illustration generously and promoted the reputations of illustrators. *The Century Magazine* and *Collier's Magazine,* together with the re-invigorated *Scribner's* and *Harpers,* became flagships of popular illustration in the United States. In the pages of these magazines can be found the work of the greats of nineteenth-century illustration: in Britain, Richard 'Dicky' Doyle, George Du Maurier, John Gilbert, John Leech, John Tenniel, Phil May and Frederick Walker; in America, Arthur B. Frost, Charles Dana Gibson, Winslow Homer, Maxfield Parrish, Edward Penfield, Howard Pyle and Frederic Remington, to name but the obvious.

In the twentieth century, editorial illustration has had to compete with the photographer's slick imagery, especially in the pages of the 'glossies'. But editorial fashion in choosing illustrators or photographers seems to swing first this way and then that, and many more opportunities that existed before have been opened to the energetic and professionally-minded illustrator through the pages of the growing number of publications catering to modern 'consumer societies'.

EDITORIAL CONTENT

Editorial illustration is the illustration of texts and covers for magazines and newspapers. Any one magazine publication carries a number of independent articles,

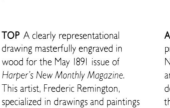

TOP A clearly representational drawing masterfully engraved in wood for the May 1891 issue of *Harper's New Monthly Magazine.* This artist, Frederic Remington, specialized in drawings and paintings of western scenes.

ABOVE These bold wood-engraved prints were published by William Nicholson in the 1890s. Nicholson and his brother-in-law James Pryde designed a number of posters under the name of the Beggarstaff Brothers all fine examples of simplified line.

TOP One of the all-time greats! As an enthusiast of pirate history, Howard Pyle knew his subject in great depth and, while perhaps this illustration is over-romanticized, it is ideally suited to the adventure story.

ABOVE For forty years John Tenniel's style was to serve him well as a contributor to *Punch*, though he is best known today for his illustrations to *Alice in Wonderland*.

editorials and reviews – in addition to its cover – that could be illustrated, and it is usual to find more than one illustrator at work in the pages of a single magazine. A few may work exclusively for one title, but it is more common for illustrators to find work across the wide spectrum of magazines.

Many illustrators today find that modern editorial illustration has a number of attractions. That most frequently expressed attraction is the sheer variety of work an illustrator can get in the editorial field. Last week it might have been a full-colour cover illustration for a high-tech magazine; this week it is an illustration for an article on the comparison of violence at sports meetings with that within the family; and next week it is a drawing to be done for a medical magazine on the effects of drugs on the interrelations between professional men and women and their clients.

As a tried and proven contributor, an experienced illustrator is likely to find editorial work a field in which art directors will give much more independence of action than in other areas, such as advertising work. There is a certain latitude for experimentation in editorial work for the professional worker whom art directors trust.

Sometimes the very frequency and exigencies of magazine publishing work to the illustrator's advantage with regard to experimentation. Often there are opportunities to try out different styles of work. A magazine – and more so a newspaper – is a near ephemeral thing usually on the booksellers' stands for a week, sometimes a month, but rarely more than this. Artwork is semi-permanent and on show for a brief time. Under these circumstances chances with style and content can be taken by both illustrator and art editor. If a new style works and looks good on the printed page all is fine and another dimension has been tried and tested; if not the embarrassment is short-lived! Other forms of illustration cannot afford the risk.

WORKING IN CONTEXT

It is the art director of the magazine or newspaper that the illustrator works with and through. In editorial work it is not usual for an agent to be involved, as the sums of money to be earned rarely warrant an agent's time and specific type of knowledge.

Editorial art directors are most inclined to call on an experienced and proven illustrator for both important work and last-minute work – depending on the

Brian Grimwood shows how an eclectic decorative approach owing nothing to literal interpretation can suit the illustration of a magazine article on wine. The roughs show the illustrator's ideas emerging and developing towards the final image (right).

Catherine Denvir's overtly decorative style has allowed her to diversify over a wide range of editorial subjects. As the illustrations show, she is equally successful both in manipulating black and white prints of her drawings (below) and in colour.

professional skill and commitment of the illustrator to get an appropriate image on the editorial desk in time.

The art director is the first person seen by an illustrator looking for editorial work. A rapport has to be set up between the two, and the means for this are an understanding of one another's jobs, and the evidence of performance as witnessed by the work shown in the illustrator's portfolio.

Some art directors have impressive reputations and powers and others are more firmly constrained by those who own or run the magazine. Most fall somewhere between these two positions. Whatever, an art director has to work under a publication's chief editor, to whom he or she is ultimately responsible, and it makes good sense to remember this. It helps you to understand, for example, why a certain illustration submitted is turned down although all parties might agree that it is good. How might this be?

Take the example of a hard-hitting article in which the journalist has written incisively on a controversial subject. It is a raw-boned piece of journalism which initially suggests to the art director that any accompanying image should be its visual equivalent. The illustration is commissioned from an artist of known ability and in due course the artwork is on the editor's desk. What is suddenly demonstrated to the magazine's editors, however, is that the combination of hard-hitting writing and uncompromising image takes the piece 'over the top'. All sorts of unwanted and unintended repercussions can be seen; will some readers be offended by the combination? Could the magazine be accused of bad taste? In these circumstances the

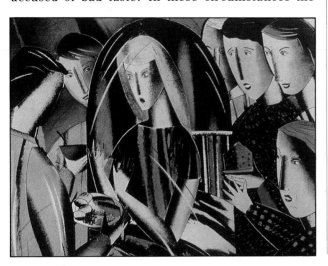

decision to use the illustration would in all probability be taken out of the art director's hands and put firmly in those of the chief editor.

Art directors are part of an editorial team to which they contribute their own and their illustrators' skills, and this contribution has to be seen in the context of the overall policy of a magazine. Everyone may have agreed, in the above example, that the illustrator had done a tremendous piece of artwork, but has reluctantly to accept that it was wrong for that particular article in that particular magazine.

PRESENTATION OF WORK

An editorial art director builds contacts with a group of illustrators known by experience to be reliable. Work is given to these illustrators because they have proven the professional ability to work to deadlines and produce good images. However, art directors are always in need of additional competent talent, and they look for it through the industry's published annuals of work, at shows, on the pages of other publications and, of course, in illustrators' portfolios of work.

The portfolio is of crucial importance. Badly presented it can destroy very quickly any expectations the art director might have had from an illustrator's original request to show work. So what makes a well presented portfolio? The guidelines are largely no more than common sense should dictate, but they seem to be often ignored, if the complaints of art directors are to be taken seriously!

An up-to-date and relevant selection of work keeps the portfolio alive and interesting. It is of no use to the art director if work is shown that is three years old and done in a style that the illustrator was once pleased with but no longer uses. If work is commissioned based on something in the portfolio that is no longer current, both parties are doomed for disappointment – and the illustrator will come off the worse! It is best to have the view that there is no such thing as a finished portfolio of work. It will, and should, be always changing and a professional will rarely be fully satisfied with the folio.

Consequently, it will be necessary to review the portfolio continuously in order to make it relevant to the magazines visited. This is not to say that experienced art directors will not see excellence where excellence is to be found: they are unlikely to miss something exceptional if they are good at the job. But they see a lot of work in the course of a week and the illustrator who judiciously puts together a portfolio of work that makes the task of looking just that bit easier for the art director will have the edge over the competition.

Generally art directors do not have lots of room in which to work and a desk top can take only so much paper before chaos results. It is sensible to keep the size of the portfolio manageable, and artwork at A2-size is the maximum. A3-size presentations are ideal. Large artwork can always be presented as prints or as colour transparencies to be viewed on a light-box, although this can become costly.

Young illustrators frequently make the error of visiting art directors with a portfolio overflowing with work. It need not include everything that has been applauded by teachers, family, and friends from the first years at art school to the present day. The portfolio should be kept current, relevant and manageable. This way a professional face is put on the presentation of work and the dialogue between illustrator and art director is made all the easier.

A portfolio with already published illustrations gives the art director confidence when looking at work for the first time. The addition of printed examples alongside original artwork demonstrates that someone has already taken a chance on commissioning and that the illustrator has some degree of experience of editorial work.

The young illustrator, unless lucky, is unlikely to have had the opportunity of getting work professionally printed. Yet the art director wants evidence of commissions successfully carried out to deadline. What can be done about this Catch-22 situation?

There appears no simple answer. Some offer to do illustrations at almost a nominal fee in order to get the first pieces of published work into the portfolio arguing that these illustrations, as promotional work, will have more than earned their real value in time. Others are unhappy about starting their career on such a note of self-exploitation. It is difficult to make this choice, but experience has shown that the existence of already published work in the portfolio encourages art directors to have confidence in an unknown illustrator.

BRIEFING AND PREPARATION

There is some variation in type and completeness of brief an illustrator will receive from commissioning art editors during a career in editorial work. Usually an article is sent to the illustrator who is expected to

LEFT An artist with his own personal style, Jean Christian Knaff will interpret a brief in an unexpected and dramatic way, but he never disappoints. Artwork and the printed version for *Marketing Week*.

read it and find his or her own visual answer in the text. Alternatively, a short abstract is sent in place: it is not uncommon that an illustrator is commissioned while the article is still in the process of being written!

When commissioning work art directors are most likely to make the initial contact by telephone – therefore an 'answer-phone' is an absolute necessity if you plan to be away from your contact address during the work day. Briefing, however, commonly involves the illustrator in a visit to the editorial offices. As an illustrator gains experience the art director gains confidence, so briefing may come to be done by the telephone, any text copy and reference material being sent on to the illustrator's studio. If a particular style or method of approach is wanted, and there is little time before the artwork must be handed in, an art director will contact the person most readily associated with that approach and commission and possibly brief across the telephone. Both parties can quickly come to an understanding of what is wanted by reference to past work and some highly successful illustration has been done this way.

It is not unusual for a commission to come from someone the illustrator has never even met. As good reputations build up so art directors get to hear about reliable professionals and will approach them with work even though they have never met face to face (a substantial amount of a well-known illustrator's work can come from abroad). Reliability and a reputation for 'delivering the goods' count for much in the frenetic world of editorial illustration.

WORKING METHODS

Although there are in theory no restrictions on what materials or techniques an illustrator can use in editorial work, there are publishing and printing practices that do, in fact, impose some necessity for forethought on the illustrator. For example, magazines and newspapers are printed on a variety of papers – from the roughest newsprint to coated art paper – and this will be a factor the careful illustrator will note when approached by a particular publisher.

Modern colour printing technologies impose restrictions on the choice of working surface. With the use of electronic scanners for colour separation – where the original artwork is wrapped round a drum to be scanned by lasers – illustrators are obliged to work on some kind of flexible surface; for example,

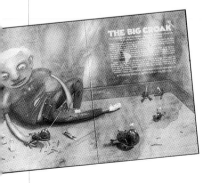

ABOVE LEFT A dramatic interpretation of a difficult theme. How do you portray pain? Here the rending apart of the stone cranium, painted by James Marsh, conveys the destructive nature of illness.

ABOVE The strength of Ed Mclachlan's illustration rests firmly in the witty assocation of graphic forms.

LEFT Ian Pollock's unique style, together with his skills of interpretation, are sought after by art directors seeking to portray challenging editorial images.

paper and not board. If an illustrator prefers to work on a stiff board it would be possible for the original artwork to be shot on to film and this used on the scanner. This is an extra cost, however, that most publishers would wish to avoid.

In black-and-white illustration specifically, it is normally best to work in a definite medium – pen and ink and scraperboard are examples – rather than attempt a fine pencil drawing. Sharp drawing with clean contrasts gives better reproduction quality across a wider range of papers than the softer tones characteristic of pencil drawings. In colour work it is possible to use a wide range of drawing and painting media, and even collaged or montaged elements, if these are appropriate to the style of work required and the reproduction methods used for print.

Keeping work 'alive' is a constant concern of the professional illustrator and many would argue that in editorial work the chance – even the need – to work spontaneously and experimentally is the best way of keeping work fresh. The opportunity for art directors to take calculated chances means that the illustrator can experiment and vary the approach. For these reasons alone it would be impossible, and even presumptuous, to lay down one professional approach for editorial illustration. What can be offered is a few general remarks.

The very speed with which editorial work is done today often precludes the submission of roughs – pencil sketches or wash drawings – by the illustrator to the art editor, which is common in publishing and design work. Roughs will probably be done by artists for their own purposes in order to sort out composition, but not unless there is lots of time available (which there usually is not) will these be seen by anyone else.

Once an idea is thought of and the first preliminary sketches have been laid down, an illustrator might telephone the art director to explain what he or she has in mind for the article. This is not only sensible – enabling the illustrator to make any alterations or additions to the drawing at the pencil sketch stage – it is also a courtesy towards the art director. Everyone likes to be confident about things they are doing and art directors are no exception. A short chat about the idea, the approach chosen and medium to be used can reassure the art director that what was expected is what is coming. Alternatively, if the brief allows for more experimental work, it prepares the art director for the arrival of something out of the ordinary.

An illustrator may be chosen for a commission because of a particular stylistic approach, another for the ability to do highly detailed and realistic work. All illustrators, however, are likely to require visual references for their work. No serious illustrator can be without personal sources of visual reference for research: most have boxes of material and shelves of books and magazines stored for use. Art directors might supply photographs for the illustrator's reference if there is time and the commission demands it – not every artist will have the details of eighteenth-century Italian opera costumes at hand, for example.

BUSINESS PROCEDURES

The fees to be earned from editorial work are generally smaller than those to be had in advertising and design. An illustrator's fee is often predetermined by the 'page-rates' in operation in a particular magazine. So much is paid, for example, for a two-column piece, or a half page, a three-quarter page or a cover illustration. Art editors are frequently constrained by these sums,

The illustrator's agent liaises between client and art director and the freelance artist on a percentage commission. He will use promotional brochures and advertisements (left) in the creative media to help obtain commissions.

BELOW RIGHT The art director at
Performance Car commissioned
David da Silva to enliven a stolid,
technical piece of text. The rough he
supplied was interpreted fairly
liberally to achieve the final
textured-look result.
BELOW A selection of artists's
portfolios stacked in an agent's
office.

which have been agreed upon by higher management.

Most creative people find talking about fees the least attractive side of earning a living from their work. It is, however, a sign of professionalism to discuss fees with a commissioning art director during the first contact. As well as information on the brief, the illustrator should clarify what payment to expect for the work.

Young illustrators getting started in editorial work must prepare for a lot of initial effort unrelated to drawing. Traditionally it means doing the rounds of targeted art directors with the portfolio. Time spent familiarizing oneself with current magazines is time well spent. Not only is a picture of what is happening in editorial illustration usefully built up this way, but further scope for work than was initially thought to exist can be discovered. Today a number of professional journals not previously noted for their use of illustration (in nursing and accountancy, for example) can be seen to have turned to the drawn image to supplement and relieve photographic illustration.

The next step is to make appointments with art directors, having got the names and addresses from the magazines themselves or through the various reference books on the industry. A telephone call is the best approach. Many art directors have a specific day in the week on which they will view portfolios and others see illustrators when they can. In the beginning, anything from four to five visits per day can be needed.

When the first commission comes along there should be one intention only; to do it well and to get it in on time. Much is riding on the young illustrator performing to expectations. It is at this point that a professional reputation begins, and if it begins badly no one can tell what the repercussions can be. Paradoxically, it is likely that this will be the most difficult illustration ever done! Neither experience nor insider knowledge is available for support and yet the necessity of performing like a professional is paramount. The only comfort to be had is that the art director saw something in both the work and the person that encouraged the commission, and that historically thousands have been through it before and not only survived but prospered.

SUMMARY

Professionally, editorial illustration is both a proving-ground and a field in which illustrators can experiment, expand and excel. But it is a professional world, and the illustrator who is popular with editorial art directors is the person with good interpretative skills – able to read in an article or hear in a telephone conversation a visual answer to a brief – and with an uncompromising attitude to supplying good work to absolute deadlines. For a professional with a healthy curiosity about the world and a commitment to excellence, editorial work can be a most exciting and rewarding field of illustration.

2/ILLUSTRATION FOR ADVERTISING

Advertising illustration is a challenging profession, involving far more than meets the eye of the contemplative consumer.

In a general sense, the uses of illustration are numerous; apart from editorial, technical and animation applications, illustration within the context of advertising is a specialist area, and has to fulfil a number of very specific functions.

Advertising illustration is above all a vital part of the one-way communication between manufacturer and consumer. The image provided by the illustration has to be one which will serve the purpose of drawing attention to the product by announcing its existence and emphasizing its desirable qualities.

Much contemporary illustration for advertising has gone way beyond the function of mere ornamentation. The advertising industry now has links with psychological research first brought to public awareness in the 1960s by Vance Packard's book *The Hidden Persuaders,* which not only identified persuasive advertising techniques already in use but forecast the psychological approach to product promotion which is commonplace today.

The illustrative image for advertising is a carefully selected, powerful evocation of the product, and is the result of a great deal of planning and forethought on the part of the client whose product is being promoted, the art director or designer who decides how the advertisement should look, and the illustrator who translates this concept into visual terms.

The saying 'one picture is worth ten thousand words' is particularly true of illustration. One illustration skilfully conceived, commissioned, and carried out, can be worth several thousand consumers.

USE OF ILLUSTRATION IN ADVERTISING

In these times of high technology, illustration for advertising faces a very real threat from the camera and computer. Yet it maintains its position as a medium of communication which has some unique qualities. Photographic and computer-generated images can be seen to be encroaching in particular upon an area in which illustration has always had a strong hold – that of surreal imagery.

The advertising industry has had links with surrealism for well over half a century. Back in 1917, artists Marcel Duchamp and Max Ernst were both developing their work through direct reference to advertising im-agery, finding within it a rich imaginative source of inspiration for the first surrealist paintings.

The situation now is reversed. Advertisers themselves owe an enormous debt to surrealism. We are daily subjected to advertising imagery which borrows unashamedly from surrealist notions and through this, illustration provides a direct means of communication.

The power of surrealism lies in its capacity to demand attention through the use of incongruity. Showing a product out of context, or in some odd juxtaposition, attracts attention. Challenging elements of surprise, amusement or intrigue appeal to the imagination. Such imagery has an intellectual appeal which flatters the consumer: a fairly elaborate system of game-playing is in operation which involves the putative consumer in decoding messages, which in themselves are not too complex. These messages invariably consist, at a basic level, of instructions to 'do this' or 'buy that' and are expressed through the illustration, which is often explicit. Usually, however, it is backed up by the use of headlines and copy.

The relatively inexpensive and uncomplicated process of illustration as opposed to the highly-priced images obtained through photography or computer generation makes it an ideal vehicle for advertising.

THE FUNCTION OF ADVERTISING ILLUSTRATION

One illustrator commented recently that 'the purpose of art is to illuminate or inspire, rather than to bewilder and confuse – to convey a message contained within a picture with as much clarity as possible . . . in this the commercial art world may have something to teach so-called fine art . . .'

Another illustrator sees the difference between fine art and commercial art as being that fine art sells itself and commercial art sells something else.

Both comments contain truths which relate to illustration used in the context of advertising, and suggest the connection which exists in a very real sense between fine art and commercial art.

Many illustrators practising today followed a fine-art training, but on leaving college decided that their work should have a less personal but more practical function. Other illustrators may have followed a course in graphic design and specialized in illustration towards the last year – and some have doubtless taken a vocational illustration course which enables them to

BELOW *Ready-made Girl with Bedstead.* Marcel Duchamp's pastiche of an early advertisement for Sapolin enamel, painted in 1916.

RIGHT A striking version of perhaps a mundane subject by Henry Ehlers, done in about 1930 for Bamberger and Hertz.

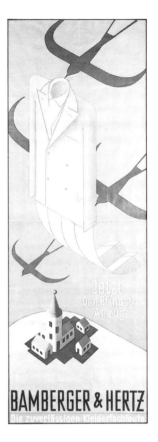

ABOVE Francis Bernard's design for this poster of 1931 uses strong and simple imagery.

LEFT Ludwig Hohlwein made dramatic use of typography as well as illustration in this advertisement of 1908.

FAR LEFT The bold lines and strong colour used by John Hassall are well suited to the message contained in this advertisement of 1908.

ABOVE AND RIGHT An exciting and challenging project for artists Julie Drake, David Sim and Martin Chatterton was this campaign for Pernod. The clients were anxious to break away from the conventional form of advertising, and the only brief given to the artists was to work in black and white with spot colour for the Pernod and the inclusion of the copy line.

deal with such specialist areas as technical or medical illustrative work. However, self-taught illustrators make up a significant proportion of those working for advertising today.

Whatever the training or background, it has to be acknowledged that fashions exist within illustrative styles which can and do dictate how an advertising concept will be expressed, and have a bearing on its ultimate success in terms of sales.

The development of an individual and recognizable style – be it fine-art based or grounded in design thinking, or the result of personal research – can help towards the securing of regular commissions from art directors who tend to associate a certain style with a particular illustrator. There is unfortunately always the possibility of becoming stuck in a rut as 'flavour of the month'. The world of advertising has a fickle side – a wise illustrator is aware of this, and realizes that one or two alternative styles are an invaluable asset.

WHO'S WHO

Besides the illustrator, a number of people have an active role in the definition, requirements, concepts and commissioning of illustration for advertising.

A graphically convenient way of presenting the hierarchy is to think of a pyramid, or triangle, at the bottom of which is the client. The client provides the fundamental requirements for the promotion and presentation of the product.

LEFT Fine detail in a highly wrought architectural style distinguishes this oblique aerial painting by Mark Hess of the Library of Congress in Washington.

ABOVE LEFT A pastiche on Modigliani proved a challenging prospect for Anne Sharp, involving considerable research. This version is the third in the series for Long John, and led to commissions for several editorial projects.

ABOVE In the painting for Nilverm by the same artist the brief was to express a sense of well-being.

LEFT George Underwood was asked to fill his picture with as many rabbits in as many colours as possible, to work around the type and to make the composition adapt to a vertical as well as horizontal shape.

FAR LEFT ABOVE This scraperboard illustration by Paul Sheldon was worked from a photographic reference and thus to a very tight brief.

FAR LEFT AND LEFT Dynamism, power and visual punning executed with style by Larry Learmonth.

Mike Terry is renowned for his characterization, and his skill in interpreting a fairly loose brief requiring a number of different 'types' is evident in this painting. After submitting the initial rough (left and below) he produced artwork (opposite) which was returned with comments from the agency for him to finalize and polish on the finished artwork (inset, opposite).

Next, a little higher up, is the designer or art director, to whom the client presents the basic brief; the art director, often working in close contact with a copywriter, devises the concept for the promotion of the client's product.

Above the art director, and the client, is found the artists' agent who may have been approached by the art director to give the commission to an illustrator. It is the illustrator who in this analogy occupies a position at the top of the pyramid.

Returning down the pyramid, in terms of what happens next, the artists' agent, if one is involved, presents the artwork to the art director. Linked in with the headline and copy, the illustration makes up the advertisement which is then submitted to the client, who is waiting at the bottom of the pyramid for the sales success story of all time.

The simplistic analogy of a pyramid to demonstrate the advertising scenario in no way takes into account the numerous inevitable slips 'twixt cup and lip which tend to imperil the success of any advertising campaign, however meticulously organized.

THE WORK PROCESS

The role of the advertising illustrator is best defined as being interpretative. The analogy of the advertising pyramid deliberately omitted the target – the consumer, who occupies a theoretical position somewhere near the apex of the pyramid, within receiving range of the advertiser's message, as interpreted by the illustrator.

Interpretation of the brief is the main task of the illustrator, who translates the ideas of the art director into artwork, in a style that has been agreed. The expression of a concept outlined by an art director on behalf of a client demands imagination and skill.

If an illustrator is to be successful, a professional attitude is essential. Professionalism in advertising requires a full understanding of the brief, an ability to interpret it through appropriate rendering skills, together with a realistic and reliable approach to the meeting of inevitable deadlines. A capacity for resilience in the face of seemingly capricious adjustments to the original brief by the art director or client is as necessary as a confident and pleasant manner. At the bottom line, a sound drawing ability, and a sense of

humour combined with an imaginative and witty approach to the brief are basic prerequisites.

As interpreter, the responsibility of the illustrator is not only to him or herself, but to the art director and copywriter, and ultimately to the client.

WORKING IN CONTEXT

If approached in a sensible and intelligent way, advertising illustration can form the basis of a satisfying and rewarding career. The opportunities for self-expression in terms of imaginative interpretation of the brief are there for the taking. Image manipulation and visual punning are the stock in trade of the advertising illustrator, who frequently has to liaise with the copywriter in the production of sympathetic work.

Illustration for advertising demands a high level of ability in problem solving. Working in a group can provide the chance for ideas to be exchanged and developed, although many illustrators prefer their own company, and work in comparative isolation. Membership of a professional association can be a valuable asset. Such bodies exist to promote illustration, to pro-

tect the rights of illustrators and artists' agents, and to bring illustrators (possibly working as individuals) together socially. Membership may be open to anyone involved with illustration – agents, clients, teachers, students, as well as practising illustrators.

Artists' agents can also offer the illustrator a good deal. Working on a commission rate of around 25 per cent of the artist's agreed fee, an agent's representative can save the illustrator time and money by taking work round to prospective clients. This has the additional advantage of reducing the illustrator's sense of personal rejection should work be refused.

The agent has numerous professional connections and takes responsibility for obtaining work for the illustrator not only in his or her own country but also abroad, if appropriate. Part of the commitment to the illustrators whose work the agent handles is to ensure that portfolios, or 'books', are kept in excellent condition, and are up to date with examples of recent and outstanding work by the illustrator in question. The agent also handles publicity and promotional arrangements and financial affairs.

BELOW David Juniper was selected from a number of artists who had submitted visuals to copy lines supplied by the art director. His initial rough was much simpler than the final designs, which became more complex and elaborate.

BOTTOM LEFT Dramatic use of visual punning by Larry Learmonth

BOTTOM RIGHT Although the typography is by one artist, Maggie Lewis, these two paintings for After Eight Mints are in fact by different artists — (left) Colin Hadley and (right) Pierre Tan.

BELOW This dramatic image is an accurate representation, as Mike Terry's brief was to make the animal as recognizable as possible within the limitations of the design.

BOTTOM Anne Sharp's realistic style is well suited to a brief which required attention to detail.

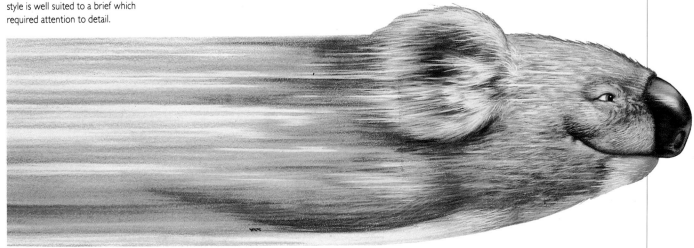

3/FASHION ILLUSTRATION

Photography is responsible for the demise of fashion illustration over the past thirty years. With its technical development and the very creative ways it has been used during this period, it has almost killed off the use of hand-drawn illustration. Before this, fashion illustrators were as famous as photographers are today – names such as Erté, Georges Lepape, Paul Iribe, Eduardo Benito, Drian, Helen Dryden, and many more. Many of them began their careers with the *Gazette du BonTon,* the French fashion journal of the 1900s. This was the beginning of the fashion magazine, quite different from what we have today: the drawings were printed in line and then each one hand-coloured. It was later followed in the 1920s by *Vogue* and *Harper's Bazaar.* These also featured the leading artists of the day and made them famous. With each issue the artists became known and identified with various publications: Erté with *Harper's,* for example.

By the fifties there was a steady decline in fashion illustration, but new names have come up with each decade, especially in the USA. The late Antonio López, whose work first became known in the sixties, was probably the most internationally famous artist of the post-war period. One of the reasons for his staying power was that, as well as being an excellent artist, he was able to adopt new styles, each as successful as the last. Other names to come out of the States during the sixties and seventies are Steven Stipleman, Barbra Pearlman, Robert Passantino, Albert Elia, Robert Young, Kenneth Paul Block, and Stravinos. Many of these were associated with *Women's Wear Daily,* the American fashion trade paper.

Illustration could and should be used more, along with photography, either combined in single pieces of artwork or as a collection of both throughout any publication which requires pictures. The visually exciting Italian magazine *Vanity* uses a good mixture of both in its spreads. Fashion illustration should not have to be judged by the standards of photography. It is a different medium and therefore can be criticized or praised on its own merits, separately.

STYLE AND CONTEXT

It is vitally important that students who desire a career in fashion illustration be aware of all the past innovators of the subject. Look at their techniques and styles to see how they solved the problems of drawing the figure for fashion. Also look at fine artists, both contemporary and classic, for inspiration. Be a serious student of life drawing and anatomy, as well as fashion, for this is essential and will only help your own creativity and style. As fashion covers the body, it is essential to know how to draw the body properly before developing a method which abstracts, exaggerates or elongates. Learn the actual proportions of men, women and children, before adapting them to an illustrative style. If illustration is to be taken more seriously and come to be used as much as photography, then it has to be more exciting and based on an excellent standard of drawing, not reliant on gimmicks.

Fashion illustration is used in many areas of the industry as a whole, so there are many potential outlets for artists' work, as long as it is good, in design, newspapers, magazines, advertising, book promotions and fashion forecast agencies. General illustration work sometimes goes to fashion illustrators; if the draughtsmanship is good, there is no reason why the work can't be used in areas other than fashion. Here again, sound drawing ability is of great advantage.

6

FASHION DESIGN

Designers use drawing as a method of putting down their ideas when working on a collection. These need only be working drawings, sketches that convey the 'look' of the clothes and giving, most important of all, the proportions. The designer starts with a drawing before making a toile or cutting a pattern. The finished garment may change a great deal from the initial drawing, but it is the basis of the designer's ideas. Young designers working for a fashion house may sit and draw all day; then their sketches are taken and interpreted for the style of the fashion house. This may include all or part of the original idea.

In this area of fashion drawing it is important that the ideas are put down in clear line, with all the details of how the garment might be cut, constructed and finished, i.e. seaming, stitching buttons, zips, pockets, etc. These aspects are more technical, but the drawing should still have a flair for fashion, and a feeling for style and the use of fabric – a personality. This sort of illustration is also used for fashion forecast agencies, who are in the business of predicting styles and other related information to manufacturers. As the information they are providing is not yet realized in terms of real garments, drawing is the perfect medium. It usually takes the form of precise line drawing showing shape, proportion and detail, with an indication of colours and fabric textures.

FASHION JOURNALISM

In fashion journalism, where items from the latest collections are reported in the daily papers, a looser, more sketchy style of drawing is used. A drawing can illustrate the information more accurately in newsprint

1 and **2** Georges Barbier, known also for his theatrical illustrations, and André Marty, both worked for the *Gazette du Bon Ton* in the 1920s.

3 *The New Yorker* carried stylish fashion advertisements in its heyday of the 1930s.

4 Rough sketches by Cecil Beaton, photographer, designer, writer and illustrator, for a play by Saki.

5 and **6** A stylish and elegant illustration by Erté, and another by the same artist for *Vogue*.

7 Francis Marshall, a prolific illustrator for *Vogue* in the 1940s and 50s, gives a flavour of late 40s New York life as well as fashion.

8 and **9** Jenny Lock's spare lines contrast with the work of Clare Smalley for fashion designer Galliano.

5

7

9

8

than a photograph, because a strong black line is more powerful than the greys of photography, giving the correct information economically and more effectively. The artist can emphasize a certain proportion and the important details in a collection, drawing the viewer's eye to these significant features, which in some collections may be very subtle. This clearly shows the designer's direction; for example, a full skirt can be made fuller, a tight waist smaller. But the drawing must be based on the facts. The illustrator is free to use his or her own style and imagination, but if this distorts the design, the result will be rejection of the work and perhaps a long wait before any commissions of the same kind come in.

ADVERTISING AND EDITORIAL WORK

Remember that the main purpose of fashion illustration is to sell either a look or a product. It is an advertisement, so it must be appealing and attract the attention of potential customers.

In selling a look, the artist may only be required to give an impression of the clothes; not to show all the details, but to express with a few lines the whole feeling and style of a collection of clothes, and the mood it creates. For selling particular garments, the artist is required to illustrate them in more detail. This is not always a glamorous job: in some cases an illustrator is commissioned to do the artwork for an advertisement because the actual garments are dull or lacking in personality, so it is hoped that with a bit of imagination and style, the illustrator can make them look quite appealing.

Editorial work for magazines is the most prestigious for the artist, and probably less lucrative because of this. However, it is like a shop window for the work. Everyone reads the latest magazines, so from here the artist can get a lot of personal publicity for work in other areas, such as advertising which is the best paid. Here, too, the most innovative ideas and styles are used. With high-quality reproduction processes, almost any medium can be used – pencil, inks, watercolours, markers, pastels, mixed media, collage, letratone, paints, etc.

The style of drawing can be strong and individual. It is important to give the figures in the drawings an attitude that goes with the clothes. For example, for glamorous evening wear, the poses can be sophisticated and the models the kind of men or women that would wear the clothes. For young designer-label clothes, perhaps the mood should be more relaxed and the models young and fashionably presented by current tastes. The faces in your drawings are important, as people want to identify with the style and you want to make them feel attractive: so make them as attractive as possible, and interesting, having character. The drawings should also have movement, as stiff figures and clothes like cardboard cutouts don't give a real impression of the garments. This may make it difficult for you to sell your work. This is where good practice in drawing will help: if you can't find a life model, draw yourself or the objects around you, training your eye and experimenting with different types of media, so you become familiar and confident with them.

OBTAINING WORK

When starting out with a portfolio, this is a very insecure time and it is natural that you are not going to be sure what will sell. The best way to deal with this is to

(1) The watercolour by Clare Smalley was designed for a wall in a boutique, while Jenny Lock's sketch (2) for a shirt company was for an exhibition.
Antonio Lopez justifies his renown for versatility in this Surrealist design for *Vanity Fair* (3). The watercolour by Howard Tangye (4) conveys a relaxed and youthful impression, in contrast to the more mannered pose of Clare Smalley's (5).

stick to what you do best. Don't be tempted to fill your portfolio with many different styles and techniques. It is likely that some will be weaker than others and should be left out, to be developed in your own time. By keeping your best work for the book, with a clear sense of style, the drawings will look stronger and give the potential clients more confidence to commission work. Their confidence will improve when you start to get printed examples to add to the portfolio as well.

Fashion covers lots of categories, starting with the basic divisions of menswear, womenswear and children's clothes, and within these categories, evening or day wear, sports clothes, suits, separates, accessories, and also hair and beauty. There is no need to do all of these just to fill the portfolio – be selective, and if you can't be self-critical, get some objective but constructive criticism before you decide what to show.

Try to be as professional as you can about the business side of things. Make appointments, don't just turn up. Keep a record of whom you call, and of dates and times for calls and appointments. After interviews, make notes on the comments raised. Get yourself a business card, perhaps printed with a drawing so clients can refer to it in the future.

When making appointments it is also wise to consider where your work is most likely to be well-received and accepted. For instance, if your portfolio shows a very contemporary approach to the style of both drawings and garments, it may not be acceptable to a middle-of-the-road publication. Art editors and potential clients are inclined to judge solely by what they see in front of them, and it may be difficult at first to convince them that you are capable of adapting your style.

Once you are commissioned to do a job, make sure that a price is fixed before you start. The client should give you an order or contract for the work with the price, delivery date and a stated rejection fee for work not accepted: this is usually half of the full price for the job. Many artists have agents to represent them, leaving them free to do the artwork: for this service, the agent takes a percentage of the fee for each job, and this varies from 15 to 30 per cent. But agents have the contracts and the business experience, and it is in their interests, too, that you should get work. If you feel unable to represent yourself, this is probably the best way of working.

Fashion illustration is not an easy occupation, and may be slow to start; but if it is what you want to do, don't be put off by any difficulties at the beginning.

5

4/NATURAL HISTORY ILLUSTRATION

Zoological and botanical illustration are areas in which it is inappropriate to have a fixed idea of progress in style or technique. In a sense, no image has ever bettered the cave paintings, and there are many masterpieces of the past which still set a standard of excellence for modern illustrators, such as the grasses and wildflowers of Albrecht Dürer and his detailed study of a wild hare vibrant with life. Great works such as Audubon's *Birds of America* stand alongside the illustrations of Beatrix Potter, whose well-loved and unsentimental animal characters in her children's books are matched by her distinguished botanical studies. The Reverend John G. Wood in the nineteenth century made a significant contribution to popularizing natural history in England and America.

This is an important time for the natural history illustrator. We are living at a time of unparalleled destruction of the natural world and witnessing a rapid rate of extinction of plants and creatures. Artists who make their living out of nature have a heavy responsibility to try to protect it. Many things which today we consider quite common may become extinct, or may be found only in one or two pockets of tiny populations where conditions have not been entirely destroyed. Illustrations can convey the joy we find in these creatures with sympathy, and perhaps even humour. An illustration can express feelings and commentary on the subject in a way that a photograph does not.

WORKING IN CONTEXT

Improved technical methods of reproduction are the significant difference between natural history illustration now and the remarkable examples of earlier artists. The fields of opportunity are in zoological and botanical books, scientific publications and museum work, in popular natural history books, magazines and partworks, posters and information graphics, some graphic illustration for television, and new opportunities in animation work. Various aspects of publishing offer a wide range of approaches, from decorative children's books to serious scientific studies.

Most illustration of this kind is done on a freelance basis; major publishing projects sometimes employ illustrators on an extended contract until publication is complete. The best way to identify the area of work which you would like to be involved with is to go to a large bookstore and look at all the natural history books. Ask yourself which you would love to illustrate,

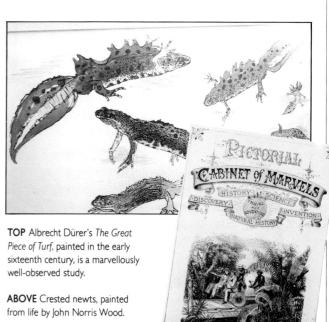

TOP Albrecht Dürer's *The Great Piece of Turf*, painted in the early sixteenth century, is a marvellously well-observed study.

ABOVE Crested newts, painted from life by John Norris Wood.

RIGHT Cover from the Victorian *Pictorial Cabinet of Marvels*.

RIGHT Stamps by Barry Driscoll, probably influenced by the Thomas Bewick wood engraving shown below.

BOTTOM This lithograph of a typical tortoise is by Edward Lear, a fine landscape painter and superb zoological illustrator.

16ᴾ Highland Cow

26ᴾ Hereford Bull

20½ᴾ Chillingham Wild Bull

and which you would do best. It's important that these two considerations go together.

Your reputation will rest on your portfolio of work, which at the outset necessarily contains original work rather than printed samples. To build up the collection of work, frequent drawing from life is essential. Make drawings of plants and animals in their habitats, and in their various attitudes. However, it's useful to get to know a particular subject very well and get a feel for it, rather than end with a lot of unrelated drawings lacking depth. The illustrator should be obsessed by drawing, working at every possible opportunity. Keep masses of sketchbooks and fill them to overflowing: all material you collect is valuable reference for the future. Where it is difficult to get firsthand experience of rare or exotic specimens which may interest you, look for the less common subjects in zoos and botanical gardens, and special plant collections or wildlife sanctuaries.

Reference materials are another important aspect of preparation for a career in natural history illustration. Collect cuttings of work you admire, seen in magazines and journals. It may also be useful to keep samples of

LEFT This watercolour of sycamore leaves by Clare Roberts formed part of a thesis on the dispersal of seed, and combines accuracy with sensitivity.

ABOVE AND BELOW John Norris Wood painted these West African snakes and the flatfish for use in textbooks, where accurate information is needed. The giant toad, however, is a friend of the family — beautifully expressed in this watercolour.

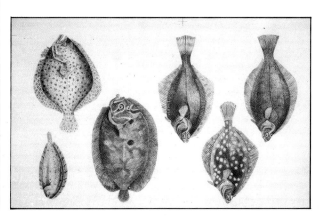

BELOW AND BOTTOM An illustration from *Jungles — Hide and Seek*, one in a series of children's books written by John Norris Wood and illustrated jointly by him and Kelvin Dean. The bat was drawn, also by Wood, in crayon and a little watercolour, for a magazine.

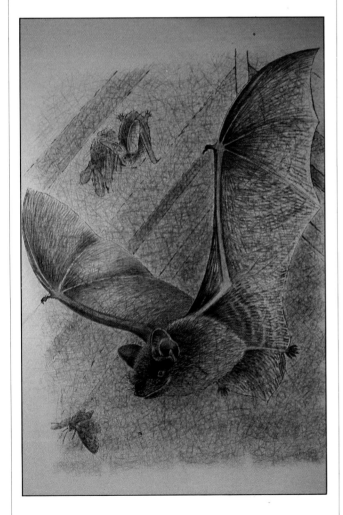

work you consider unsuccessful, as a warning of how not to do it. Read as much as possible about your chosen subjects, as well as studying them in the field, and build up a personal library of well-produced books as you can afford them. Be cautious, though, about relying on photographic reference. Straight copying of photographs has a lifelessness which is visible in the work, and the camera can distort the subject.

You will be working at home or in your own studio premises, and it is important to have a well-sized room with good light, though not direct sunlight. You will need magnifying glasses – those with a lighting strip surround are useful – and perhaps a binocular microscope, if you are studying tiny things. As well as drawing different subjects, experiment with a range of media and be experimental – use coarse bamboo pens to loosen up your style, for example, as well as fine dip pens and drawing pens for detailed work. Papers and boards are a matter of personal choice, and when you try out a new surface always do some rough doodles before embarking on the full artwork. Trying out unfamiliar materials may reveal a different aspect of your style, keeping the work fresh. In the words of John Ruskin: 'There is no general way of doing any thing, no recipe can be given you for so much as the drawing of a cluster of grass.'

BUSINESS PROCEDURE

It should not be forgotten that there is a growing number of natural history artists and there are more illustrators than there is work. Rates vary incredibly from job to job and you should approach every commission as a different problem. Work out an hourly rate for your time, and expenses for such items as drawing and painting materials and reference needed. Half the time, on a natural history project, can be taken up in finding the right reference. You need to know how much time is required of you overall, and what is involved in the actual work, as well as taking into account the resources of the client.

The professional illustrator with good specimens of work in his or her portfolio should not agree to do unpaid samples. To avoid disagreements, always get your brief in writing, with full conditions and stated fee, and an agreement on a rejection fee if applicable. If you are providing illustrations for a book, consider whether it may be a steady seller and try to arrange a royalty payment rather than a flat fee.

5/MEDICAL ILLUSTRATION

The pictorialization of 'medical' matters can be traced back into antiquity, but true medical illustration associated with genuine scientific enquiry really began with Leonardo da Vinci in the fifteenth century, who, at a time when research on the human cadaver was unlawful, undertook his own clandestine dissections on which his superb anatomical drawings were based. Leonardo of course was unique in that he combined so many extraordinary talents. Subsequent medical illustration developed on the basis of a partnership between scientist and artist; a partnership which is exemplified in the magnificent drawings produced by the Dutch artist Calcar for the anatomist Vesalius in the sixteenth century.

THE ROLE OF MEDICAL ILLUSTRATION

Today's technology permits us to see and record images within virtually every body cavity, and superb pictures of organs and body sections can be built up by computers acting on 'information' created by the magnetic manipulation of the atomic structure of body tissues. It may appear strange that in this context the work of an artist in medicine is still in demand and medical illustration continues to thrive and expand. This is due to the fact that as mechanical methods of recording have developed, the medical illustrator has adapted to the role of interpreter and communicator of scientific information; a role in which understanding of medical science and communication psychology, and imagination, are perhaps of greater importance than artistic skills. The sensitive nature of the work makes this a particularly demanding area of illustration, requiring extended specialist training.

The interpretative nature of the medical illustrator's work can be most easily understood and observed in the illustration of subjects in which a 'photographic' recording, while being both accurate and truthful, may be virtually unintelligible; for example, body structures and surgical procedures. By using existing knowledge, with visual and tactile examination, and the study of microscopic preparations, radiographs etc., the artist is able to reconstruct a 'three-dimensional' visualization of the anatomical subject.

In illustrating a new surgical operation, scores of sketches are produced in the theatre. Later, with the aid of anatomical and technical knowledge, these are distilled into pictures in which vital structures and tissues are enhanced and differentiated; blood, secre-

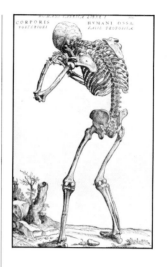

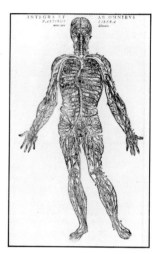

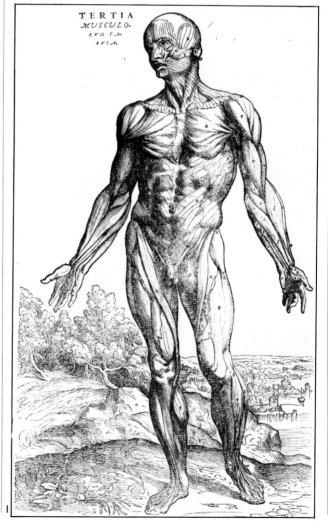

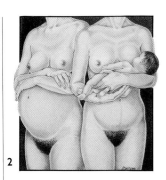

1 Illustrations by Jan Van Calcar for Andreas Vesalius' *De Humani corporis fabrica*, the first scientific book on anatomy, published in 1555.
2 and 3 Illustrations for medical magazine articles on cancer of the bowel and ante-natal and post-natal conditions by Philip Wilson.
4 Bryony Cohen succeeds in demonstrating complex structures as well as interpreting the different components in this drawing of the temporo-mandibular joint.

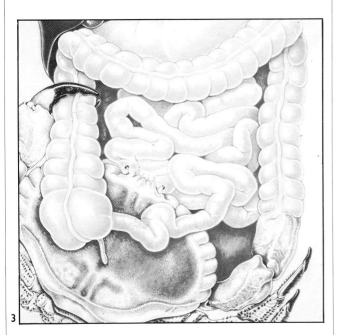

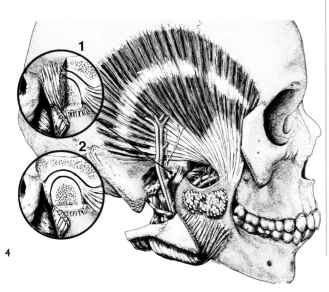

tions, towels, swabs, instruments, the operator's hands and other unnecessary obscuring factors are removed and the technical procedure, perhaps lasting many hours, is condensed and explained within a short sequence of 'frozen' images.

In the two foregoing examples, the illustrator is concerned with the interpretation of things which can be 'seen'. The task of the illustrator, 'teacher' and 'learner' in interpreting, communicating and understanding respectively, is made somewhat easier by the fact that they can all draw on real experience and observation.

This is not the case, however, when dealing with information which has no real observable form, such as a physiological process, a concept or a theory: for example, in providing a visual explanation of the chemical structure of DNA, how it replicates itself within cells and its role in the transfer of genetic information. This requires the artist to employ symbolism and pictorial analogues, and to 'sense' pictorial images where none exists in reality. This type of illustration now forms a large and increasing part of the medical illustrator's work in the wake of advances in scientific knowledge and the redirection of interest from the macro- and microscopic to the chemical and atomic structures, metabolism and other body processes.

The quantity of existing knowledge in medical and science is now enormous and growing at an accelerating pace. Thus the task for the prospective doctor of acquiring the basic facts and, when qualified, keeping up to date, is formidable. Modern medical education makes great use of the new technologies of communication, and this is one of the major factors accounting for the continuing growth of medical illustration in the provision of teaching materials. Imaginative illustration and good design play an important role, both by way of explaining facts, and as a means of 'oiling the wheels' of communication by presenting information in a stimulating, digestible and pleasurable form.

In addition to growth of knowledge, the increasing size of the communication task and the media employed have also been responsible for a change in the character and style of much modern medical illustration. It is no longer sufficient simply to make knowledge available; in the quantities we now possess, it needs to be regarded as a 'marketable' commodity and as such subject to marketing techniques involving psychology, colour, good design, etc. Even the cartoon, though not the most

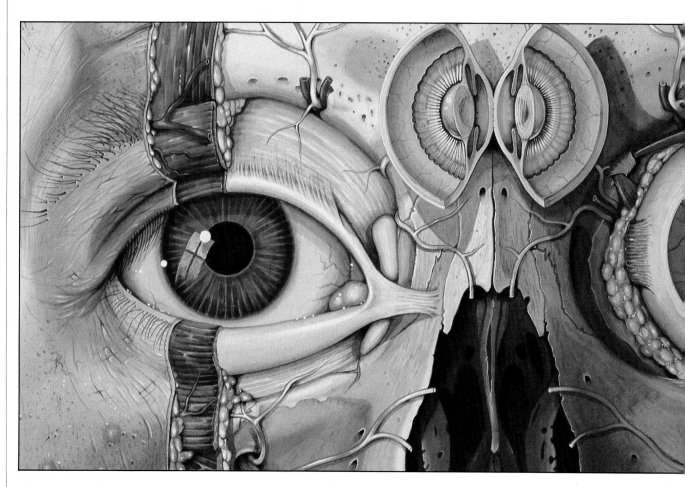

elegant of art forms, by appealing to different emotions, can not only provide light relief but indelibly imprint salient facts and ideas in a most effective manner.

WORKING IN CONTEXT

Until comparatively recent times, the medical illustrator provided a service which was almost exclusively confined to meeting the requirements of the medical practitioner, the researcher, the medical teacher and the student. Now, however, this activity spans the whole spectrum of health care. For the patient, the illustrator provides a wide range of informative and instructional materials, from booklets on ante-natal care, for example, to the more sophisticated audio-visual programmes assisting those about to embark on home-based renal dialysis. In the field of preventative medicine, he or she is responsible for the conception and design of informative and persuasive materials, from the simple poster to a full-scale health education campaign.

Obviously a substantial proportion of such work does not make great demands on the illustrator's knowledge of anatomy, physiology and the like; however, deep involvement in medicine is vital, for it enables the illustrator to interpret correctly the needs and objectives of the communicator and assess the right approach to, and the reactions of, those on the receiving end.

Medical illustration has often been described as being essentially non-creative, in the sense that it requires of the practitioner a disciplined adherence to established facts, principles and ethics; whereas the fine artist has enormous latitude in ways of expressing ideas. Despite this absence of licence, medical illustration offers the practitioner great satisfaction in employing knowledge and imagination on the one hand to successfully elucidate complex scientific phenomena to students of medicine, and on the other to bring about greater awareness or a change in attitudes in the cause of improved health.

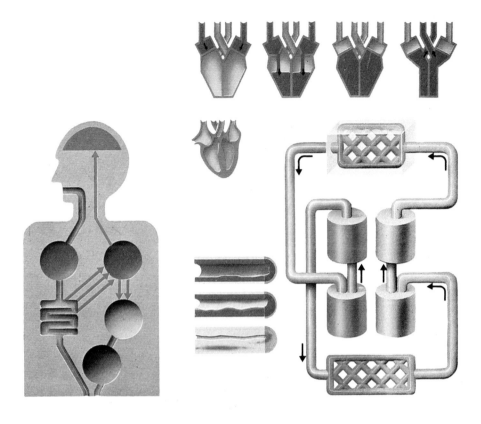

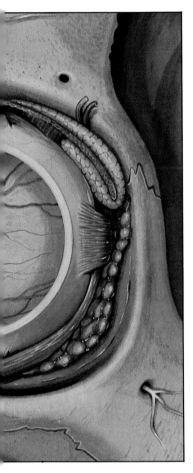

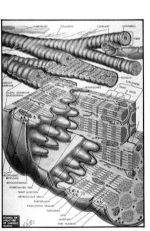

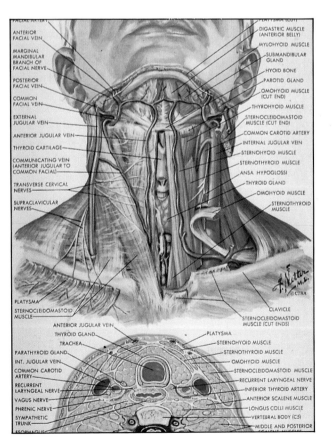

ANTERIOR FACIAL VEIN
MARGINAL MANDIBULAR BRANCH OF FACIAL NERVE
POSTERIOR FACIAL VEIN
COMMON FACIAL VEIN
EXTERNAL JUGULAR VEIN
ANTERIOR JUGULAR VEIN
THYROID CARTILAGE
COMMUNICATING VEIN (ANTERIOR JUGULAR TO COMMON FACIAL)
TRANSVERSE CERVICAL NERVES
SUPRACLAVICULAR NERVES

DIGASTRIC MUSCLE (ANTERIOR BELLY)
MYLOHYOID MUSCLE
SUBMANDIBULAR GLAND
HYOID BONE
PAROTID GLAND
OMOHYOID MUSCLE (CUT END)
THYROHYOID MUSCLE
STERNOCLEIDOMASTOID MUSCLE (CUT END)
COMMON CAROTID ARTERY
INTERNAL JUGULAR VEIN
STERNOHYOID MUSCLE
STERNOTHYROID MUSCLE
ANSA HYPOGLOSSI
THYROID GLAND
OMOHYOID MUSCLE
STERNOTHYROID MUSCLE

PLATYSMA
STERNOCLEIDOMASTOID MUSCLE
ANTERIOR JUGULAR VEIN
THYROID GLAND
PARATHYROID GLAND
INT. JUGULAR VEIN
COMMON CAROTID ARTERY
RECURRENT LARYNGEAL NERVE
VAGUS NERVE
PHRENIC NERVE
SYMPATHETIC TRUNK

CLAVICLE
STERNOCLEIDOMASTOID MUSCLE (CUT ENDS)
PLATYSMA
STERNOHYOID MUSCLE
STERNOTHYROID MUSCLE
OMOHYOID MUSCLE
STERNOCLEIDOMASTOID MUSCLE
RECURRENT LARYNGEAL NERVE
INFERIOR THYROID ARTERY
ANTERIOR SCALENE MUSCLE
LONGUS COLLI MUSCLE
VERTEBRAL BODY (C5)
MIDDLE AND POSTERIOR

OPPOSITE PAGE A progressive dissection of the contents of the eye sockets by Peter Cull relating the structures as if in the living body.

ABOVE These airbrushed cutaways help to rationalize physiological functions and make them accessible to the general reader.

LEFT AND FAR LEFT Professor Frank Netter's famous collection of several thousand paintings for CIBA are remarkable not only for the vast medical coverage but also for the clarity with which difficult scientific concepts and processes are explained, as in the dissections of the structures of the neck (left) and the cardiac muscle (far left).

6/TECHNICAL ILLUSTRATION

Illustration of any kind is simply a means of communication, either to enhance the written word or, as is often the case with technical illustration, as a language of its own. Technical illustration as we know it today developed with the advent of industry and mass-production, and the need for people to learn more about their environment and how things work. It is now a broad area of illustration associated with various specialized disciplines.

Some impetus for the development of technical illustration came from the unusual conditions of World War II. In Britain, for example, there was a sudden need for arms production on a massive scale: with many skilled industrial workers called to join the armed services, this presented a great problem. Training of unskilled people was achieved to a large extent by the use of perspective drawings and exploded diagrams which had to be clearly understood by non-specialists. This led to the development of servicing and spare parts manuals, all of which were, and still are, profusely illustrated.

In the post-war period in Britain and the USA, the development of the aerospace industry and vehicle manufacturing involved artists working in industrial drawing studios. These set an extremely high standard of technical illustration in areas of product development and marketing which is maintained in current practice. The tradition of instructional illustration typified by work done for maintenance manuals also has wider application, in different forms, in such areas as museum work and educational publishing. Illustration is today as necessary as the written word in communicating the complex subjects which are the everyday currency of the modern world.

AREAS OF WORK

Technical illustrators work mostly on a freelance basis, though some are employed in specialist areas such as design studios or museums, publishing, advertising, architecture, manufacturing and the film industry. Twenty years ago and more, the technical illustrator was trained through work in the commercial world. Today, however, various institutions offer specialist courses dealing with technique and forms of presentation, but it is still true to say that whatever art training the technical illustrator has received, there is a great deal to be learned from commercial practice. Working as part of a team and coping with deadlines set by clients are just two of the areas that schools or colleges have difficulty in simulating effectively.

Line work, airbrushing and painting are the primary techniques of technical illustration. With each of these techniques, it must be assumed that the artist is able to draw well freehand and has a good working knowledge of graphic design, typography, photography and printing processes. The ability to interpret plans (orthographic drawings) and to employ systems of projection and perspective is also essential.

There are particular conventions in technical illustration used to present all aspects of a specific product. Exterior views show the overall appearance, while exploded drawings explain the relationship of parts. Cut-aways and ghosted illustrations provide detail of inner components and workings normally concealed by the outer structure of the object. The technical illustrator may also be required to construct diagrams showing mechanical and electrical functions.

The skills of the illustrator must contribute to the all-important task of communicating clearly to the client the ideas that are proposed. Glossily finished artwork is no substitute for poor drawing and lack of understanding of the subject matter.

WORKING FOR INDUSTRY

Assume a freelance illustrator has been commissioned by a small firm to contribute drawings for the launching of a new food processor. Before company directors approve any new design they will require, apart from costs and projected sales estimates, some idea of what the product will look like. The brief for this task could be given to the illustrator by the engineering design department, who at this stage may only have produced rough drawings of the general arrangement of the product. After agreeing a fee, the illustrator's first task is to produce a series of technically correct roughs which are then presented to the engineers for approval. The next step is to finalize a presentation visual to submit to the Board of Directors.

Assuming all goes well and the product is put into production, the next stage is to produce repair manuals and publicity material.

REPAIR MANUALS

These are essentially publications for use by professional engineers, and are consequently free from publicity or sales coloration.

In a small firm, there is probably only one tech-

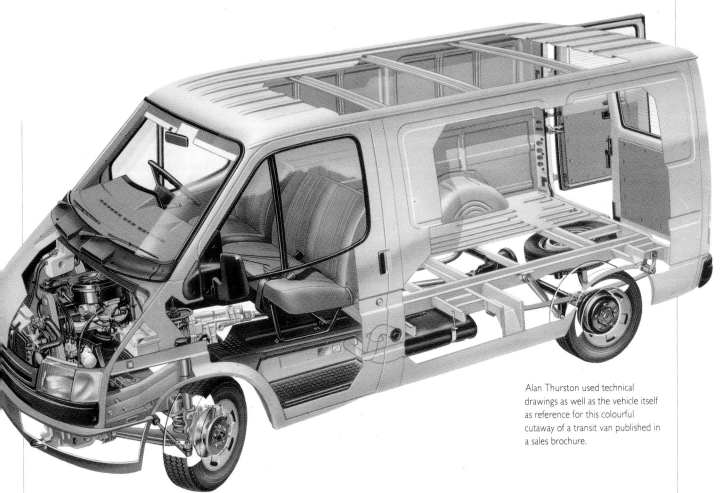

Alan Thurston used technical drawings as well as the vehicle itself as reference for this colourful cutaway of a transit van published in a sales brochure.

nical author employed, who may previously have worked specifically as a service engineer. This implies limited graphic and illustrative competence, hence the need to employ a freelance illustrator. In order to influence the graphic content of the manual, the illustrator should ensure that a close working relationship is quickly established with the writer. Not only can a good illustration take the place of many words, but when both are necessary, a verbal description can be much reinforced and expanded by apt illustration. Most of the conventions of technical illustration are used in work for repair manuals.

Costing is important, as always, and it is probably best to negotiate an hourly rate if possible; if an overall price is preferred, a limit must be set to the number of illustrations required. The author and illustrator must work out a flat plan so that each knows where the separate areas of responsibility lie.

PUBLICITY

Most companies use advertising agencies for their publicity, in which case the agency briefs the technical illustrator. As these agencies always work under pressure of time and competition, they may well give the

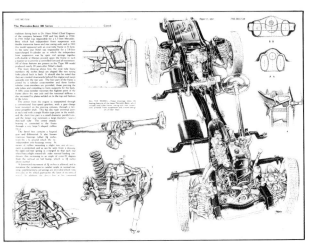

A Mercedes 200 drawn for *Motor* magazine in 1952, giving car enthusiasts a clear picture of the basic mechanical components.

1 Airbrushed cutaway of a locomotive engine for a general railway reference book.
2 and 3 A rough and final illustration by Joe Lawrence. In this type of illustration, technical detail is the paramount consideration.

4 and 5 Fine technical illustrations such as these examples by Joe Lawrence can be used creatively for promotion and advertising to emphasize the quality and reliability of the product.
6 In this cutaway of a watch by John Harwood, which was used in magazine advertisements, skilled draughtsmanship and airbrushing show what the eye cannot see, demonstrating the superiority of illustration over photography.
7 This cutaway by Paul Thurston was adapted to provide an illustration of both right- and left-hand drive.

RIGHT This finely finished pencil drawing by Rob Garrard is the end-result of several sketches which were needed to achieve the final colour illustration. The exploded view is a demonstration of the possible combinations of Lego materials.

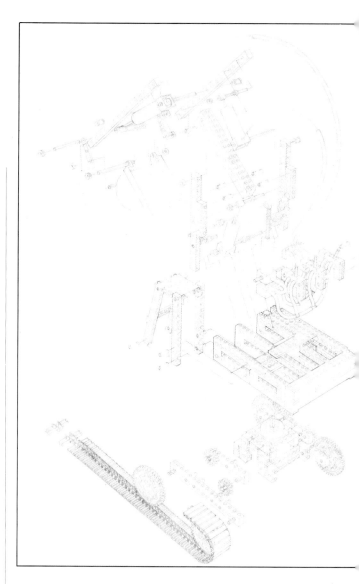

impression of desperate urgency, but there is usually no need to be intimidated if you believe good work must take a little longer.

It is worth noting here that most clients will only commission work if they can see something near (in style, at least) to what they require. A portfolio showing the scope of work and kept up to date is a must. It is of value to take photographs of current work, since it may be many months before the work is published and printed examples can be added to the portfolio.

The brief is usually given by the art director and includes visual roughs giving relatively precise guidelines for the image required, although style and interpretation are left to the illustrator. Highly finished techniques such as an airbrush rendering are favoured for technical subjects in advertising, but there is always a demand for a freer approach in descriptive artwork where an environment and figures may be included.

Costing should be on the generous side, as acceptance of the work often depends on its aesthetic appeal to more than one person, with the obvious contingency of changes or complete reworking.

WORKING FOR PUBLISHING

There are three different areas to consider in publishing: educational books aimed at schools and colleges; the range of general illustrated non-fiction and more elaborate or specialist publications; and magazines and journals. Although publishing in general is not the most highly paid area for an illustrator, it can be challenging and both rewarding and worthwhile. School books, in particular, are produced in small print runs and the price must be kept as low as possible; although this limits the amount of work feasible it does not detract from its interesting nature and educational value.

Publishers typically use freelance illustrators and writers, although often employing their own specialized staff for editorial work, book design and production. Normally the editor is responsible for commissioning illustrators and writers for educational books, while for titles in which the design content is a more significant element, it is the graphic designer who carries greater responsibility for this commissioning. Again, commissions are only given to illustrators after presentation of a suitable portfolio, but once established, a long working relationship can take place.

Monthly magazines tend to build a network of regular contributors, and often employ in-house artists.

This does not, however, eliminate the freelance artist as there is always a demand for new material and fresh ideas to maintain readership interest and improve circulation. It is obviously imperative that deadlines be scrupulously adhered to, since the chain of production and sales depends on this.

MUSEUM WORK

Major museums employ an exhibition design team which includes exhibition and graphic designers and also illustrators. However, most of the illustration for a large exhibition is given to a freelance artist or outside studio. The work is varied and interesting; it gives scope for creativity and offers the opportunity to work on a much larger scale than is possible in any other commercial area.

Exhibitions are initiated by the director of the museum with guidance from curators and exhibition design staff. At an early stage, plans are drawn up to show structures that it may be necessary to build, and to detail areas where specific subject matter is to be shown and illustrated. By the time the freelance illus-

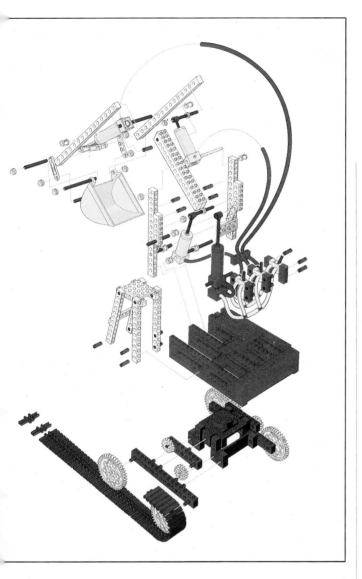

trator is called in, work on the structure is usually well under way and the place often looks more like a building site than a museum.

The brief is normally given by one of the members of the in-house design team, jointly with the curator of the subject area. It is usually in the form of a verbal discussion, together with a visit to the display site. Many things not encountered in other fields of work have to be taken into account in any exhibition: the fact that over a period of time, thousands of people will be touching and rubbing against the surfaces; the size of type to be used and graphic detail both needing to be legible from the appropriate viewing point; and the lighting appropriate to the exhibit and its structure. All these elements must be considered at the initial briefing.

Co-ordination of building and display exhibits is not only a problem for the museum; it also affects the illustrator's work schedule. But notwithstanding the many obstacles that can arise before completion of the work, it is most rewarding to have a part to play in what is often a long-lasting and educational show. The type of work here required of the technical illustrator in-cludes line diagrams, line perspectives, airbrush perspectives, paintings showing technical subjects in their environment and scientific discoveries depicted in the same way.

FILM INDUSTRY

This is in many ways similar to exhibition display, but does have special techniques of its own, such as glass-painting, and perspective layouts used to work out camera positions and distortions of set design.

Glass painting is used when action shots are required to be superimposed on still-life scenes. A painting is done on a sheet of glass with areas left clear in order to allow shots to be filmed through them.

It is not easy to obtain work in the film industry, as few are needed to do this type of work and the profession tends to train its own people.

BUSINESS PROCEDURE

Quoting for any form of artwork is never easy; quite apart from the initial discussions which can take some time and involve expense in travel, there are often unforeseen situations.

The following must be taken into account: how long the work will take; the cost of the necessary materials; contingencies such as changes in the brief after some work has already been done; and the number of times the work is to be used by the client.

The client will have an idea of the budget for this work, but may not divulge it. The artist must ascertain the type of finish required – for example, whether airbrush work or line drawing – as the client may not realize the difference in cost. The artist should also make it clear from the start that if changes are made to the initial brief after work has been done, a reassessment of the cost should take place.

Prior to undertaking any work, a written commitment or an official order must be obtained. The order often gives the date by which the work is required as well as unit cost and invoice instructions such as reference numbers, etc. It may also contain a legal passage which should be read before signing.

Anyone intending to work freelance in this field would do well to find a local accountant familiar with small concerns and freelance individuals' accounts. He or she can give the best advice on how to keep books and will fill in tax returns. Book-keeping can be basic, but it must be kept up to date.

7/ILLUSTRATION FOR INFORMATION

A designer, an illustrator, a typographer, a mathematician; and a creative thinker as well. Illustrating information requires many more skills than merely the ability to draw well. Yet it is the use of these combined qualities which makes the task not only demanding but interesting, and also fun.

It is a task which is in increasing demand. The twentieth century has seen a deluge of information. A wide range of bodies from government departments and international organizations to private companies and individuals collect the flood of statistics and technological data which assail us at every turn. Interesting, sometimes essential information; but how much of it is palatable? Too often it is discarded because it looks boring, heavyweight and impenetrable: our brains reel.

The job of the information designer and illustrator is to make information visible and therefore accessible to the reader. Firstly, the task is to attract attention; secondly, to make clear 'at a glance' the subject matter of the information; and thirdly, and perhaps most importantly, to explain the information, however detailed or complex, clearly to the reader. A good chart not only succeeds on all these counts, but via a creative visual narrative embellishes and emphasizes the statistical purpose of the information.

HISTORY AND BACKGROUND

There has always been a need to communicate information. Before the advent of general literacy, pictorial representation was one of the main options. Painted or carved friezes described how a battle was won, a king buried, an ambassador received. The need to explain things in exact detail accompanied the developments in science. More information was being collected, more theories explained; people wanted to know how things worked. Inventions in mathematics, and especially geometry, started to provide a basis for plotting certain information. René Descartes, in 1637, outlined the form of the graph in a footnote to his book *Discourse on the Method of Rightly Conducting the Reason and Seeking Truth in Sciences*. The graph, with its grid of criss-crossing lines against which information is plotted, is well-known today. It's easy to forget that it was the first of its kind.

Descartes' theories were developed by other mathematicians, but it was a Scotsman named William Playfair who, towards the end of the eighteenth century, started to make practical applications of the theories. It

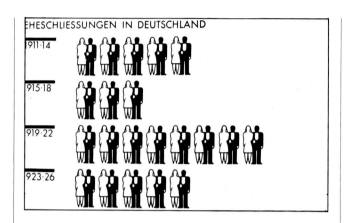

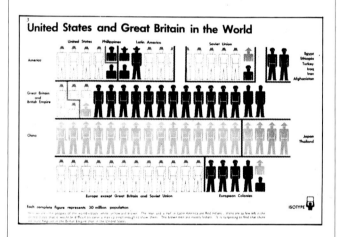

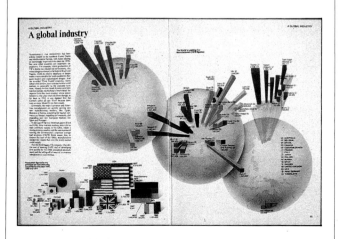

TOP AND ABOVE Bar charts using Otto Neurath's picture language called 'Isotype'. Each symbol represents one unit, and is repeated in accordance with the statistics.

ABOVE An abstract and pictorial bar chart, using 3-D, and representing car production.

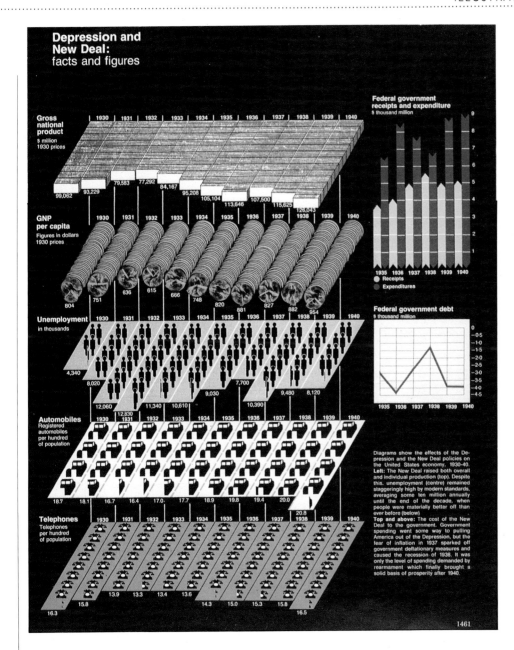

Depression and New Deal: facts and figures

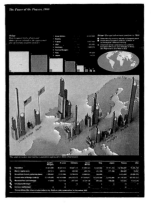

is to him that we attribute the invention of the bar chart, the line graph (also called fever graph, by association with temperature charts) and the pie diagram. His first inventions appeared in his *Commercial and Political Atlas,* published in 1786, which contained 44 charts, including the first bar charts and line graphs. As the charting method was new to people, Playfair was extremely careful about explaining everything and even included the raw statistical information as well. His charts dealt with imports and exports, the effect of war on Britain's National Debt, the population sizes of Europe's capitals and so on. In 1805 he published the first pie diagram in his *Statistical Account of the United States of America.* Delicately hand-coloured, it shows the proportional size of each of the states currently in the Union. It is inscribed: 'This newly invented method is intended to show proportions in a striking manner.'

As the new century progressed people began to collect more and more statistics, but it wasn't until the early twentieth century that the next leap forward was made by Dr Otto Neurath of the Vienna Museum of Social and Economic Studies. In the 1920s Dr Neurath devised a system of pictorial representation called 'isotype' (International System of Picture Education). The system was extremely logical and was very strictly applied to the statistics. The diagrams contained no decorative or distracting elements. The symbols used were simply drawn and always repeated as units to show quantity. Devices such as enlarging the symbol or using 3-D images were outlawed.

Since Playfair and Neurath, diagrammatic conventions have developed considerably. As the reader has become more familiar with these we don't need to repeat information as laboriously as Playfair did. And perhaps, despite Neurath's insistence on chart discipline, we look for more visual excitement and variety today.

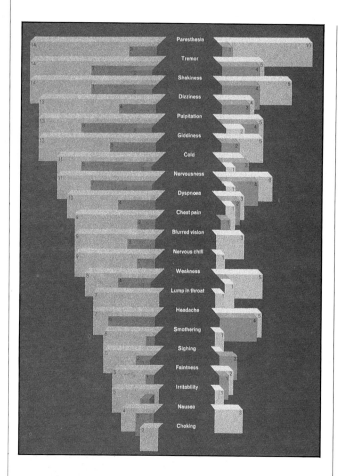

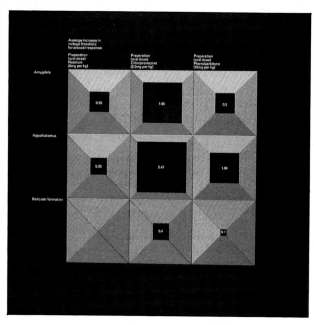

QUANTITATIVE INFORMATION

This section deals with statistical information. The four ways of translating figures into charts are:

1. The bar chart.
2. The pie diagram.
3. The line (or fever) graph.
4. The table.

It's important to remember when designing charts and diagrams that you must assess, right at the start of any assignment, into which of these categories the raw information must naturally fall.

THE BAR CHART. *Definition:* Specific quantities are each represented by a bar corresponding in height or length to the amount stated.

Uses: Bar charts are used to plot figures so they can be compared. A wide variety of information can be shown by this method. Comparisons between two or more sets of figures can be drawn within the same chart. The actual figures are either placed adjacent to the 'bar', or are plotted against a scale.

Misuses: Do not use a bar chart when there are so many figures the bars would become too thin in the available space: a table is more appropriate if space is limited. Also, it should not be used when the 'flow' of figures needs to be clearly seen: in this case a line graph is more appropriate.

Creative notes: As with all types of charts in this section the form can be either abstract or pictorial. If an abstract form is chosen then the distinctive features of the charts rely on the style and colour of the form. 3-D bars can be used, but in this case, ensure the reader is in no doubt about which part of the image represents the calculations.

If, on the other hand, a pictorial treatment is favoured then there are several options. The image can be repeated as in the isotype technique; a suitable image can be extended to correspond with the calculations, or an overall image may be chosen and the constituent parts varied to carry the information. As with all design and illustration work, the skill lies in finding an image which not only represents the subject matter but also reflects the meaning of the information.

THE PIE DIAGRAM. *Definition:* In this diagrammatic convention, a whole shape is divided into segments representing the statistics.

Uses: The pie diagram is used when a total statistic is

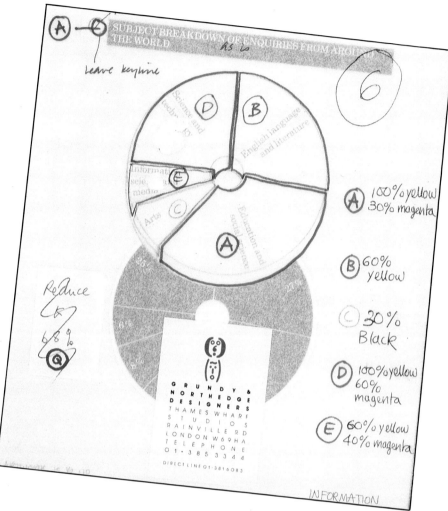

BELOW Here we see a combination of bar and pie charts.

BOTTOM The circle used for this pie diagram is easily divisible, and a shadow underneath is used to carry part of the statistical information. The version on the left shows instructions for colour printing.

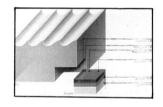

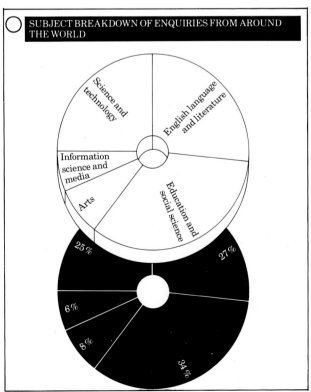

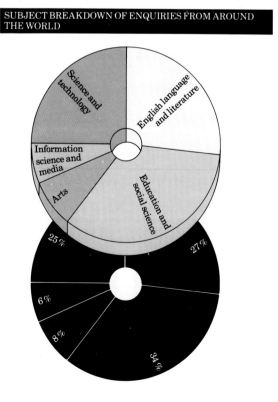

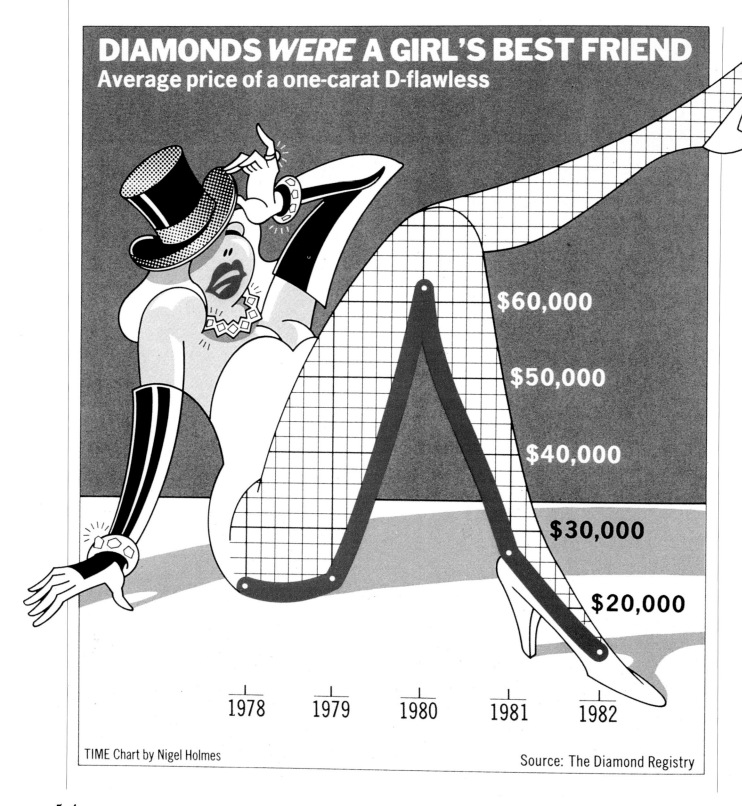

DIAMONDS *WERE* A GIRL'S BEST FRIEND
Average price of a one-carat D-flawless

$60,000

$50,000

$40,000

$30,000

$20,000

1978 1979 1980 1981 1982

TIME Chart by Nigel Holmes

Source: The Diamond Registry

SICK SYSTEMS *total passengers in millions/adult cash fare*

	1950	1955	1960	1965	1970	1975	1980
New York†	2,334/10¢	1,778/15¢	1,782/15¢	1,830/15¢	1,667/30¢	1,469/35¢	1,327/60¢
Chicago	1,325/15¢	990/20¢	847/25¢	792/25¢	661/45¢	650/45¢	692/80¢*
Philadelphia	828/12¢	622/18¢	568/22¢	419/25¢	274/30¢	314/35¢	330/65¢
Boston (subway; bus)	494/15;10¢	288/20;15¢	256/20;15¢	265/20;10¢	254/25;20¢	245/25;20¢	280/50;25¢
Detroit	332/15¢	216/20¢	130/25¢	112/25¢	112/40¢	77/45¢	70/60¢
Los Angeles	321/10¢	187/17¢	167/15¢	193/25¢	199/30¢	218/25¢	353/65¢
Baltimore	288/15¢	168/18¢	125/25¢	116/25¢	78/30¢	127/30¢	115/50¢
Pittsburgh	272/15¢	137/20¢	94/27¢	104/30¢	104/35¢	110/40¢	106/75¢
San Francisco	250/10¢	200/15¢	202/15¢	198/15¢	201/25¢	170/25¢	295/50¢
Atlanta	N.A./10¢	91/15¢	74/20¢	71/25¢	65/35¢	75/15¢	119/50¢
U.S. TOTALS	17,246	11,529	9,395	8,253	7,332	6,972	8,228

†Does not include transfers
*January 1, 1981
▼1951 figure

Source: American Public Transit Association
and local transit systems
TIME Chart by Nigel Holmes

FAR LEFT This line, or 'fever', graph is a fine example by Nigel Holmes showing how the shape of the plotted graph can create the image itself.

LEFT Here a potentially uninteresting list of figures has been turned into a lively chart by the same artist. The combination of information and appropriate imagery captures our attention and keeps us reading.

subdivided into categories by means of percentages. The circle is the most accurate mathematical device to use, as with the aid of a protractor the segments are calculated and the proportions of the information become immediately apparent. The percentages can be added either directly or by means of a key.

Misuses: Do not use a pie where the information has very many subdivisions. This leads to the segments being impossibly small, causing difficulties with labelling.

Creative notes: Although a circle is the most widely used form for pie diagrams, other devices can be used: for example, a semi- or quarter-circle could be employed. Pictorially, any shape which the reader can recognize as finite can be used, but it's important that the shape chosen can be subdivided accurately; an irregular shape leads to the information being distorted. If a series of percentage statistics are to be compared, the shapes must all be exactly the same size and height so that direct comparisons can be drawn.

THE LINE GRAPH. *Definition:* Statistics are represented by a line on a grid. The grid has two axes; one represents time, the other quantity.

Uses: A line graph is used when the flow, or rise and fall, of the figures over a period of time is the most important factor. It can be used for any one set of statistics, or comparisons can be drawn between two or more sets in the same graph.

Misuses: This presentation is inappropriate when there is very little variation in the statistics or when a sudden great increase would provide difficulties with the scale. In this case, a table is more suitable. Tables should also be preferred to graphs when there is too much information to be clearly plotted in the available space.

Creative notes: The line graph can be either abstract or pictorial, two- or three-dimensional. An image can either contain a straightforward graph or, more interestingly, become the chart itself. The grid can be treated in a way relevant to the subject matter. It's good to explore all the possibilities.

THE TABLE. *Definition:* A series of statistics typeset in columns.

Uses: The table can be used for all the information which can be presented in the above charts, and indeed for many other types of information too. It is often used for statistics which are too disparate or too close in scale to be visualized; where exact numbers have to be read; or where space is too limited for a visual.

Misuses: It is a shame to use a table when there is an opportunity to make the statistics immediately visible by using one of the other methods described.

Creative notes: Tables can be made more appealing by using an illustrative element creatively: the table can be contained within an overall illustration, symbols can be used either in conjunction with or in place of type, 3-D abstract shapes can be employed, and so on. It is essential to have good typographic skills when tackling this one. An accurate type specification will save hours in the paste-up stage.

NON-QUANTITATIVE INFORMATION

This section looks at diagrams which are not concerned with statistics but are more to do with explaining things. They divide roughly into the following four types:

1 Flow diagrams.
2 Chronological charts.
3 Relationship charts.
4 Maps.

FLOW DIAGRAMS. *Definition:* A flow diagram describes a process. It progresses from a start to a finish, although the movement may be cyclical.

Uses: It can be used to describe a physical process; for example, a manufacturing system or an event in nature or science. It can also be used as a decision-making aid. Where there are complicated instructions for carrying out a procedure, a flow diagram showing the steps and options can assist the reader much more than a paragraph of text.

Creative notes: As with most charts, either abstract or pictorial images can be used as appropriate. Where the subject matter is a process in nature or industry, a pictorial approach will naturally assist the reader. However, it is important in this case to eliminate superfluous pictorial information.

Decision-making charts are usually designed with abstract imagery. Here the layout and typographic skills of the designer or illustrator are critical.

CHRONOLOGICAL CHARTS. *Definition:* Chronological charts are concerned with the progress of events where the time period is a significant factor.

Uses: The most well-known application is the historical time chart. Against a grid representing the time-scale the events, either natural or manmade, are plotted. However, the chart may be concerned with the development of scientific or philosophical ideas rather than physical events.

Creative notes: Historical time charts lend themselves to a pictorial treatment, as do some scientific theories, for example, the development of ape to man. It is important to ensure the time-scale does not get lost among the imagery and the reader can easily relate it to the events. Some subjects are suited to an abstract treatment.

LEFT A pictorial flow diagram showing the beer-making process.

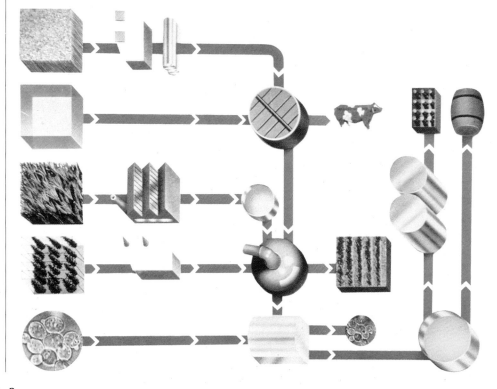

BELOW An abstract chronological chart with an enlargement using 3-D and airbrush to show a certain section of time.

BELOW MIDDLE AND BOTTOM These flow diagrams use pictorial imagery to achieve a degree of realism. The diagrams of car production show two solutions to the same problem, both using the 'conveyor belt' to maintain the correct sequence of events.

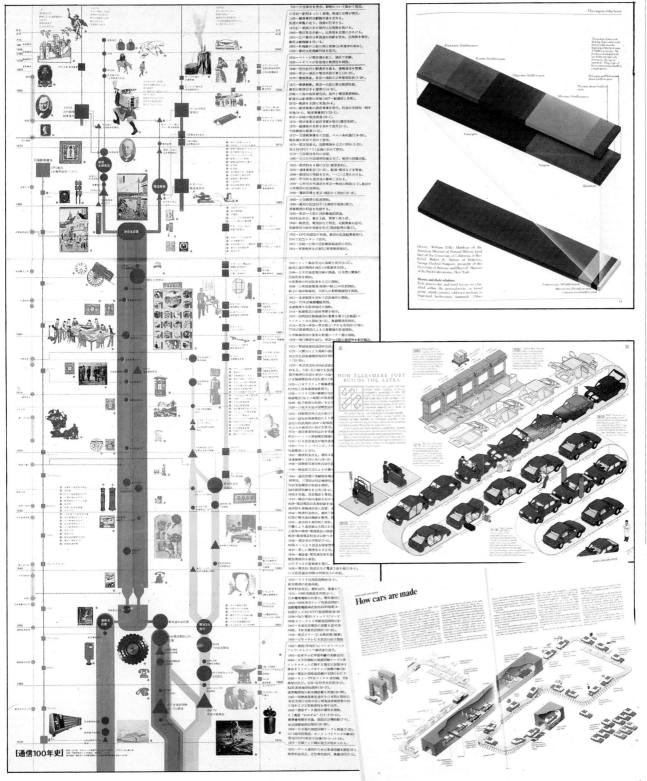

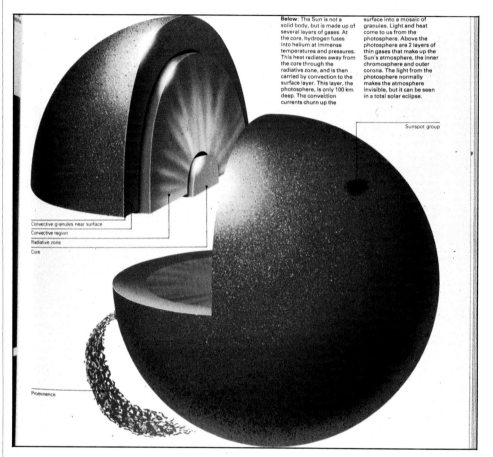

Below: The Sun is not a solid body, but is made up of several layers of gases. At the core, hydrogen fuses into helium at immense temperatures and pressures. This heat radiates away from the core through the radiative zone, and is then carried by convection to the surface layer. This layer, the photosphere, is only 100 km deep. The convection currents churn up the surface into a mosaic of granules. Light and heat come to us from the photosphere. Above the photosphere are 2 layers of thin gases that make up the Sun's atmosphere, the inner chromosphere and outer corona. The light from the photosphere normally makes the atmosphere invisible, but it can be seen in a total solar eclipse.

Sunspot group

Convective granules near surface
Convective region
Radiative zone
Core

Prominence

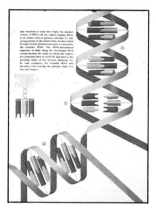

ABOVE The use of airbrush helps to convey the distinctive molecular structure of DNA.

LEFT A cross-section in 3-D to show the relationship betwen the various constituent parts of the sun.

RELATIONSHIP CHARTS. *Definition:* These charts show the connections between different people or groups of people.

Uses: The most widely-used form is the 'family tree', one of the most familiar types of diagram. This chart begins with one or two people and spreads out as marriages are made and children born. Another type of relationship chart, which is less well known, is the organogram. Here the internal departments of an organization (often a business) are shown in relation to each other. Emphasis may be laid on the number of staff employed, or where the power of decision-making lies. Diagrams can also show the relationship between businesses; for example, the client and the supplier network.

Creative notes: These charts can be treated as abstract or pictorial but often they are much more fun if the latter style is chosen. When planning the diagram, ensure enough room is left for all the captioning and this is not squeezed in as an afterthought.

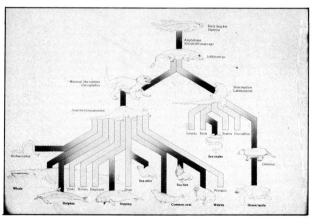

ABOVE A 'family tree' using airbrush and pictorial imagery.

BELOW AND RIGHT This diagrammatic map of the London Underground (inset below), designed originally by Henry Beck in 1933, broke all earlier traditions. The world map uses geography to identify the countries but not their location. On the stylized geographic map advertising a business park, visual interest was added with small graphic devices.

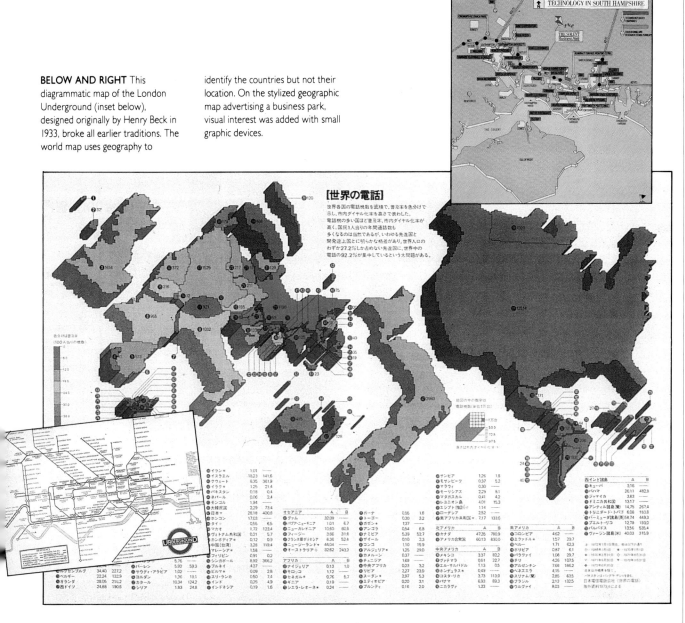

MAPS. *Definition:* A two-dimensional representation of a geographical location or a system.

Uses: Maps have various uses. The most obvious one is for direction-finding. These maps may vary from localized street plans, through transport systems, to maps of entire countries, continents and oceans. The other main use is to give information about a location: this could be its external connections or data about the place itself; what it produces, consumes, its population size, and so on.

Creative notes: When designing direction-finding maps, many considerations have to be taken into account. What sort of person is going to use the map and under what physical conditions? Will there be good lighting? Will the map be in their hands or on a wall? In some circumstances a truly accurate geographical map is unnecessary, a useful example of this being the map of the London Underground rail system.

Information maps subdivide into two categories: geographical and cartograms. In the former, the map may be accurate to the geography or abstracted to any degree considered appropriate. Statistical information can be plotted on the maps in the form of symbols: these can vary in size according to the statistical information. Bar or pie charts can also be integrated with the map. However, extremely careful planning is required so that the geography is not obscured by the information.

In a cartogram the size of the country is changed in proportion to the statistical information it represents. For example, a cartogram of comparative world population sizes would show a huge China compared to a small Australia. A cartogram can be used to represent two sets of statistics. In this case the size of countries would depict one set and the countries could be represented three-dimensionally for the other set. Again, extreme care needs to be taken that one country does not obscure another. Cartograms require very careful mathematical calculations and arrangement so they still resemble the countries they are representing.

WORKING METHODS

In this section we look at all the stages of carrying out a project from taking the brief to delivering the artwork. This is illustrated by various stages of an actual commission carried out by Grundy and Northedge for *Design* magazine.

TAKING THE BRIEF. A project usually begins with a phone call from a client. Before arranging a meeting, find out over the phone whether the job will suit your skills and if you can complete the work in the period required: this might save you and your client a wasted meeting.

However, assuming the job is suitable then the briefing meeting is one of the most important stages. It is essential to gain a clear idea of the project requirements in order that the next stage, the presentation rough, fully answers the client's brief. Follow a checklist of the important points:

The brief: Is the person who briefs you experienced at commissioning? An inexperienced client may not have drawn up a proper brief, and may not be aware of all the work stages involved. In this case it is the designer's or illustrator's task to write up the brief after the meeting, and it's often useful to send this to the client. Make sure the client understands the stages of work you will be going through, and provide a schedule of the points at which checking or approval is required.

Presentation of roughs: Some clients are unused to seeing roughs, so it's important these do not lead to misinterpretation. More experienced clients, who may themselves be designers, will not require such finished presentations.

The function of the artwork: Who is the end user of the diagram, and do they have any prior knowledge of the subject?

Information: Is the client supplying all the information, or will you need to do research yourself? Try to obtain all the material you need, including picture reference, from the client, as you can then be sure it is correct. Go through it all at the meeting to be sure you understand it; this saves phone calls later on. If the information is not available complete at the time of the briefing meeting, make sure the client is aware that the delivery date for the artwork may be affected. If you are involved in research, don't forget to charge for this.

Technical details: Check the reproduction size of the diagram and ask for a page grid. Note whether the diagram is black-and-white or colour, and discuss how the artwork is to be done: for example, full colour or black-and-white with tints specified. Get details of the printing process to be used. Ask if you are to handle typography for the diagram (which is preferable) or whether the client organizes this. Is there a specified type style to follow and are you responsible for ordering the type?

Timing: Agree with the client dates for showing the rough, the accurate tracing (if necessary) and the final artwork.

Fee: Don't feel rushed into agreeing a fee. Sometimes the client has a price in mind, but you should consider this in your own time and feel sure that it is fair for the work involved. Alternatively, if you are asked to quote, say you will ring later with a price: don't forget to include cost of materials. Follow this up with written confirmation.

Orders: When the budget is agreed, obtain an order before starting work. Discuss payment terms, that is, how long between invoicing and payment, and check who will own the copyright on the work. This may seem a lot of detail, but it marks a professional approach and is essential procedure.

PRESENTATION ROUGH. Once you are ready to start work, the first job is to analyse the information. Sort out the information logically and make notes on its structure. Clarify any points with the client if you need to. Consider into which of the diagram categories the data most naturally falls. What are the points which need to be made and how will the diagram bring these out?

Next comes the conceptual stage. Are you constructing the diagram with abstract or pictorial imagery? Is there an appropriate idea to hold the information, or will the data dictate the imagery? You may need to start drawing up one or two ideas roughly to see if they will work. Once the approach is selected, progress to plotting the information. Consider what degree of finish is required in the visual shown to the client. You may not need to demonstrate the whole chart plotted, but you must be sure it is all going to fit.

DEVELOPMENT WORK. When the rough has been approved, progress to the tracing stage. Consider the appropriate size for the artwork. You need to take into account not only the size you are happy to work at (generally ¼- or ½-up on the reproduction size), but also reproduction factors. For example, if you are doing full colour artwork which is to be scanned direct at the printers, the

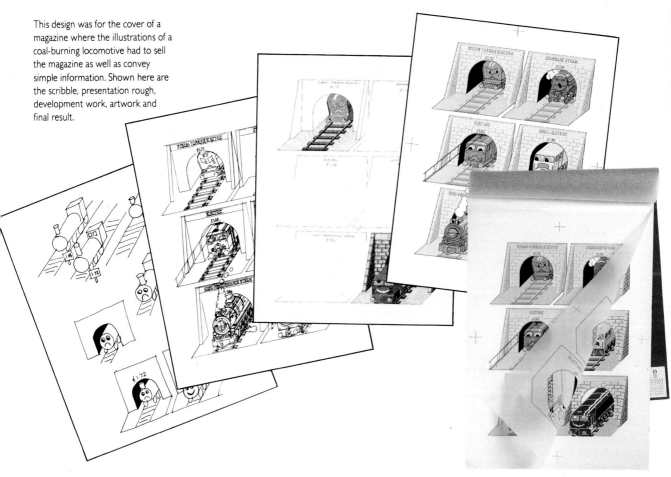

This design was for the cover of a magazine where the illustrations of a coal-burning locomotive had to sell the magazine as well as convey simple information. Shown here are the scribble, presentation rough, development work, artwork and final result.

artwork must be sized to fit the scanning drum. Also, ensure you can obtain all the artwork materials you will need. Once the accurate tracing is finished, it is a good precaution to let your client check it.

ARTWORK. First order your typesetting. This will enable you to progress the artwork while the setters are setting the type. The copy can be proof-read by the client and any revisions ordered as necessary.

The method of doing the artwork depends on your own particular style. It may be full colour artwork, painted, airbrushed, crayoned, collaged or even montaged. It could be black-and-white with a tint specification for the printer to lay the colours, or simply monochrome. Before taking or sending it to the client, photocopy it together with any printers' instructions so you can refer to the copy later should a query arise. Leave your client enough time to check the artwork and get back to you with corrections if necessary. If they are author's corrections (i.e. not your mistakes) do not be afraid to charge for making them.

A FINAL NOTE

Designers and illustrators beware! Diagrams are not just pretty pictures. The information they carry deserves to be accurately represented, otherwise every-one involved, including the reader, is wasting his or her time.

With statistical information, it is all too easy to misrepresent the data in the search for an eye-catching visual. The diagram has to be successful at all levels; the initial attraction of the reader; the 'at a glance' explanation of the main points; and the 'in-depth' study. If it fails in any of these, diagrams will come to be mistrusted by people and the opportunity is lost.

One of the most common faults in chart-making is changing the scale of pictorial symbols. It has been shown that Dr Neurath repeated his symbols to repre-sent quantity. As long as the symbols remain the same size, this is clear enough. However, often we see charts where the symbol has been enlarged in height to cor-respond with the statistic. The factor the designer has overlooked is that the width of the image has also in-creased. This gives a false visual representation of the relative percentages.

The designer and illustrator, aware of the respon-sibility for accurately conveying information, should be in continuing demand by today's producers of raw infor-mation. It is essential for competitive industries, govern-ments and organizations to communicate effectively. As members of the design profession we must ensure we are given the opportunity to carry out that task.

2
DESIGN

Introduction by
F.H.K. Henrion

INTRODUCTION TO DESIGN

Design has become a growth industry or, more accurately, a growth profession. There seems to be an ever greater demand for design, and college graduates who a few years ago might have found considerable difficulty in getting a job now find themselves in a seller's market. If they show a modicum of competence, talent and application, employment is no problem.

This book deals with most aspects of graphic design. All of them come under the heading 'Visual communication', and if this concept is properly understood, it becomes apparent that there are certain common denominators among the various specializations. This commonality of purpose ought to have priority in consideration of all the subject areas described in the following chapters. The concept of visual communication divides into three main elements: communication, methodology, and visual ecology.

COMMUNICATION

Advertising, corporate graphics, publishing of books and magazines, packaging and promotions, film, television and computer graphics, visual signing – the common aim of all these media is to communicate something to a certain audience, or target public. This may be the general public, or a selected audience such as professional, ethnic or political groups, or sections of the audience targeted by age, for example, teenagers or senior citizens. Considering the enormous variety of these groups, it stands to reason that any message sent to any audience must have a considered approach and form. A children's book must look different from a school textbook, which in turn has an appearance very different from that of an engineering manual.

In communication theory, there is a sender who determines the message (the client) and a recipient to whom the message is addressed (the target public). The designer stands between these two to encode the message. If the code of the message is such that the recipient is unable to decode it, the message is obviously lost – the designer has failed in his or her task. This failure makes an important point; namely, that the designer's skill and ingenuity in devising codes (design ability) is wasted if he or she does not know and understand the characteristics and peculiarities of the target public.

Therefore it is imperative for designers to have empathy, i.e. the capacity to put themselves into the mental and physical conditions of the persons to whom

This view of Hong Kong is an example of visual overkill: so many messages are thrust at us that it is impossible to single out the important ones. As a photograph it conveys a fine sense of excitement, but the designer of each shop front or advertisement might have wished for more neutral surroundings.

they address their messages, in order to look at the world in the way the target audience does.

In commercial terms, empathy has become marketing – which means analysing, qualifying and quantifying a market, or market section. As design, the methodical application of empathy, has become the most important marketing tool, in all its many manifestations, it is very clear that it is necessary for the designer to understand it and its requirements.

The message itself always contains some sort of information. In fact, every visual medium conveys information. Therefore, the designer's job is to create attention, achieve comprehension and make this information memorable. A unique, original approach combined with the greatest clarity and simplicity will achieve these objectives. These principles apply equally whether the information communicated is a fairytale, a flight timetable, a listing of stock exchange values, a political election appeal, the announcement of a cultural event, or the contents and instructions for use of any type of product.

Visual appearance – form, colour, texture and typography – are entirely conditioned by the information to be conveyed and by the target public.

METHODOLOGY

Long experience in the practice of all the various design areas has proved that if the design activity is seen as problem solving, a certain sequence of procedures will help towards the eventual solution, and ensure that the solution is the best and most appropriate answer to the problem.

The first steps in this design procedure are:
- Statement of problem;
- Survey of problem area;
- Analysis leading to the brief formulating the problem, including a list of objectives or goals, of criteria, constraints and parameters. The sum of all constraints and parameters defines what to avoid and what not to do. This points the direction in which to aim, and thus formulates the goals to be achieved.

Rudolph Arnheim, the author of *Visual Thinking*, states: 'Man exploits his mental endowment more fully if he not only acts intelligently but also understands intellectually why he acts as he does, and why his procedures work.' This means that a body of theoretical knowledge helps the designer in his or her work, and that thinking is in itself an essential part of the work. To

Company identity is one of the major areas of graphic design, with the profileration of logos in the past 20 years or so symbolizing the growth of the 'design industry'. Nowadays a company begins to think in terms of corporate identity almost as soon as it is formed, whether it is a small or a large concern, and the logo must express something of this as well as being visually memorable.

Chrysler Corporation, USA; Lippincott & Margulies

Häberli, Möbeltypen, Sweden; Marcel Wyss

Haslett Corporation, USA; Robert Pease

Handelsgesellschaft, Germany; Anton Stankowski

Bayrische Motorenwerke AG, Germany; Wappen von Bayern

Nuclear Disarmament, UK; Hugh Brock/Pat Arrowsmith

Intergastra, Germany; Peter Wehr

Alitalia, Italy; Walter Landor

design is to have a plan before it is carried out: in design the thinking process must at all times precede the doing.

It can be said that all design activity is an ordering process, and the measure of order depends upon the amount of simplification and unification achieved in given circumstances. As Mies van der Rohe put it: 'Design is doing more with less'. This much-quoted maxim holds a lot of general truth, and can almost always be used as a valid criterion for comparing design solutions: it is common that the designer will reject one solution in favour of a simpler alternative – one which does more with less.

VISUAL ECOLOGY

Everything which is not organic is manmade, and has been designed – however badly. We can speak today of visual ecology – as the organic ecology suffers from the destruction of rare animal species and vegetation, and is damaged by pollution of water, air and environment, so we also suffer from visual pollution through over-production of visual 'noise'. This consists of messages which do not concern us, yet impinge on our eyes. We are all subject to the intrusion of information which does not concern us. Any relevant message must com-

pete with and rise above the others to be noticed.

A great deal of our visual environment is made up from graphic artefacts, from early morning until we go to bed at night: the packages in kitchen and bathroom; newspapers read over breakfast or travelling to work; the street and transport signs, shop fascias and hoarding posters which we see as we travel; the internal sign systems in the workplace; various types of publications; and means of communication of every kind – typewriter, telex, computer, photocopier, fax machine. In fact, everyone is exposed to constant attack from innumerable graphic signs and symbols.

But as design is indivisible, these graphic elements are set within the context of the related manmade environment – architecture and interiors, furniture and furnishings, decor and fittings. Considering all this as our visual ecology, designers have a lot to answer for. The sensitive understanding of connections and relationships between all manmade objects ought to condition the nature and quality of design.

The principle of ecology is to see the interdependence of all things, the relationships of people to people, people to things, and things to things. That every designed item must be seen in relation to all others is the reason why it is important not only to look at the special-

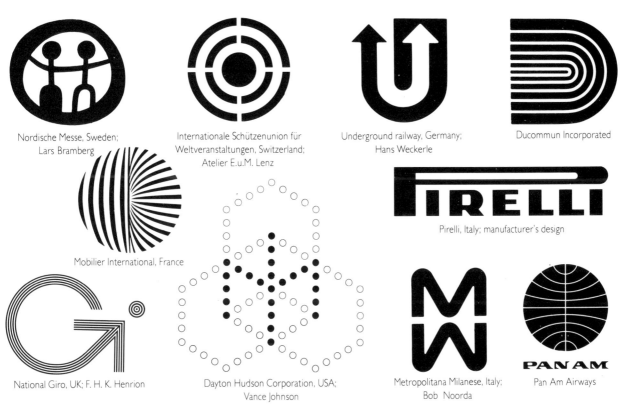

Nordische Messe, Sweden;
Lars Bramberg

Internationale Schützenunion für
Weltveranstaltungen, Switzerland;
Atelier E.u.M. Lenz

Underground railway, Germany;
Hans Weckerle

Ducommun Incorporated

Mobilier International, France

Pirelli, Italy; manufacturer's design

National Giro, UK; F. H. K. Henrion

Dayton Hudson Corporation, USA;
Vance Johnson

Metropolitana Milanese, Italy;
Bob Noorda

Pan Am Airways

ist areas dealt with individually in the following chapters, but also to see them all in their interrelationships. If one accepts the design process as one of ordering, then it becomes imperative to ensure that these ordered solutions, wherever they occur, can be co-ordinated on a somewhat higher level to achieve a sensible visual environment. Corporate identity design attempts this kind of positive and beneficial co-ordination.

Yet in context there is a function to the message which must be considered. If 'Drink Pepsi-Cola' shouts louder than 'Beware, children crossing the road', then the producers are in danger of losing their young consumers. Unless the function of each design is clearly defined, it is unlikely to perform well, but likely to contribute to the visual pollution. One function of a packaged brand of goods is to be seen on the supermarket shelf, to catch the eye of the roving customer: this happens in a matter of seconds. This pack, once purchased, may be seen and used in the kitchen, bathroom or dining room for months, where its once-only sales function becomes a daily insult to the domestic environment. This is just one example: similar instances can be identified in any design area.

CONCLUSION

So let us remember that whatever the design medium,

unless the aimed-for communication is noticed, understood and acted upon by those to whom it is directed; unless the problem is analysed, defined and resolved to ensure its appropriateness; unless the design fits happily into its wider visual ecology, in which it will be seen and used; unless all these thing come together it cannot be good design, however beautiful it seems.

Designers must act as a responsible body of people; they must be concerned that, besides solving problems successfully, they also make a contribution towards the quality of life in their society. They must also by their approach and conduct deserve the authority to be listened to by clients and have their advice on things visual followed and acted upon. This can only happen if designers are seen as professionals in the same way as are lawyers, medical practitioners or accountants. Professionals have clients whom they advise, while businessmen and industrialists have customers with whom they negotiate terms: only high professional standards, ethics and codes of practice can ensure the status of designers. Hence the importance of looking at design not as a business or industry, but as a profession.

8/CORPORATE GRAPHICS

Corporate identity is the explicit management of the ways in which a company's activities are perceived. All organizations have an identity, but how is it defined?

When a company is new or small, or both, its identity emerges, naturally and spontaneously, around the owner's idea of the way it should do business. The identity of a hairdresser, for example, inevitably is focused around what the owner wants the business to be, what his or her interests are, whether he or she wants to deal with young people, older people, men, women or both. The way the shop is designed, fitted out, what it is called, where it is located, how it is staffed, all directly derive from the owner's ideas and perceptions.

When an organization becomes bigger and more complex, when it is based in a number of different locations, carries out diverse activities, even operates perhaps under a number of different names, its identity can no longer be so simple and spontaneous. The need for an identity policy to hold, shape and present the whole organization becomes greater, but the ability to project a policy implicitly and spontaneously disappears.

At some stage in an organization's life, as it grows and becomes more complex, it becomes necessary explicitly to control or manage the ways by which the organization's activities are perceived. This is what is usually called corporate identity.

THE COMPONENTS OF CORPORATE IDENTITY

Corporate identity is concerned with four major areas of activity:

Products/services – what you make or sell;
Environments   – where you make or sell it;
Communication   – how to describe what you do;
Behaviour   – how people within the company behave to each other and to outsiders.

Corporate identity involves a number of disciplines, most but not all of which are design disciplines. The design disciplines are product design, architectural and interior design, and graphic design. Corporate identity has close links with marketing, advertising, public relations and human resource development. In addition, it has a relationship with a number of other management disciplines and resources.

The aspects of identity with which this chapter is primarily concerned are those involving graphic communication. These are sometimes, but not always, the

When products are not intrinsically different from each other and their packaging is also very similar, their identity is derived from the way they are promoted and the presentation of the logo.

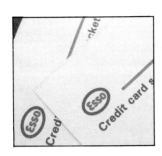

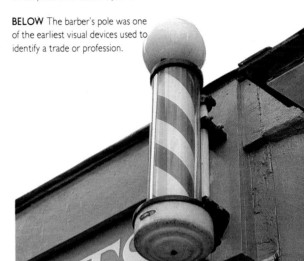

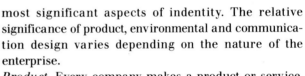

most significant aspects of indentity. The relative significance of product, environmental and communication design varies depending on the nature of the enterprise.

Product. Every company makes a product or service. Sometimes the product and how it performs is much the most significant factor in influencing the way in which the organization is perceived. It is, for example, the appearance and performance of a Jaguar car which primarily affects the way we perceive the company's identity.

Environment. Every company operates in buildings; offices, factories, showrooms. These influence the way the organization is seen and the way in which it sees itself. Sometimes, as in retail stores, the environment becomes the crucial factor in presenting the identity idea.

Communication. In some companies, products derive their identity not from what they intrinsically are, but from the packaging, advertising and other promotional material by which they are surrounded. In this case, communication, especially graphic communication, leads the identity mix.

Behaviour. In companies providing a service as opposed to products, like airlines, say, it is the way people behave that has a crucial influence on the identity. Here the visual impact of identity, although it remains crucially important, is subordinate to its behavioural aspects. It is the way the airline stewardess behaves, as much as what she looks like, which determines our attitude towards the airline which she represents.

IBM is an example of 'monolithic' corporate identity, using one name and visual system for all products.

Where a company has grown by acquiring others, it often tries to keep the acquired names, fitting them into a single visual system.

Unilever is an example of an organization that deliberately sets out to separate the company from the product.

AUDIENCES

Any organization inevitably develops relationships with the society in which it operates. It buys from, sells to, collaborates with and competes with other companies. It has factories or offices which operate within a local area. It has staff of different kinds, who also have other loyalties, to their families, to their trade union, to their sports clubs, or whatever.

The organization lives within a series of communities – these communities, all of whom will one way or another form a view of it, are its audiences.

The most important audiences are:
Staff – of all kinds, their families, and pensioners
Customers – direct and indirect
Suppliers
Shareholders
Potential recruits
Competitors
Collaborators
Government – local and central
Trade unions
Trade and industry associations
Journalists
Opinion formers

It is important to bear in mind that audiences will form a view of an organization based upon impressions received from a variety of sources. Where the impression is contradictory, the overall view will be confusing or negative.

STRUCTURE AND STYLE

Identity affects these two areas of a company's business. In terms of structure, corporate identity can play a significant role in defining and demonstrating how a company is organized. Part of the corporate identity process involves the creation of a clear corporate structure.

There are three categories into which the corporate identities of most organizations fall. These are:
Monolithic – Where the organization uses one name and visual system (e.g. IBM).
Endorsed – Where a single organization which has grown by acquiring different companies or brands, tries to keep some or all of the acquired names, but fits them into a single visual system (e.g. United Technologies).
Branded – When companies deliberately set out to separate their identities as companies from the brands which they sell (e.g. Unilever).
Although all organizations would, if they carried out an effective and thorough identity programme, fall into one or other of these categories, companies that have not carried out such programmes, and that means many, are often an unhappy and uncomfortable mixture of all three types of identity.

From the point of view of style, corporate identity is intended to project visually a clear idea of the personality of the organization; for example, whether it sells expensive or cheap products, whether it values technology more than marketing, whether it is more interested in people or process. The visual identity of an organization should clearly signal what kind of company it is to all of the audiences with whom it communicates.

DESIGN STAGES

A corporate identity programme is developed through a series of stages. These are:

Stage 1 – Investigation, analysis and recommendation leading to design brief;

Stage 2 – Developing the design idea;

Stage 3 – Refining the design, creating the basic elements and applying them in principle;

Stage 4 – Implementing the programme.

These stages may vary according to circumstances, but broadly all corporate identity programmes follow this pattern.

Stage 1: Investigation and analysis. Before starting work the designer must be clear about where, when and how, and for what purpose, the name and visual identity of the company will be applied. In order to do this, the designer carries out an investigation of the company, either alone or more usually with the collaboration of other consultants. This involves interviewing various people within the organization and outside it to determine which kind of identity structure and what sort of visual style the organization requires.

These are some of the factors which the designer has to consider:

● Is the organization exclusive and small, or does it dominate its market-place?

● Is it growing, or stable, or declining?

● If it is growing, in which direction is it growing?

● Is it in a fashionable part of the market-place, where styles change often, like clothing, or a more stable area where style is much less volatile, like chemical engineering?

● Is it local, regional, national or international in its business activities?

Visual audit. At the same time as the investigation is underway, it is essential to carry out a visual audit. This simply means looking at and then recording by video or still camera a truly representative sample of the visual output of the organization. For this purpose, as for so many others, the three categories product/services, environments, and communications are important.

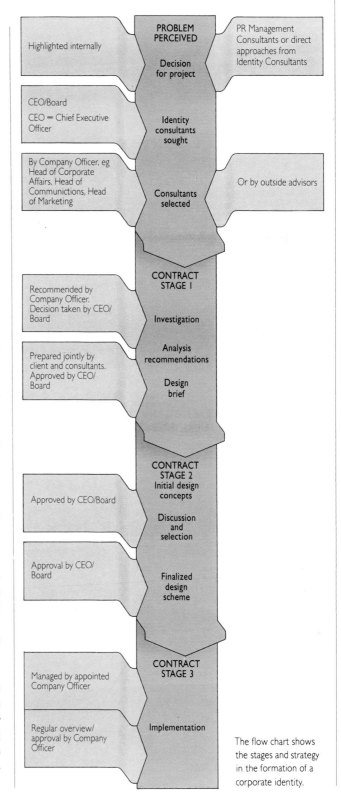

The flow chart shows the stages and strategy in the formation of a corporate identity.

Once a company has established its identity it can begin to think about its application at all levels, and for a large company like Ford these applications are many and varied. It is interesting to note the slight differences in the use of the logo according to the product or environment. The designers involved will be closely briefed on the permitted variations in colour scheme and so on of the logo itself, which is the constant factor.

The car illustrated is a Sierra XR4×4 with optional windscreen rapid de-ice and headlight wash/wipe at extra cost.

Here we see stages in the development of a brand name and symbol for Kuwait Petroleum, which has 4000 petrol stations throughout Europe. The first symbol was a falcon **(1, 3, 5)** and the second pair of Arab stallions **(2, 4, 6)**. Models and drawings were donw to show the client how these could be applied to a number of different items, but they were rejected.

1

2

3

It is important to examine and record both the visual material itself – vehicles, packaging, uniforms, signs on buildings, brochures and so on – and also housekeeping; that is, how much self-respect the organization has. Is it clean and orderly, or slovenly and ill-kempt? Or is it inconsistent, good in some places, bad in others?

As part of the audit, it is important to find out how the company currently carries out its purchasing and maintenance. For example, how often are vehicles bought and repainted? Who commissions buildings? Who buys furniture? On what basis is furniture selected? Who commissions brochures? And so on.

When the audit is complete, and the analysis and the recommendations have been presented and agreed, it is possible to prepare a design brief.

The design brief. The brief should be very short, preferably no more than one sheet of paper. It should indicate what business the company is in, what its position is within the industry, what its personality is like, how the personality should be projected, and which structure the organization is going to adopt (monolithic, endorsed, branded).

The written brief should be short, concise and comprehensive, because it is the working document on which design work is based and to which the designer should refer.

Stage 2: Developing the design idea. The name is the most important single element which distinguishes an organization. The intention of the visual system, the symbol, logotype, colours, alphabet and everything else is to invest the name or names with a particular significance, a special feeling, so that whenever the name emerges, its associations are immediately perceived.

The name Shell, for example, brings certain simple clear images to mind. Without the visual system which has been created for it, these would be much less potent. The components of such a system are:
- Prime name
- Subsidiary names – if appropriate
- Prime symbols
- Subsidiary symbols – if appropriate
- Prime typefaces
- Subsidiary typefaces
- Colours

These components are used by the designer on the basis of the design brief to produce the design idea.

The creative process is unique to each individual: most people create ideas in ways particular to them. Normally, however, a series of differing approaches are developed, shown in rough sketch or more developed form, modified, developed again, shown again at various stages and finally approved. When the basic idea has been approved, Stage 3 begins.

Stage 3: Refining the design. When the creative idea has been approved, it has to be developed into artwork. In other words, the basic elements, as listed in Stage 2, have to be created. From the basic elements, a range of applications is prepared.

Stage 4: Applications. The name and visual system have

The brand name Q8 (the pronunciation of Kuwait) and the sails device, symbolizing a seafaring nation, were accepted, and final designs **(7)** and models **(8)** were done to present to the client. The bottom illustrations **(9, 10)** show the reality — brand name and symbol on a tanker and a petr station in Belgium.

7

8

9

10

to be put together so that they can work effectively and flexibly in the widest possible range of applications. In principle, it should be possible to create a system in which differing elements dominate according to particular requirements. Sometimes the corporation will predominate, for example in an annual report or corporate brochure; at other times, however, it will be appropriate for subsidiary companies or brands to play the major role in a specific situation.

In addition to this, the visual system has to be appropriate for all kinds of materials such as:
- Print (black and white)
- Print (full colour)
- Television
- Metal
- Plastic

- Special display materials, e.g. neon, glass, or mosaic

The elements of the visual system must also be effective in different sizes. In addition to these permutations, there may be a requirement for the organization to present itself in a number of different parts of the world, where different languages, even different alphabets, are used; for example, Arabic, Japanese, Chinese, Thai, Hindi and so on.

Another factor to take into account is the differing situations in which the identity will appear. On an annual report, or the Chairman's letterhead, the name and logo will be treated with a reserve which will be very different from the way it will be treated by an advertising agency involved in a consumer promotion.

What all this means is that the applications for a major corporate identity programme are infinite, and

The design manual is vital for the implementation of corporate identity at all levels, and this will be used by employees involved in this area as well as by outside design groups working for the company, suppliers, printers, architects and advertising agencies. The very expensively produced ANWEB manual, designed by Studio Dumbar, has been extremely influential, marking new peaks of achievement in this field. Another costly example is the Emirates manual, designed by Million Design for an exclusive gold club in Dubai.

what is therefore demanded from this system is a kind of robust flexibility. In addition to the standard applications – letterhead, vehicle and so on – it is advisable to try a few applications that really test the system such as a lapel badge or a neon sign, or both. When the system has been tested and seen to work, it can be progressively applied to the organization.

THE MANUAL

As the identity begins to be implemented, it is essential that the work which is done is logged, codified and recorded.

In a sense, the design manual is simply a convenient system to collate all the identity applications as they are carried out and file them for further reference. At one level, therefore, the manual is simply a record of how the identity has been applied and a guide (which like all other guides will from time to time need to be revised) about how it should be applied in the future.

At another level, however, the manual almost invariably develops a much greater significance. It can become the book in which the corporate identity system is enshrined. In a sense, this may be desirable, because it gives the identity an authority which it might not otherwise be perceived to possess. The danger is that when this begins to happen, the manual may cease to be treated as a day-to-day working document, subject to change and modification. Great care, therefore, must be taken in design and in preparing the manual to invest it with appropriate significance.

Manuals can vary considerably in size and layout, and therefore in cost. For complex multinational companies with a proliferation of subsidiaries, they can run to many volumes, while for small companies with one name based in one location, a small slim volume economically produced may well be entirely appropriate. All manuals should contain an introduction from the Chairman or Chief Executive officially endorsing the identity project and outlining its value to the organization as a whole.

The manual should be distributed to those people inside the organization who are responsible for applying the identity at any level, in any situation. It should also go to all suppliers of the organization: printers, advertising agencies, sign makers, architects, exhibition construction designers, interior designers, product designers, and so on.

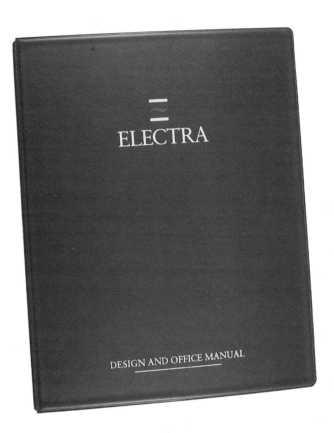

نادي جولف الامارات دبي

EMIRATES
GOLF CLUB DUBAI

كتيّب التصاميم
Design Manual

When companies which already have a strong and well-established corporate identity and logo, such as Volkswagen and Audi, merge into one group, it clearly makes sense to retain as much as possible of the identity. A special typeface was designed for the group, however, and the design manual gives specific instructions for its use and that of the V.A.G. symbol in its varied applications.

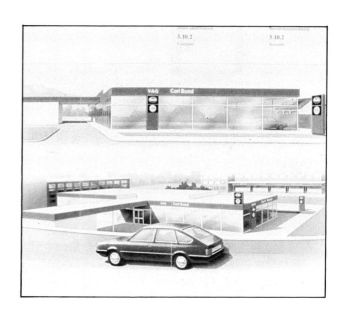

THE LAUNCH

A corporate identity programme can be launched in a number of different ways:

– a complete change – overnight from old to new;
– a controlled change taking place very quickly;
– a gradual change;
– replacement on *ad hoc* basis.

The rule here is that if the new identity is dramatically different from the old, rapid changes will be required. If, however, the identity is simply being modified, the organization can afford to replace it over a longer period of time.

The launch should always take place according to the following order:

• Own staff
• Dealers
• Outside world including customers

CONCLUSION

The identity of an organization is its most precious asset; if it has no name and no reputation, it has nothing. A corporate identity programme is a means by which the organization can make its strategy, structure and personality clear for everyone who comes into contact with it to see and feel.

The corporate identity designer has an immense responsibility which should be discharged with appropriate rigour. The designer must always remember that the designed identity is not a personal project, but structured for the organization, who may be using it for twenty years or more.

BELOW AND OPPOSITE Here we see a selection of pages from design manuals together with their practical applications. The illustrations below are double-page spreads from the Emirates golf club manual. The opposite page shows the British Telecom manual and several different applications of the logo, from a pair of wire cutters to a satellite dish. The middle illustration is taken from the part of the manual dealing with correct and incorrect uses of the logo, with suggestions for alternative colour schemes and patterns where appropriate.

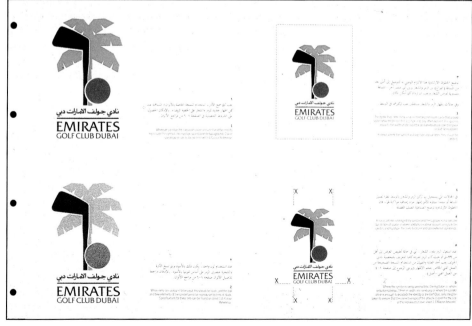

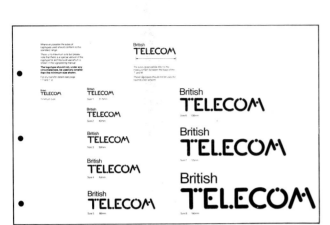

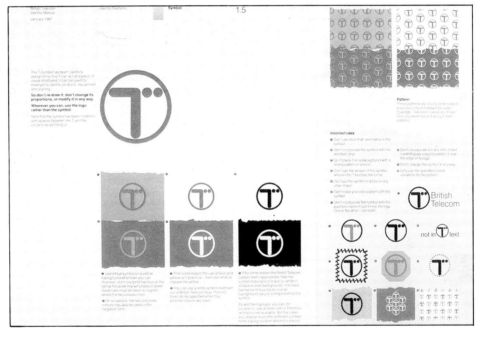

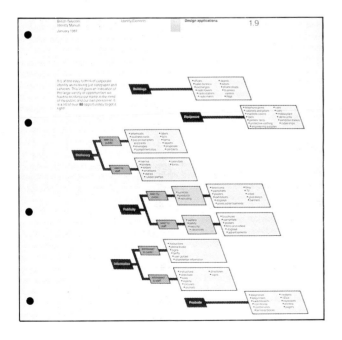

9/PACKAGING

The function of any package is simply understood, as a carrier, protector and dispenser for any given product. To be successful it has only to pass the most fundamental of tests – will it stay together and keep the product intact in transit, and will it protect and in turn lengthen that product's life? In the majority of cases, these questions are answered in a simple and unsophisticated way – a bucket, a box, a bottle. Varying degrees of technical expertise are then introduced, depending upon the product's physical makeup, to ensure the individual characteristics of the product perform satisfactorily.

If the product can also be viewed in or through its container, such as milk in a bottle, and that product's appearance is beneficial to its purchase or demand, then the efficiency of the package is even greater. But the matter becomes complicated when the manufacturer, or in the case of, say, milk, the producer wishes for individual acknowledgement, in an effort to increase sales and supply. Is the best strategy to design a new weird and wonderful package to carry the milk, or simply to put the producer's name on the bottle?

This simplistic dilemma has produced the most memorable and extraordinary packaging formats over the last century: physical pack shapes so familiar, like a Coca Cola bottle, that even when viewed in silhouette they remain instantly recognizable; name styles so synonymous with their product type, such as Oxo, that they have become generic.

There are also many cases where decades of advertising persuasion and on-shelf familiarity have kept alive an awareness for products whose packaging personality, and product type, in today's terms clearly do not fit, but which have endured the rigours of fashionability and market trends, and have been labelled 'classic'.

For the designer starting in this arena of seemingly random choice and ill-defined disciplines, with a product to package and a blank piece of paper, where do you begin? In a live marketing situation, 99 times out of 100 the target audience has been defined, the price of the product has been decided, and the level of sophistication is expected, clarified. All you have to do is think up a container shape, suitable packaging material and a few attractive graphics.

Unfortunately, as straightforward as this thought process appears, the one factor that overrules all others in the equation is the consumer. Someone is going to have to pay money for this piece of design, not to mention the product it contains, and it has to be designed to make

LEFT Where the shape and contents of the package are similar, or sometimes identical, the consumer must be persuaded to choose one product rather than another by the style, impact and message contained on the package, which provides a back-up for any promotion or advertising.

BELOW The design of own-label packaging is an area now considered vitally important by retailers faced with ever-growing competition.

them do it. Where packaging design crosses over from a purely functional task to the art of subtle persuasion is what this chapter is all about.

MATERIALS FOR PACKAGING

It is said that the egg is the perfect package, ergonomically shaped, with an exterior both indestructible and at the same time brittle. But it is the manmade structures that carry the egg that are equally surprising. The different use of materials begins to symbolize the origin of the egg itself. The traditional fibre-pulp box, once the only form of egg packaging, is now equated with free-range eggs. The 'natural' quality of the pack has become a metaphor for tradition. As if in an attempt to avoid deception, supermarkets have adopted clear plastic or polystyrene to carry the battery-farmed produce.

It is this consumer perception which inevitably governs the final decision as to a packaging choice. Milk is the other commodity example where reason works in reverse. Brought up on receiving the daily pint

packaged behind glass, and later weaned on to the more economic carton, the consumer is accepting the suggestion that even technologists thought ludicrous, that liquid could be carried in paper. But this relatively incongruous way of packaging is apparently acceptable for such an ancient and natural product. The choice of inappropriate packaging materials can also be demonstrated with milk. Should a producer decide to market the product in a can, the perception would swing towards an unnatural interpretation of milk, condensed or powdered. Yet the transportation of pure milk from farm to pasturizing plant is in just such a fabric, the traditional milk churn, and further through the process, transporters that can be seen thundering the motorways safely despatching their produce, are also a familiar sight.

So why are some materials suitable for certain products and not others? Custom and tradition often play a large part, and as in the case of the egg, material can suggest something intrinsic to the product's personality. Glass, for instance, once the most common of bottling materials, is being replaced by newer, more flexible materials. PET, the lightweight plastic now commonly used for drinks packaging, has transformed the bottle by extruding into a light, durable carrier, virtually replacing any large soft-drink container. And of course so it should; it's cheaper than glass, therefore reducing any price premium passed on to the purchaser, and its appearance isn't far short of the real thing, without the bulk – a very important consideration when you're doing the week's shopping. But there the similarity stops. Despite its flexibility it cannot begin to imitate the complexity of shape that glass can suggest.

This, as with any packaging material, is really the skill. Once you have learned the basic personality of the material, its very nature dictates what products it is suited to. The apparent uniformity of finish for PET means that to package a vintage champagne in such a manner would be marketing folly. But the reality is that the material could not only handle the rigours of such an explosive product, but because of the cost of the existing glass, which has to be strengthened to endure high pressure, PET would dramatically reduce costs.

So begins the inevitable struggle between the packaging buyer and the marketing department, one pulling for economies of plant, the other pushing for quality perception at the point of purchase. The consultant's role is to add reason to the two.

PRINTING PROCESSES

GLASS
Onto paper labels
- Lithographic
- Gravure
- Letterpress
- Silkscreen

Onto PVC shrink sleeves
- Gravure   reverse printed
- Flexographic   reverse printed

PLASTIC
Onto paper labels
- Processes as for glass
Shrink sleeves
- As above
Stretch labels
- As above
In mould labelling
- i.e. special type of pre-printed label inserted into bottle mould. Bottle is formed so label is fused to bottle surface.
Therimage
- Heat transfer labels. Gravure and screen print. Dry-offset.

CARDBOARD
- Lithographic
- Flexographic
- Screenprint
- Gravure

PLASTIC
Direct onto plastic
- Screenprint
- Flexographic

FOIL/FILM LAMINATES
- Flexographic
- Gravure

CAN/METAL
- Dry-offset print
- Reprotherm — transfer system for full-colour photographic image

FORM AND FUNCTION

Structural packaging fulfils a number of important functions in the modern retail environment. Most products require some form of container in order that they can be handled, sold and transported to the home. A pack often needs to protect the product which it contains from the environment, either from actual physical damage or from deterioration caused by exposure to an environmental condition that would be detrimental to the product. An obvious example is to preserve the condition of food products. In some instances it may be equally impor-

tant to protect the environment from the product, as in the case of toxins and medicines.

Packaging also provides a means of obtaining a pre-determined measure of product. The pack is then a measured unit either by weight, volume, quantity or size.

Packaging is both a vehicle for and a means of communication about the product. Often the shape and format of the pack can allude to the particular qualities of the product or its method of use. Colour, texture and surface finish also communicate messages at a subliminal level about the product and often the target consumer. Blue, for example, has been often associated with bleach and other aggressive cleaning products. Certain colours become standards for particular markets where competitive products try to associate with the brand leader through colour; pink signals a particular leading brand of window cleaner, for example.

Structural packaging has grown and is continuing to grow in importance, and is represented by the increasing diversity of pack types and their sophistication. The basic reasons for this growth can be traced to changes in technology and patterns of consumption. Manufacturing technologies change and new materials with advanced performance characteristics for specific applications are developed. An example is the development of multi-layer co-extruded plastics which made possible the squeezable plastic ketchup bottle. The bottle is made up of several layers of different plastics which in total provide the necessary barrier against oxygen getting into the pack. Glass is an excellent oxygen barrier but is obviously very heavy, it shatters when dropped and it cannot be squeezed to dispense product like a plastic bottle.

Increased affluence and disposable incomes, changes in the roles of men and women, work and leisure patterns, and lifestyle in general, together with the proliferation of the supermarket and hypermarket have contributed to an increased demand for choice and variety. There is now a greater diversity of product types (market

LEFT The shape of pack is determined by a combination of functional attributes (ie holdability, use of product, merchandising, machine-handling) and appropriate visual imagery. A product may become instantly recognizable by virtue of its pack shape, an example being the Toilet Duck.

PACKAGING MATERIALS

1 Total graphic coverage, optimum print quality and image are all possible here. Board type and pack construction can be tailored to meet the physical protection requirements of the product.

2 PET is a lightweight and shatter-proof alternative to glass. It can be produced to provide an acceptable barrier against the loss of carbonation in fizzy drinks.

3 Foil provides an excellent barrier against moisture entering the pack as well as giving protection from ultraviolet light and oxygen. Durability and strength is built in through polyester coating on the outside surface allowing pack to be vacuum-moulded into block shape for shelf stacking. Polythene coating on the inside surface facilitates heat sealing.

4 Pack capable of very high speed and volume tinning and handling. This is very durable, and can be processed at high temperatures to preserve the contents. It also provides a high level of protection against contamination after processing.

5 Glass is a relatively low-cost packaging material offering product visibility and excellent protection from contamination. Contents can be preserved through high-temperature processing and sealing the lid to the jar via the vacuum created inside the jar.

6 Paper, foil and polythene lamination. The foil provides a moisture barrier; the polythene gives heat sealability; and the paper excellent print quality.

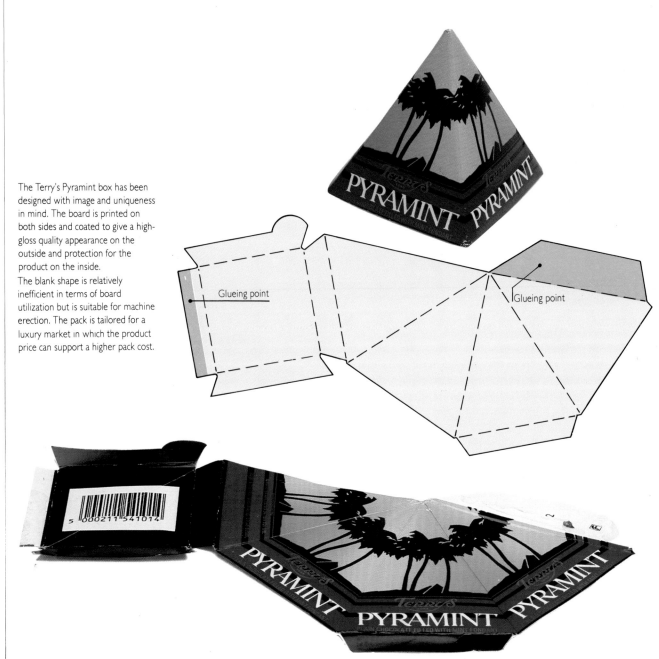

The Terry's Pyramint box has been designed with image and uniqueness in mind. The board is printed on both sides and coated to give a high-gloss quality appearance on the outside and protection for the product on the inside.

The blank shape is relatively inefficient in terms of board utilization but is suitable for machine erection. The pack is tailored for a luxury market in which the product price can support a higher pack cost.

Glueing point

Glueing point

segmentation) and a growth in products offering added convenience and utility.

Retailers are increasingly important in determining the development of packaging, both in terms of own label products and in setting down requirements which the brand manufacturers need to comply with. The retailer is interested in factors like efficient shelf space utilization where the profitability of the store is related to the amount of product that can be displayed on shelf. The issue of shelf life is also an important one. Products with a short shelf life need to be sold quickly to avoid waste, therefore it is more convenient for the retailer to extend life wherever possible. However, consumer preference for fresh foods, and for reducing the amount of artificial additives in food, including preservatives, means that retailers must gauge product turnover and distribution more accurately or find alternative means to keep products fresh and maintain shelf life. The gas flushing in

form-fill-seal packs which removes oxygen is one way of increasing the shelf life for fresh products such as meat, without adding preservatives.

There are legislative requirements to be aware of too, especially in the packing of foods and drugs. The inclusion of child-resistant closures on detergent products has become an issue through consumer pressure. Similarly, consumers prefer packs to have some form of tamper evidence, that is a means by which they can tell if a pack has been opened and possibly tampered with.

CONSTRUCTING THE PACKAGE

Structural packaging design has traditionally been the domain of technical experts and engineers, generally as part of the pack manufacturing process though occasionally undertaken by the product manufacturer. Graphic designers have also been involved in work on structural packaging, though usually as part of the

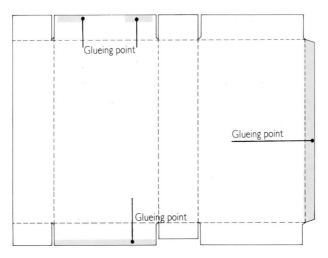

Glueing point

Glueing point

Glueing point

The cornflakes carton has been developed to be a highly efficient and cost-effective pack, the product being extremely price sensitive. The carton blanks are tailored to obtain the most efficient utilization of board and ease of handling by high-speed automatic carton cresting machines. The material specification is critical to obtain the right degree of stiffness both for machine handling and to maintain product image on shelf (ie to prevent the product 'bulging' through the carton and crumpling at the back when the packet is picked up by the consumer). The medium-coated, white-lined, folding box board provides an acceptable white print surface, which is printed with gloss inks obviating the need for gloss varnishing.

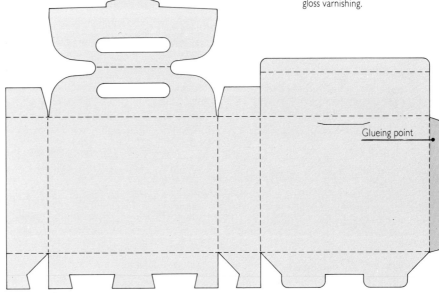

Glueing point

A premium luxury product like the Bonsai Garden requires a packaging which reflects its special quality. Good-quality stiff board and print are used to make the pack look and feel good as well as to support and give protection to the products. The carton is machine erectable, but is primarily designed to be hand erected with an easy-looking base and top tuck-in tab, appropriate for low volume, small runs.

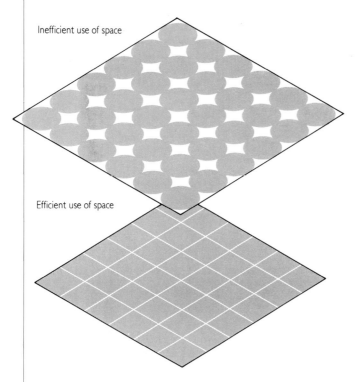

Inefficient use of space

Efficient use of space

Direct Product Profitability
The shape of a pack can determine
how much product can be displayed
on a fixed area of shelf space. In
principle a given number of packs
with a square plan section occupies
less space than the same number of
round packs of the same sectional
area. Space utilization relative to

product volume affects product
profitability at every stage from
manufacture, warehousing,
transportation through to stock
holding and merchandizing in store.

biased. Invariably the pack requirement will be to respond to or initiate a change in one or both of these areas.

It is important to understand the reasons behind a
new packaging brief in order to give the correct emphasis
later on during the course of the design project. It may be
a new product development, in which case the project
probably requires the broadest perspective. A product
reformulation may also require a wide approach, though
often many of the parameters will be pre-determined.
Changes to existing pack format or shape for purely
visual updating, or as the result of a technical development, require the designer to work within much more
closely defined criteria.

Taking the brief, as in all areas of design, is the most
critical stage of a project, and above all requires good
listening ability. It is at the briefing that the parameters
are established, the fixed and variable criteria ascer-
tained. Very often nuances in what the client is saying
provide the real insight to the problem for which the
design solution is being sought. Frequently the client will
be speaking in terms of his or her professional bias, be it
technical or marketing, which the designer must trans-
late into the language of design.

Following the briefing, a proposal or synopsis of the
work to be done is written. A commonly used format for
this is to restate the essential points of the brief and then
to relate this to the design objectives and provide an
outline of the process by which the desired result is to be
achieved. A project is usually broken down into stages
allowing the client to check progress, select design
routes and approve the work at the end of each stage.
Timings and design fees are related in manageable por-
tions to the various project stages.

graphic design process carried out by design and advertising agencies.

Increasingly, the structural side of packaging is
handled by industrial designers, whose training is essentially in three-dimensional design. The industrial designer is well equipped to provide the design solution to a
packaging problem by drawing upon a technical and
functional understanding, combined with an aesthetic
sense, within a broad framework of market awareness.

The briefing. The packaging brief comes either from a
product manufacturer, or from a packaging manufacturer, or from a retailer. Depending on the source, the
project emphasis will be either technically or marketing

Design stages. A carbonated drinks bottle development
provides a useful case study of a typical structural packaging design project. The brief is to determine the
appropriate pack format and size, then to develop a pack
shape that reflects the marketing objectives behind the
new product launch.

A 2-litre custom-design PET bottle is recommended
on the basis of competitive pricing, retailer preference
for PET over glass, and the general movement of the
market towards PET.

Having agreed a PET bottle development with the
client, the next stage would be to establish a unique bottle
shape. This must be carried out within a clearly defined
marketing framework and understanding of technical

THE PACKAGING BRIEF

A good packaging brief should tell you the following:

I Market background. What's going on in the marketplace.
2 Why a new pack is needed.
3 Background to the product and its past performance.
4 The image properties of the product. If a name brand, what people know, feel and believe about it.
5 What aspect of the packaging is sacrosanct. Anything that has to be retained - the corporate logo; the background colour etc.
6 Consumer profile. The backgrounds of the people who buy the product — sex, average age, social group, main motivations for buying.
7 Pack use. How, where and how often is the product used. The needs and wants of the consumer.
8 Communications task. Is the intention to attract new users; to raise quality expectations; to modernize product image?
9 Pack format. Printing process; number of colours; size of type; product compatibility; product volume; product technical requirements.
10 Distribution. Environment; means of transport (trays, cases, pallets, shrink wrapping etc); storage conditions and space utilization.
II Filling. Hot or cold; automated; filling speeds; machinery parameters; post-fill processes (heating, freezing etc).
12 Cost. Speed; lead times; related components and compatibility, machine requirements and parameters.

supermarket shelves, bottle diameter for compatibility with standard base cups, bottle stability (the relationship of height to base-stand width), neck and cap requirements for filling and capping machinery, need to be considered at this early stage.

A selection would then be made with the client from typically between 10 and 20 bottle shapes. Selected bottle shapes may then be drawn to the correct volume and rendered in detail for later evaluation in market research. Upon presentation of these, it may be decided to make accurate three-dimensional solid models of the selected designs to accompany the renderings in market research.

The models may be made in PVC and spray painted in the required colour if the bottle is to be opaque. With clear bottle designs, acrylic is normally used and then tinted if necessary to represent a tinted bottle, or the product colour.

The next stage, and again typical of most pack developments, would be to produce a detailed technical drawing of the one bottle design chosen after any market research. A 'detailed technical drawing' is what the toolmaker uses to either make the tool directly from or as a basis for his own working drawing. It is at this detailed drawing stage that all the technical requirements are re-checked and built in.

Many of the requirements will have already been covered, such as the nature and state of the product and its compatibility with packaging materials, how the product is filled, hot or cold by hand or machine, filling line speeds and conveyor requirements. But the detail of ensuring that the bottle can be machine-handled through all the various filling, capping and labelling stages is finally specified here. A label size is specified, though often the pack must be designed to accommodate a label of a predetermined size.

Consideration must also be given to how the packs are to be transported and ultimately displayed on shelf. In the case of PET bottles, they are generally packed in sixes into board trays which are overwrapped with neat shrinkable polythene. Alternatively, bottles may go into full board cases. These trays or cases then go on to pallets in several layers and the pallets are themselves wrapped round with polythene. This whole process is often fully automated and the pack implications on all these stages needs to be understood. Pallet efficiency is an important issue, that is, to ensure that the maximum number of packs can be accommodated on a standard

parameters. In the case of a new product launch a clear understanding of the target consumer is required and any product associations that need to be incorporated. Factors such as age, gender, socio-economic group and product marketing values will help to give shape to the design thinking. For example an approach may be to create and overtly masculine image with harder, straighter lines, and incorporating design elements associated with the male environment for a product that is clearly targeted to appeal to men.

Surface texture, embossing and colouring of the base cap (the plastic injection-moulded base piece attached to PET bottles) may be considered. Technical parameters such as maximum bottle height to fit within

Scenes from a manufacturer supplying high-quality specialist printed products, folded cartons and labels in a wide range of uses. Printing is by litho sheet process on paper and board.

1 Making the forme, the body of type.
2 Guillotines.
3 Making a mould for a fitment in a gift box.
4 Vacuum forming the mould.
5 Blister card packing.
6 Self-adhesive labelling.
7 Inspecting labels on the Web.
8 Quality control: humidity testing.
9 Quality control: weight checks.
10, 11 Inspecting the painted boards for colour.
12 Knocking out cartons ready for glueing.

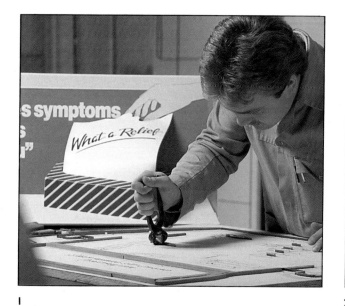

1

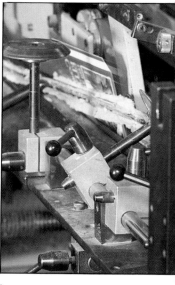

2

3

4

5

6

9

11

12

pallet and such that the total configuration with several layers of packs provides a stable structure.

Obviously the product must reach the retailer in good condition, while the appearance of the pack itself also needs to be maintained. Time, storage and transport condition all have an effect. The packs themselves or additional protective transit packaging must therefore be designed to withstand the particular conditions to be encountered.

The detailed component drawing is often not the end of a design project. Ideally the designer should retain involvement in a new pack development right into production, thus ensuring that the design work is correctly interpreted and executed by the packaging manufacturer. The designer should therefore be in communication with all the parties involved, be ready to solve problems as they arise and to check the first-off production items.

PACKAGING GRAPHICS

It is a very exciting time to get into packaging design. Packaging awards for mass marketing products prove that no longer is design excellence confined to a sophisticated few. The driving force of this change has been the supermarket, and self-selection of products by the consumer. In the past, the neighbourhood grocer could expect to know the customer and could reach to the shelves for the staple products required and recommend new products for trial. Graphics had little more to do than identify the product name and contents. In this limited role, packaging tended merely to reflect the graphic style of the time. Today, packaging has taken over from the grocer, and is itself the spokesperson for the product or brand.

The consumer society, whatever you may think of it, is dedicated to variety and choice: a myriad products to suit your needs, whims or indulgences. As choice of product makes a statement about you, there are almost as many product presentations as there are personalities to match. The demand for packaging design seems almost insatiable.

The growth of supermarket shopping has introduced an important distinction in packaging design, between brand name products and supermarket own-brand labels. Famous brands – names like Kellogg's, Heinz, Bird's Eye, or, in other fields, Shell, Hoover, Black & Decker – all have in common a reputation for quality and a specific personality. You trust them and can relate to them almost as people: that is to say, you can describe their particular personalities versus those of their competitors. You hold certain expectations about any product that carries the name. Their reputations have enormous commercial value, which is one reason why the guardians of those reputations – the brand managers – are cautious about actions that could place them in jeopardy. This tends to lead to a safe approach to packaging – perhaps to freshen up the appearance of the product rather than change its image or style.

Own-label packaging is different from that for brands in ways which make it easier for supermarkets in design terms. No individual product carries with it a

Some of the visual options presented to the client for the packaging of an own-label breakfast cereal, together with the printed result.

reputation in which vast sums have been invested, for the supermarket itself is the brand. One product failure will not ruin a supermarket chain in the way it could ruin a brand manufacturer.

Packaging design has witnessed a remarkable revolution in the past few years now embraced by almost every supermarket chain. Manufacturers are concerned that however ugly their duckling may be, it is familiar, known and loved. Supermarkets have no such restraint and have taken good design as their point of difference, with remarkable effect. Brands have lost market share significantly to own-label products, and are now looking at the role of design in this effect. The need for points of difference between products, in home and export markets, is more widely recognized and supported. Good design is seen not only as the way to make these distinctions, but also as an active selling point: good design sells better than bad. That is why it is an exciting time to be getting into packaging design.

Design features in packaging. Packaging and print are different. The designer who believes that designing a pack is like designing anything else is deluded. So is the designer who believes that packaging is just shelf impact. Both myths exist and have some truth in them, but you have to dig deep to appreciate the subtleties as to where your talent may be best utilized.

The pack designer and the print designer dip into the same stockpot for an original and relevant idea, supported by balanced typography and appropriate execu-

tion. Both have to communicate a message successfully to a target audience, but herein lies the difference. In broad terms the print designer's audience is receptive, the pack designer's unreceptive. The recipient of print is already sympathetic before judgement is passed. For example, in a bank the literature picked up is located inside the brand, which is the bank. The consumer encounters product packaging head on, with no buffer in between. The mood is unsympathetic, the environment most certainly competitive.

Packaging must communicate from a distance, and then at progressively closer levels. It has to make an immediate statement and then reveal its secrets in logical order. The immediate statement is often abused, merely to shout loudest. Good news for designers is that there is a new accent on impact called tone of voice – a very competitive weapon.

A good pack designer is able to distil creativity to the very essence of the product projected. The design has to be manipulative. The consumer may not want to buy, have no obvious need for the product, be loyal to the competitor: to enjoy packaging, you have to enjoy this little battle on the shelf. Form and graphics have to be considered as one. Competitors' stance and repeat facings influence design decisions. Product and brand personality have to be balanced with creativity.

Packaging and print are now moving closer together. The rise of the retailer as the 'walk-in brand' has reduced the noise on the shelf. Today's consumer enters the store, like the bank, aware of the corporate message.

BELOW RIGHT Styled to appeal to a sophisticated, health-conscious market, this packaging for a low-caffeine coffee stands apart from traditional coffee packs.

BELOW The design concept for Vetiver bath products, as with all Crabtree & Evelyn packaging, goes back to the nostalgic, friendly, earthy and very traditional look with warm coloration.

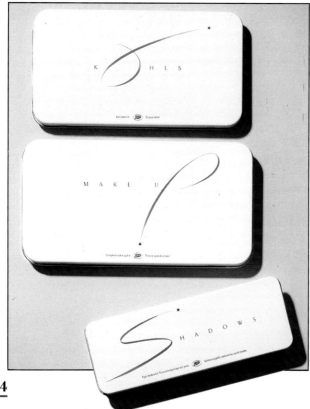

ABOVE AND LEFT In sharp contrast to the mass-market range (above) these toiletries, produced with a minimum budget and designed by Lewis Moberly, were targetted specifically at the thirteen-year-old girl imitating her older sister.

BELOW AND BELOW RIGHT
The values of traditional brewing are
evoked in the own-label stout,
designed by Lewis Moberly, and a
combination of serious typography
and discreet corporate branding was
used for the rum, designed for a
young and sophisticated market.

ABOVE AND RIGHT The oil and
vinegar and shortbread, further
examples of Crabtree and Evelyn
packaging, are in the same friendly
style as the Vetiver products opposite.

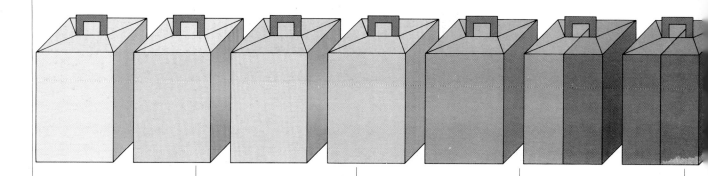

With packaging there is usually a lot of money at stake — not so much the cost of the packaging itself as the cost of the product it contains. It often runs to millions of dollars. Packaging projects are therefore quite elaborate, with one or more research stages to make sure that the new design is communicating effectively and to help reduce several options to one. Shown here are the basic steps with typical timings. Each box represents two weeks.

ASSIMILATING THE BRIEF *(1-2 weeks)* Prerequisites to any design project are a written brief from the client and a visit to the retail environment in which the packaging has to work. Take photographs; buy products. Bring them back as reference.

The fuller the brief the less chance of misunderstanding later. Challenge aspects of the brief you do not understand or agree with: the client should make all previous research available and welcome your opinion. However, there must be a strategy agreement before you start work. Your main priority is to discover the two essentials — who you are talking to and what you are trying to say.

FIRST DESIGN CONCEPTS *(3-4 weeks)* What is essential is that your ideas are relevant and communicate. Providing they do that, you can fly as high as you like — the more unexpected the better, but they must hit their target. Ideas, however, are only half the battle: the other half is crafting them. A good idea can be killed at the craft stage, but craft skills can never cover up the absence of an idea.

Design direction and deciding what gets presented to the client are the responsibility of the creative director. Typically, between three and seven ideas will be presented on a major project. Standard of presentation varies from one design company to another but with the availability of rub-downs, the standard of finish tends to be high. Most clients judge what they see; it's a false economy to make it hard for them.

RESEARCH MOCK-UPS *(2-3 weeks)* There are two kinds of research — qualitative and quantitative. The first consists of a discussion group of six to eight individuals selected from the target market. The discussion is led by an expert, often a psychologist, and lasts for about 1½ hours. One research exercise might consist of six such groups taking place in different parts of the country.

This kind of research can be very useful to the development of creative ideas. It's quite fascinating, if a little nerve-racking, to attend such groups, and you learn a lot about how designs are perceived.

Research mock-ups for this exercise will probably be one-offs. Acetate film kills your colours, and photography is also a problem and must usually be rendered as illustration.

Quantitative research, on the other hand, is all about numbers, with a minimum sample of a hundred. For his you need fully printed mock-ups, which involve the preparation of artwork. This kind of research, which is based on the questionnaire technique, will give you statistically significant answers: A is preferred to B by a certain percentage, etc. But it is less helpful in telling you why, or what to do about B to make it better.

The store's ethos creates the buffer between consumer and product. Understanding the new climate is important, but so too is the strength of the name brand, still alive and well, slowly and often painfully adjusting to its cavalier competition, own-label.

WAYS OF WORKING

As a packaging designer, you have the choice to join a company or work freelance. Big, small, multi-disciplinary, specialized – there is a profusion of practices with which you may try to identify. A large established company offers a degree of security; a small company where systems are still being developed includes a risk factor which can encourage insecurity. This is also a factor to consider if you decide to work alone, but the advantage of freelancing is your freedom to work on the projects you choose.

When looking to join a company, you must take into account the approach to projects, imposition of house style, if there is one, and the scope for experience in a broad range of products or a specialized area of packaging design. The conditions of work vary enormously:

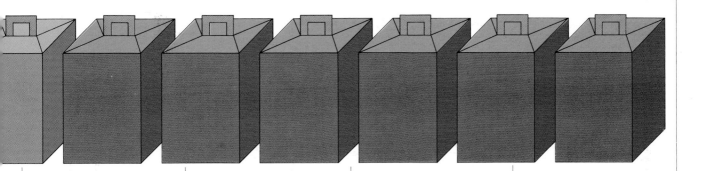

DEVELOPMENT *(2 weeks)* The client will probably choose two or three ideas to go forward for development. Not only will you want to take account of client reactions, but you will be now have your own views on how to make your work even better. Designs are like babies: after they are born, they grow up, and this is a very important process. Don't fall in love with the first thing you put down on paper and be precious about it. Learn to let go; it can always be made better.

POST-RESEARCH DEVELOPMENT *(1-2 weeks)* Some lessons are likely to be learned from the research exercise which will mean minor developments to your design. Research, however, is only as good as the person who interprets it and this is where so often the power of an idea can be destroyed by the fear of offending someone. Stand firm if you are confident of your approach.

ARTWORK *(2-3 weeks)* Again, like the research, the printed result can only be as good as the artwork supplied. Most design companies have a separate artwork studio or use one trusted supplier. As designer, you may be expected to art direct the artwork, not to do it yourself, although some designers do design and artwork in tandem.

Your control comes through your artwork trace, which must be impeccable, as also must be your specifications to the printer. Remember this: paste-up artists and printers work to your specifications. They only do what you instruct them to do. Never leave room for judgement. Everything you require must be clearly indicated with precision.

QUALITY CONTROL *(4-12 weeks)* All your painstaking care to date may now be wasted if you do not follow through. With print work, the design company will often place the print order; with packaging hardly ever. So it is vital the client understands that you expect to brief the printer and require to approve the proofs. Your standards may be higher than the client's.

Packaging covers many more print processes than design for print — lithography, gravure, rotary letterpress, flexo, therimage, etc. Your technical knowledge must be of a high standard. To achieve the results you want you must be prepared to visit both the colour separation house and the printer, and remember, the job is not finished until you have pristine samples of your printed work safely in your hand.

some companies operate a distinct junior/senior structure with the emphasis on training by observation and practice; in others you will be thrown in at the deep end – but you will only have been offered a job if you are thought to be capable of dealing with the situation.

The freelance designer must create the self-discipline and motivation to learn the job and take control of the projects. As a freelance you must accommodate all the factors that a company can take care of for the designer: difficult clients, finance, overheads, finding the work. On the other hand, the freelance can choose the projects to work on and the clients to work with, and an experienced freelance is a highly respected and necessary member of the design profession.

Freelances who offer a specialized skill are the most secure; the generalists tend to be first to lose out when opportunities are limited. It is a good compromise to develop your design skills and identify your strengths while working for a company, before moving to freelance work when you feel confident of what you have to offer, or feel a real need to operate alone.

10/DESIGN IN ADVERTISING

We're living in a very noisy marketplace. In the aftermath of the population explosion we now face a media explosion that's bombarding us with new products and advertising campaigns. Every day, the average big-city commuter is exposed to as many as five hundred advertising messages. Of those only a handful make any impression, and discounting the subliminal effects of those that remain lodged in the subconscious mind, it becomes clear that a primary function of advertising design is to gain the consumer's full attention.

Quite simply, if an ad isn't noticed it might as well not exist. (The client would be better off if it didn't.)

At the same time it's essential that the design of an advertisement makes it quickly and easily understood. Most campaigns endeavour to reach the audience with a simple proposition and if this is obscured by intrusive and irrelevant imagery and design elements, the message will be lost and the space wasted.

However, in addition to visibility and comprehensibility, there's a third principle of advertising design that's of ever-increasing importance – style. In the early years of advertising manufacturers concentrated on product descriptions and price – what you get and what you pay for it. But with the proliferation of so many 'me-too' products (those which have no real advantage over one another), style has become an all-important factor in purchasing decisions. Often the only competitive edge a product has is its style as perceived through its advertising and packaging. Style is also the means by which an advertising campaign identifies its audience. If the juxta-

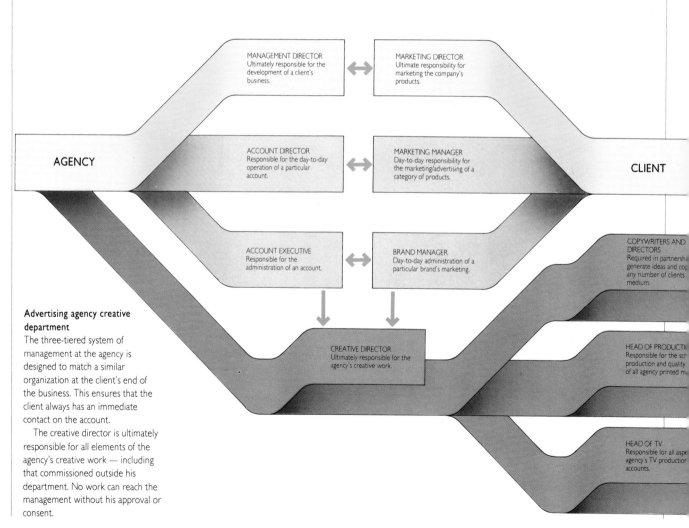

Advertising agency creative department

The three-tiered system of management at the agency is designed to match a similar organization at the client's end of the business. This ensures that the client always has an immediate contact on the account.

The creative director is ultimately responsible for all elements of the agency's creative work — including that commissioned outside his department. No work can reach the management without his approval or consent.

MANAGEMENT DIRECTOR
Ultimately responsible for the development of a client's business.

MARKETING DIRECTOR
Ultimate responsibility for marketing the company's products.

AGENCY

ACCOUNT DIRECTOR
Responsible for the day-to-day operation of a particular account.

MARKETING MANAGER
Day-to-day responsibility for the marketing/advertising of a category of products.

CLIENT

ACCOUNT EXECUTIVE
Responsible for the administration of an account.

BRAND MANAGER
Day-to-day administration of a particular brand's marketing.

COPYWRITERS AND DIRECTORS
Required in partnership generate ideas and cop any number of clients medium.

CREATIVE DIRECTOR
Ultimately responsible for the agency's creative work.

HEAD OF PRODUCTIO
Responsible for the sch production and quality of all agency printed m

HEAD OF TV
Responsible for all aspe agency's TV productio accounts.

position of words and pictures carry an advertiser's message, then style is the accent or 'tone of voice' that makes the right people listen and take notice.

As a very basic guideline (there are no hard and fast rules) one can say that advertising design has three functions – to make an ad noticed, to make it easily understood and to present it in a style that flatters both product and consumer. Easily said, but who does it and how?

THE CREATIVE DEPARTMENT

You won't find anyone in the creative department of an advertising agency calling themselves 'the designer'. You will find a team of art directors, copywriters, typographers, TV producers, art buyers and traffic controllers working under a creative director.

It's becoming increasingly unusual for creative directors to be actively involved in the writing and art direction of the agency's campaigns. The administrative demands of the job are time-consuming in the extreme, and the creative director will most probably devote his or her attention to assigning the correct personnel to a project and then using personal experience to judge and modify the work before it is presented to the client.

THE CREATIVE TEAM

The first people in line actually to solve a creative problem are the art director and copywriter. It has become a worldwide tradition for writers and art directors to work in teams. These 'marriages' have both practical and emotional value and are frequently long-lasting, with the partners moving together from one agency to the next. Certainly, in the business of generating ideas, the synergy of two minds and two disciplines – pictures and words – is very productive, and also comforting when the pressure is on.

Because advertising is a multi-media exercise the role of the art director is something of a Jack-of-all-trades. He or she is required to exercise critical judgement over concepts, layouts, typography, photography, illustration, film-making, retouching, reproduction and printing, and even to come up with the occasional headline when the copywriter is struggling. In turn copywriters, who may be art-school trained, contribute a great deal of the visual thinking of the campaign. In fact, in working practice the division of the two roles is extremely blurred and varies from project to project.

However, once the team has 'cracked' the initial idea, it can call upon the more specialized skills of the rest of the department to get the job into production. This process invariably starts with the arrival of a creative brief.

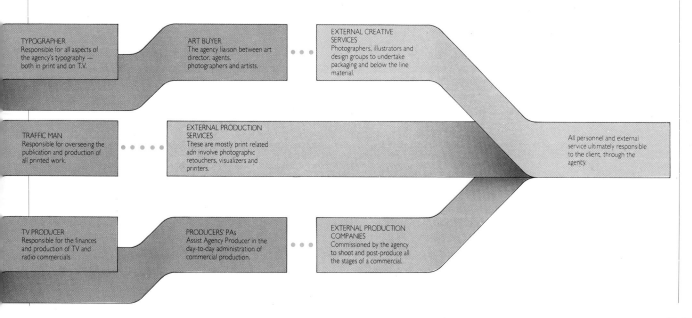

TYPOGRAPHER
Responsible for all aspects of the agency's typography — both in print and on T.V.

ART BUYER
The agency liaison between art director, agents, photographers and artists.

EXTERNAL CREATIVE SERVICES
Photographers, illustrators and design groups to undertake packaging and below the line material.

TRAFFIC MAN
Responsible for overseeing the publication and production of all printed work.

EXTERNAL PRODUCTION SERVICES
These are mostly print related adn involve photographic retouchers, visualizers and printers.

All personnel and external service ultimately responsible to the client, through the agency.

TV PRODUCER
Responsible for the finances and production of TV and radio commercials.

PRODUCERS' PAs
Assist Agency Producer in the day-to-day administration of commercial production.

EXTERNAL PRODUCTION COMPANIES
Commissioned by the agency to shoot and post-produce all the stages of a commercial.

THE BRIEF

In most cases the brief is a synthesis of ideas from the client's marketing people and the agency's planning, research and media departments. Before it lands on the creative team's desk it will have to meet with the approval of the creative director. After that, overall co-ordination of the project falls into the hands of the account management department, whose principal role is to act as a conduit between agency and client and ensure the smooth running of the business.

A good brief will contain eight pieces of information:

1 A description of the product and its marketplace.
2 The objectives of the advertising.
3 The target audience.
4 The key thought or proposition of the campaign.
5 Relevant facts to support the proposition.
6 The media in which the ads will appear.
7 Guidelines on the tone and personality of the advertising.
8 The budget allocated to production.

Using the brief. Whenever possible it's best to start work on a campaign by getting first-hand experience of the product. If that's out of the question you'll have to rely on the brief to give you a succinct description. It must also identify the target audience, and should suggest the media and tone of voice you use in addressing them.

Two questions remain – what do you say and how do you say it? The single most important point is item 4 – the key thought. It's the main input of the brief and must be the main out-take of the advertising. Most successful campaigns work by continually restating the same key thought in different and dramatic ways.

There are many modes of expression in advertising. These include demonstration, comparison, celebrity presenters, analogy, hyperbole, before and after comparisons, and emotional cues that range from humour to sentimentality and nostalgia. But there are no hard and fast rules as to how you can and should use them. This is where the problems start.

Cracking it. Much has been written about the creative process and yet it still remains mysterious and frustratingly elusive. Certainly there are no formulas for producing a new idea – formulas lead to the predictable, which is the last thing you want in an advertising campaign.

However, one thing is certain, ideas don't come out of thin air. They seem to occur when two relevant but unconnected thoughts collide. (Arthur Koestler called this 'bisociation', but it's usually known by Edward de Bono's term 'lateral thinking'.) The best way to encourage this is to fill your mind with as much relevant material as possible and then pull out a few thoughts and push them around on a layout pad. It's a hit-and-miss process but keep the key thought in mind and with luck you'll soon know that you've cracked it.

THE FIRST PRESENTATION

In these initial stages the creative director judges only one thing – the strength of the idea. For this he or she requires only the simplest of felt-tip drawings. An idea that works rarely requires more. (Look at any outstandingly effective advertisement and you'll see it can be described adequately in a very rough form.)

In making a decision, the creative director probably uses the simple criterion of the 'relevant-unexpected'. If an idea is relevant and therefore dramatizes the key thought, you are halfway there – you're saying the right thing. If it is also unexpected you are home and dry, because you are saying it in a way that is both noticeable and memorable.

The next step is to convince the client.

DEVELOPING A PRESS CAMPAIGN

Clients tend to be less 'ad-literate' than agency people and need the reassurance of more highly finished roughs or 'scamps' at the presentation. So while the copywriter is working on the body copy, the art director starts making decisions about layout, typography, illustration and photography.

Layout. Mercifully, as far as most accounts are concerned, the days of rulebooks for advertising layouts seem to have passed. Back in the 1960s, for example, David Ogilvy, chairman of Ogilvy and Mather, insisted on a particular configuration of elements – squared-up picture, headline beneath it and copy beneath the headline. He didn't allow headlines to be reversed out (set in white against a coloured panel or picture), or set in sans serif, or only in upper-case (capital) letters. In the same decade a company called Eye Scan conducted fairly scientific research into the way in which a reader's eyes would dwell upon elements of a layout, so that it could be redesigned to encourage more immediate and therefore effective communication.

These attempts to formularize layout have left their mark. Even today some companies enforce the strict maintenance of a house style. Generally speaking, though, the rules have all been successfully broken and only guidelines remain.

One such guideline is to ensure that the picture and layout are not doing the same job. To test this cover up the picture and see if the ad still makes sense. If it does, then the picture is in part superfluous and one or other of the elements needs to be changed; the most involving communication occurs when the message is found in the interaction of visual and headline. Once this principle is in effect you can choose which element will dominate. In this respect good ads are rarely evenly balanced. They are either picture ads or headline ads, with the emphasis going to the element that is inherently more dramatic.

There remains one golden rule. Before developing a layout, always consider the medium in which the ad will appear. Make sure that it will stand out and not be lost in a kaleidoscope of editorial and advertising graphics.

Typography. It's not essential for typography to be resolved at this stage. However, it may be helpful in selling the campaign, particularly if there is no photograph or illustration involved and the selling copy is pre-eminent.

Working together, the art director and agency typographer will use layout and typography to establish a style and format for the advertising that is distinctive and yet suficiently flexible to accommodate new ideas as the campaign develops: without this flexibility it will be hard to maintain graphic consistency for any length of time.

There are literally hundreds of typefaces available but relatively few are commonly used in advertising. Once the art director is happy with the style of the chosen face, it is usually left to the typographer to experiment with different ways of setting it. All typefaces can be modified at this stage. Most are available in bold, medium and light; they can also be condensed or expanded photographically at the typesetting house. Even after setting, the face can be letter-spaced by the typographer before the ad is pasted up.

Sometimes an art director may decide to integrate the picture with the copy, or even forsake photography and illustration for the 'creative' use of typography. It's then that the technical skills of the agency 'typographer' will prove invaluable.

As is the case in all areas of advertising design, legibility remains a serious concern. Some art directors take this to the extreme of believing that 'the best typography is never noticed'. The suggestion here is that the reader absorbs the information of the advertisement without being distracted by the actual letterforms. This may well be true, but it should never be forgotten that typographic style is a major component in the overall style of any piece of advertising.

Illustration or photography. The deciding factors in this debate are style, reproduction method and budget.

Illustration is an infinitely flexible way of executing a visual idea and, unless you enlist the services of a particularly famous artist, tends to be less expensive than photography. Anything that can be imagined can be drawn in just about any style.

Photography, on the other hand, offers the realism that only an airbrush artist could hope to approach by other means. This realism, however, is more flexible than one might imagine and the camera can be made to lie. Advances in photographic and darkroom techniques have brought photography closer to illustration. Retouching and photocompositions, or 'stripping-in', enable the photographer to make the most fantastical images appear convincingly real and therefore of greater impact. Unfortunately the expense of these techniques can be prohibitively high.

When choosing between illustration and photography the art director must consider the possibility of reproduction problems in the press. Black-and-white newsprint ads are particularly susceptible to inconsistent inking, and print-through from the other side of the page. Such problems ruin a delicate half-tone photograph. One option is to use a bolder illustrative style. Another is to treat the photograph with a special screen to strengthen its chances of survival.

Presentation material. As soon as the art director and typographer have made their decisions about layout and typographic style, the campaign can be briefed out to an art studio. Such studios specialize in producing magic marker roughs of the campaign and will finish the work to whatever standard is required. Drawing styles range from cartooning to complex mixed-media illustration, and headlines can be either drawn in or set by a type house on to a clear acetate overlay. Copy is usually indicated with squiggly lines or set Greek text.

Whenever possible, it's best to opt for a minimalist

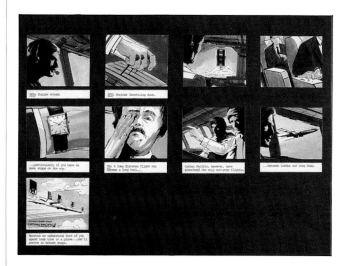

style in presentation roughs. Otherwise there is the danger that the studio will include inaccurate or irrelevant details in the drawing which then become red herrings in your discussions with the client. The best brief to a studio artist is 'when in doubt leave it out'. Most clients are sufficiently well versed in the visual slang of marker drawings to understand what the art director intends.

HOW WILL THE WORK BE JUDGED?

Clients usually make the same demands of creative work as do creative directors, but with added concerns and different priorities. The average client might have a mental checklist that reads as follows:
1 Is it a good idea? (i.e. relevant/unexpected)
2 Is the style flattering my product?
3 Is the tone of voice right for my target audience?
4 Is it easily understood?

5 Is it well branded?
6 Can I afford it?
Point 5 generates so much anxiety with clients that it's worth looking at in greater detail.

Branding. In any category there are usually products that are every bit as good as that marketed or manufactured by your client. But the campaign must sell this product, and not the others. So it is essential that when people recall the advertising, they remember the correct brand name.

This requirement often leads to conflicts between the client and the creative team. Some clients feel an ad is better branded if the headline contains the brand name – a requirement guaranteed to upset the copywriter. Others insist on increasing the size of the logo – guaranteed to upset art director and typographer.

The only effective solution to the problem is to

make sure that the style and graphics of the campaign are distinctively dissimilar to the advertising for products in the same category. Continual exposure will then make the campaign a memorable and identifying property of the brand.

PRODUCING THE CAMPAIGN

Most large agencies employ an art buyer whose role is to recommend and help choose an appropriate illustrator or photographer, and then handle the administrative side of the job – contracts, scheduling, and fee-bargaining in the event of the work being rejected. A good art buyer is the first to know of any new talent on the market and is therefore invaluable to the art director, who probably can't devote so much time to seeing artists' agents and reps.

Commissioning artists. There are literally thousands of artists to choose from. Fortunately the decision is made easier by the fact that they usually specialize – particularly photographers who tend to work mainly in one field such as fashion, still life, landscape, room sets, portraiture or reportage.

As soon as a decision has been made, a meeting is arranged between the artist, the art director and the art buyer. In the case of illustration, it's often the artist's agent who takes the brief. This poses no real problem for the art director, who will insist on seeing an accurate trace of the drawing before work can proceed. This trace can then be used as reference by the typographer for setting of the copy and headline.

With photography, it's more likely that the art director will talk directly to the photographer. There are no roughs or traces in this process and if the client doesn't want to pay for a test shoot, the brief must be clearly understood at the outset.

Retouching. As soon as the drawing or photograph has been approved by the agency it will be 'duped' (copied) on to a large format, usually as a 10 × 8in (25 × 20cm), transparency. The image can now, if necessary, be retouched – colours changed, highlights added, elements removed, other images added. This is a very flexible and creative process and success depends entirely on the skills of the retouching studio. When the work is complete a final dupe is made for the printers.

The mechanical. When all the elements of the ad are at hand – finished transparency, set copy, set headline and logo – the agency typographer assembles them into

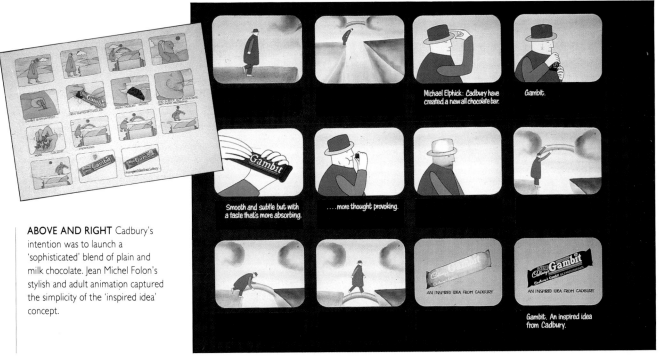

ABOVE AND RIGHT Cadbury's intention was to launch a 'sophisticated' blend of plain and milk chocolate. Jean Michel Folon's stylish and adult animation captured the simplicity of the 'inspired idea' concept.

LEFT This 48-sheet poster is part
of a campaign by Bulmers to
redefine Woodpecker as a more
alcoholic, more street-credible drink.
The changes between rough (above)
and finished artwork represent the
art director's attempts to simplify
and strengthen the image.

a 'mechanical'. This is simply a black-and-white paste-up of the ad that is sent, with the transparency, to the printers. Its purpose is to guarantee the accurate positioning of the elements, and before it leaves the agency it is signed by the key personnel on the account.

It is while assembling the mechanical that the art director and typographer can fine-tune the design – type sizes may change, the cropping on the picture can be altered, and often the body copy is partially rewritten so that the words fall more neatly on the page.

Proofing. Before the ad appears, the printers run off a few proof copies on the appropriate paper stock so that the art director can compare the reproduction with the original transparency and mechanical.

In the case of colour artwork the printers also run off some copies of the separated plates, called 'progressives'. These show individually the four colours – yellow, magenta, cyan and black – which will be printed one after another to recreate the full colour image. At the proof stage the art director can change

the colour balance of the ad by increasing or decreasing the inking of one or more of these 'process' colours. It makes the decision easier to look at separate prints of each. This is also the last opportunity to eradicate any blemishes on the printing plates before the ad appears in the publication. As with the mechanical, the final proof is signed by the key personnel.

The traffic department. There are many people with specific responsibilities involved in the production of an advertising campaign. That they should work together so efficiently would be improbable were it not for the services of the traffic department.

As soon as a campaign goes into production it is the traffic person's job to co-ordinate everyone involved – both inside and outside the agency. This means liaising with printers, retouchers, poster contractors, the art buyer, the art director, the copywriter and the account management team. Even after the work has started to appear in print, the traffic department keeps an eye on the publications to make sure there is no loss of quality.

DEVELOPING A POSTER CAMPAIGN

Designing a poster poses many of the same problems as designing a press campaign. Advertising in both media is judged on the same criteria and the production processes are virtually identical. So what are the important differences? Quite simply, size and situation.

The smallest outdoor poster measures 60 × 40in (1.5 ×1.2m) and is called a 4-sheet. It's in portrait format and has a big brother called the 16-sheet which is four times the size. In the landscape format, there is the 12/sheet (three 4-sheets side by side) and the 48-sheet billboard which measures 10 × 20ft (3 × 6m). There's also a 96-sheet poster known as the 'Supersite'.

It would be easy to assume that, because of its size and lack of copy, the poster is an art director's medium – a theory ruled out by any number of successful copy-based poster campaigns. However, the siting of posters does pose problems that favour a visual solution.

Unlike press advertising, where the medium captures the audience, posters have to fight to be noticed in crowded streets where people are on the move.

People on the street and in moving cars have little time to study advertising in detail as they might in a magazine. Consequently, poster headlines tend to be short, rarely as many as thirteen words, and set in a bolder type face than for comparable press advertising. Legibility, comprehensibility and style are critical if the poster is to succeed and, as there's no copy, the strategy must be unequivocally single-minded.

Occasionally, you see posters with copy displayed at bus stops and on railway platforms. The reason for this apparent transgression of an advertising law is that bus queues and waiting customers are captive audiences with time on their hands. They can get close enough and stay long enough to study the ad and probably welcome the diversion. These sites, usually 4-sheets or 16-sheets are the exceptions that prove the rule.

Poster specials. In 1985, the London agency FCO came up with a stunning idea to advertise adhesives for its client Araldite. They stuck a Ford Cortina to a 48-sheet poster site on one of the main arterial roads into London. The headline read 'It also sticks handles to teapots'. This extraordinary visual hyperbole with understated headline was the talk of the town. Since then other agencies have followed suit and it's clear that the 'poster special' is here to stay.

Although ideas for these sites are generated by the agency, the execution is in the hands of a specialist company. Obviously there are a restricted number of suitable sites and the expense is considerable, but sheer pulling power and drama make it a viable medium.

POINT-OF-SALE MATERIAL

Point-of-sale material is literally an advertising device that appears in the place of purchase – usually a shop. In many product categories point-of-sale is extremely important because the purchasing decision is made while the consumer is browsing through a selection of competitive goods. If a product is 'front of mind' it stands a better chance of being purchased.

The golden rule of point-of-sale is to use devices that recall the proposition of the advertising campaign. Apart from that anything goes, as long as the shop is prepared to display it.

DIRECT MAIL

Direct mail is a flexible medium because it consists of anything the client can afford and the post-office is prepared to deliver. Its real advantage is that, given the right list broker, the targeting can be very precise indeed. However, people in some professions, particularly doctors, receive so much direct mail advertising that they tend to throw the whole lot away

One answer to that problem is to send the target audience something that not only conveys the style and proposition of the advertising campaign but is of lasting value or interest – hence the number of safety posters in doctors' surgeries that bear a pharmaceutical brand name.

DEVELOPING A TV CAMPAIGN

Good TV commercials involve their audience with ideas that are relevant but unexpected, and executed in a style that suits the product and appeals to potential consumers – the same principles found in press and poster work.

A common mistake is to believe that on TV one can ignore the need to be single-minded. Usually people can retain only the central proposition of a commercial and, if the script is good, the name of the product. Branding is of particular importance on television where even the best-loved ads can be attributed to the wrong client if a popular slogan or jingle doesn't actually include the brand name.

1

2

3

4

5

6

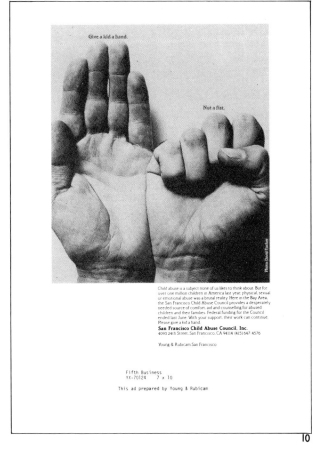

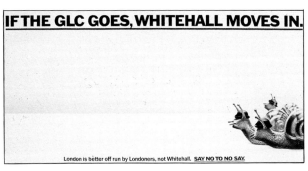

11

The posters for Boris Becker and the GLC **(8, 9, 11)** show clearly how the combination of two thoughts can create an idea. Coq Sportif and Sainsburys **(1, 3)** are differing exercises in style — one in fashion, the other in quality and reassurance. Araldite **(4, 5, 6)** is one of the all-time product demos, and Heineken **(2)** a much-loved hyperbole. Hard-hitting copy and strong images make a good combination in selling art **(7)** and funding for child care **(10)**.

Another threat to TV advertising is the 'Video Vampire' – agency slang for irrelevancy of visual execution which dominates the commercial to the point where the product message is totally forgotten.

To combat these problems creative teams often use mnemonics – devices that trigger the memory. Over the years there have been many famous ones such as the Colgate Ring of Confidence or the Esso tiger. Probably the most common technique has been to animate the company logo or symbol in a way that relates to the theme of the advertising.

The script. Scriptwriting is as much the activity of an art director as of a copywriter. It's a very different discipline from writing headlines and copy, but has to achieve many of the same ends.

As soon as the art director and copywriter have developed an idea it is scripted and storyboarded. Advertising scripts are not transcribed in the format of a play. The visuals are described in one column and the soundtrack (voices and sound effects) in another. This separation is useful as it makes it easy to study the two elements in isolation and see exactly what each is communicating.

When the script has been written it can be briefed to the studio for a magic marker storyboard. This is simply a presentation rough in comic strip form with the words and sound effects written under each frame. Some teams avoid mounting the frames on a single board and use a flip-over that reveals one at a time. The advantage is that it prevents the client from racing ahead to the end of the script while the writer or art director is still explaining the details of the first frames.

Two events must precede presentation to the client. The scripts must be sent to the appropriate regulatory body for approval, and the agency production department must check on the cost feasibility of the project.

Animation or live action. As Walt Disney has shown, animation is a wonderful medium for developing unusual characters and visual effects, and over the years advertising has used it very successfully to create brand personalities. It's a medium in which nothing is impossible and the stylistic variations are endless – unless, of course, you require photographic realism.

Live action filming is becoming increasingly expensive. It can come in at over three or four times the cost of an animated film of the same timespan, even before the actors have been paid their 'repeat fees' (the royalties that the principal characters earn every time the film goes on the air). However, live action remains the most popular of the two media – photographic imagery is more credible, has greater emotional range and can show the product in the most flattering light. But the two can work together: art directors often use animation to illustrate product functions or features that can't be filmed and then insert these sequences into a live action commercial. Currently there's a fashion for combining live action and animation simultaneously – a mixing of the real and the imaginary that's visually arresting.

CHOOSING A PRODUCTION COMPANY

The creative team and agency producer base this decision entirely on the director's style, the production company's experience and the cost. Directors tend to specialize in different styles – comedy, action, food, technical or close-up work (often referred to as table-top) and it's quite usual to discuss the project with several companies to be sure of getting the most competitive price. When a decision has been made the production company producer submits a detailed quote for client approval, and the pre-production phase begins.

Pre-production. During this phase the agency team and director hammer out the details of the shoot. A freelance art director is appointed by the production company to handle set design, brief model-makers and supervise styling and props. Also on the director's team are a casting agent who helps to find the right actors and a wardrobe lady who finds the right clothing. If it's an outdoor shoot they are joined by a location finder.

Once these details have been resolved to the satisfaction of the creative team, a full presentation is made to the client. If all goes well in this meeting, the agency should get the go-ahead.

The shoot. On average a commercial shoot lasts for one or two days and the agency team will be there to make sure they are getting the shots they want. Ideally, though, all variables will have been removed in pre-production and the creative team will have very little to do.

Post-production. On the day after the shoot there is a screening of the 'rushes'. These are ungraded prints of the director's favourite takes. The film editor attends this meeting and helps to choose the shots needed to cut the film together, then over the next few days assembles a rough cut for the agency to view – usually on the cutting bench or 'Steenbeck'. When the creative team are happy with the edit they can then commission any optical effects required – fades, dissolves or special effects.

Special visual effects can be added either to the film or to a video copy of the film. TV commercials don't suffer in video post-production, but cinema commercials have to be finished on film. In either case the work is done by specialist companies and briefed by the director and creative team. Film effects can sometimes take weeks to achieve, during which time the agency can only wait and hope for the best. Video effects, on the other hand, are immediate and allow director and creative team to be actively involved throughout the process.

Video post-production systems such as the Quantel Paintbox allow each frame of the film to be altered with exactly the same flexibility as colour photography re-touching. The potential of this device is vast.

Dubbing. When all the visual elements are in place the film or video transfer is taken to a dubbing studio where the soundtrack is married to the picture. Voice-overs, and sometimes music, are recorded live in front of the picture at the studio to ensure that they synchronize perfectly. Sound effects are usually taken from the studio library, but occasionally have to be specially recorded.

Grading and titling. The finished film is sent back to the lab to be graded. This is a photographic process that ensures that the colours on the film remain consistent throughout the commercial. When this has been done the end-title, or 'super', can be added to the final frames. The art director and typographer set the super on to flat artwork and it's then superimposed on to the picture.

As is the case with most aspects of post-production, grading and titling are easier to do on video, but many agencies and clients prefer to have the finished production on film. As soon as the titles are in position the film is transferred to master video tape and is ready for transmission to the TV stations.

PRODUCING AN ANIMATED COMMERCIAL

Because of the complex nature of the processes involved, animation production takes several weeks to achieve. Yet it's very much cheaper than live action and more flexible – the creative team can monitor each stage and the cost

of re-shooting sections is never very high.

From the creative team's point of view the procedure is very straightforward. The first decision is to choose an artist whose style of drawing is right for the animation. The second decision is to choose a production company whose animation techniques and experience are right for the artist. As with live action there are the pre-production hurdles of securing the client's agreement on style, cost and script details.

Key frames. Stage one is to brief the artist to draw several key frames. These must provide the animator with all the visual reference he or she requires to then animate the storyboarded scripts in a style that exactly resembles that of the artist. In this initial phase there will be much discussion between the animator, the artist and the creative team about style and execution. Once those issues are resolved the artist's job is virtually over.

Line tests. Using the key frame reference, the animators produce a line-only version of the film – with no colour and virtually no tonal detail. When this line test is completed the creative team can judge whether the elements are working properly and make changes as they wish. A certain amount of experience is needed in judging a line test as the characters often appear to move faster than in the full colour version of the film. A mistake now would be problematical, as the next stage is to shoot the finished film.

Post-production. When the colour film has been shot to everyone's satisfaction it is dubbed and graded in exactly the same procedures as a live action commercial. Titling can be done in the same way but it can sometimes be more consistent with the graphics of the film to let the animator introduce the titles in the artist's style. As soon as the title is on, the film is ready for transmission.

SUMMARY

Despite the many different processes and procedures in advertising design the underlying principles are simple, few and constant. An advertising message must be presented in a way that is intrusive and relevant, in a style that flatters the product and appeals to the consumer, and in a form that is immediately intelligible.

Given those elements, the right media and the required budget, even a weary commuter might pay attention.

11/PROMOTIONAL LITERATURE

In recent years manufacturing companies have gradually become more aware of the immense value of good design. They have learnt that design can simplify manufacture, reduce costs, improve functionality and give marketing appeal to their products. All manufacturers and providers of services need to explain their wares to their potential customers. Just as companies have learnt the benefits of good design in the manufacture of their products, so they are also learning the benefit of good design in the presentation of their product and service literature.

The range of product and service information includes:
- Product brochures
- Exhibition catalogues
- Holiday brochures
- Mail-order catalogues

As well as achieving a sale, it may be necessary to supply technical information. Then there may be a need to communicate information about the company itself – to customers, to staff, to shareholders or to financiers.

Some publications are required simply to convey information for entertainment or education – for example, guides to stately homes, parks and nature reserves. So here are several other examples of literature to add to those which directly sell products and services:
- Technical information
- Corporate brochures
- Annual reports and accounts
- Company flotation documents
- In-house staff magazines
- Visitor's guides

There is a choice in the type of format in which information in this category can be published. Much of it will be in the form of booklets; some of the less detailed items may be simple leaflets. But there is a range of alternatives, including:
- Mailing shots with complex folds/perforations
- Folders with gussets and pockets to take inserts
- Ring binders with loose-leaf pages

All these items and formats constitute the area of promotional literature, an area which represents a large part of the work of graphic designers. For the sake of example, all these products will be categorized into two groups – marketing literature and support literature – and explained by the specific examples of a travel brochure and a visitors' guide respectively.

MARKETING LITERATURE

Literature produced for the purpose of promoting the sale of products and services must be seen as one part of the total marketing effort. It may need to link in with packaging, advertising, point-of-sale material and public relations activity. The designer is a member of the total marketing team and should be involved at the earliest stages of the planning of the marketing strategy.

Those early stages may involve a number of specialists from areas such as marketing, advertising and research. The designer has to be able to recognize the particular market sector being addressed. Once a direction is agreed he or she must develop a design which meets all the technical requirements, but at the same time holds an attraction for the target market. This is true of all product categories. The reader must identify with the product on offer in order to become a potential customer.

Taking a travel brochure as a typical example of marketing literature, there are four distinct stages for the designer to work through. Firstly, deciding on the structure of the brochure, developing various creative solutions to the design brief and producing sketch visuals for each approach. Secondly, the adaptation of those visuals and working up into finished visuals for the cover, key introductory spreads and typical resort or hotel pages. Thirdly, the production of detailed layouts for each individual page of the brochure, showing descriptive texts and photographs. The last stage is for the designer to supervise translation of those layouts into final colour proofs.

Structure of the brochure. The first area to tackle is the structure of the brochure and the production specifications.

What page size should the brochure be? The vast majority of holidays are sold through travel agents, and their displays are these days geared to displaying A4 size brochures. A brochure larger than A4 will stand out among its competitors and give greater scope for the layout of individual spreads. However, if you produce anything other than A4, there is a danger that the brochure will be left out of agents' display systems. For a small operator this would be disastrous. A large operator could perhaps afford to supply a purpose-made brochure dispenser and thus secure a prominent position in the agent's display.

The range of literature promoting product or service is wide, and the brochure may be the only means used by a company to publicize its activities. The importance of good design cannot be overstated in a competitive marketing age. Shown here are examples of annual reports, product and corporate brochure, mail-order, guides and exhibitions and holiday brochures.

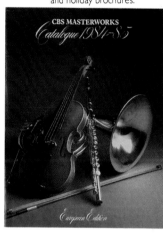

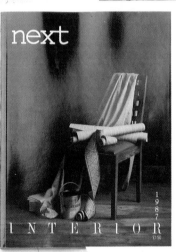

Should it have full colour printing throughout? In the last 20 years the cost of colour printing has steadily dropped in real terms, as technology has advanced. It is now common for the vast majority of promotional literature to be printed in full colour process. Only specialist, small-scale operators are likely to produce brochures in single or two colours. Once the print run exceeds 50,000 the difference in cost between single and full colour is not excessive, and the public has become used to and expects colour brochures.

Is the brochure to be subdivided into sections, by country, region, etc.? Many travel brochures run to 100 pages or more and some division of the content is necessary to make it manageable to the reader. Operators usually offer holidays to more than one country, so this is an obvious division. Others may offer holidays of only one type, or to only one country, in which case some other division may have to be evolved. One way of making these sections clear is to use single or double page introductions to each section, so that the flow of the brochure is broken by occasional pages of a different nature, introducing the next section. These pages should have a different layout, perhaps with background colour so that they can be picked out during a quick browse through the brochure. Each section can be colour coded, or identified in some other way, to establish discreet entities within the brochure.

What production methods are to be used? It is important to establish these in conjunction with the client at this early stage. Webb offset lithography or gravure printing can be used and each has its distinctive characteristics. The reproduction method may also affect the designer. Some electronic page makeup systems are not particularly good at tackling certain requirements, such as angled type. However if electronic page makeup is to be used it may allow certain design techniques which would be prohibitively expensive if carried out by conventional reproduction planning methods.

The binding method to be used affects the layout of individual pages. Brochures of up to 100 pages are likely to be saddlestitched, i.e. secured with two wires through the spine from the covers to the centre spread. Due to the bulk of the brochure, the inner pages will be over-trimmed by comparison to the outer pages – maybe as much as an extra 3mm (⅛in) off each page. To overcome the danger of the foredge trim getting too close to the text area, or even cutting some of it away, it is usual to shift the text area towards the spine. Each print section has its text area shifted by a different amount, resulting in a constant foredge margin but a diminishing gutter as you get closer to the centre pages of the brochure. This technique is a major restriction on designers, as it precludes the use of images bleeding across the spine of the brochure.

For brochures over 100 pages it is normal to use perfect binding techniques. This entails the print sections being stacked one on top of each other, rather than one inside each other as for saddle stitching. A small amount is routed off the spine and the pages are then glued inside a 'drawn-on' cover. This binding technique restricts visibility into the spine and this has to be taken into account when planning the page grid. Unlike a saddlestitched brochure, use can be made of the spine of the brochure to carry the title or a sales message.

Creative work. The initial creative work is aimed at developing various approaches to the problems defined in the brief. If this is the second or later year of a holiday product, the client will have identified areas of the design which are not working satisfactorily. It is for the designer to solve these problems and to establish a visual style for the brochure.

Establishing an individual style for the brochure is an important part of creating the identity of the product. Consideration should be given to whether illustration is appropriate to the product, perhaps large feature photographs are called for, or some special technique of presenting information.

At this stage of the design thumbnail sketches may be useful to begin to work up the feel for the layouts. Once an appropriate style is identified then work should transfer to full size.

Attention now transfers to the detail of the design: the choice of typefaces and sizes, the page grid, maps, colours, symbols, price and departure tables, etc. The design detail of such brochures is of vital importance as they have to communicate effectively the variety of information relevant to choosing a holiday. If a brochure is not easy to follow then it will not be used by counter staff in travel agencies and will soon be discarded by the travelling public.

Typefaces should be clear and legible, but also need to be suited to the atmosphere of the holiday. It may be that several are required to meet these needs. A decorative face can be used for large text introductions, but a clear and precise face is required for the small sizes and complex tabular matter usually found in the price and departure tables.

The page grid of a travel brochure is strictly functional. It has to accommodate a large amount of information packed into each page, with hotel descriptions and photographs displayed clearly. The grid needs to be flexible and there are arguments for using quite complex grids, perhaps with asymmetric columns. For example, the large amount of detailed tabular information required in a ski schedule can usefully be placed in a narrow column outside the main text area.

The style of any necessary maps can be a very useful way of emphasizing the individual identity of the brochure. Maps can be tint-laid in flat colours, they can be airbrushed or painted; they may be simple two-dimensional street plans or complex three-dimensional views. They can be used to bring in some illustration to reinforce the theme of the brochure design.

The choice of appropriate colours is an important part of creating the overall design style. However, the choice of colours cannot be made on a wholly subjective basis. Thought has to be given to the use of colours for small type, for black text being legible when printed over a panel of the colour, and for text reversed white out of the colour also being legible.

There are many aspects of holiday information which can best be communicated through the use of symbols; for example, special facilities available at resorts and the grading of hotels. There are other aspects which the operator will want to promote heavily and these too may be featured by the use of symbols; special offers, new hotels, etc. The designer has to create symbols which convey the information and stand out clearly on the page, yet at the same time are sympathetic to the overall brochure style. It is also important to develop appropriate ways of featuring the symbols on the page. To scatter them randomly is likely to be unsightly, yet to place them in too ordered a manner may defeat their very purpose.

The designer's typographic skills are exercised by the price and departure tables which are such a major feature of travel brochures. More often than not, these are placed one on each double page spread and usually give the departure dates, flight details, seasons, prices and any special supplements. In some cases they may be placed all together in one section at the back of the brochure, or even as a pull-out supplement. This gives the advantage of reducing the work and cost involved in last-minute price changes just before the brochure goes to press, but has the disadvantage of making it considerably less convenient for the potential client to refer to prices. Considerable care is needed with the typography of these 'P&Ds'. They contain a great deal of detailed information which has to be capable of being read without any ambiguity.

First presentation. To complete this initial work the designer needs to prepare sketch visuals for presentation to the client. This includes magic marker sketches of all the visual elements worked on so far, an annotated grid and samples of typefaces and sizes.

In presenting this initial stage to the client the objective must be to ensure that the design is progressing along the lines intended in the brief. A wide-ranging discussion can take place in an informal atmosphere. The client will be able to express opinions about the suitability of various alternative ideas.

The designer will be able to guide further work according to the outcome of the meeting. The next stage is to work up the ideas to their final form, to complete detailed design work on the various elements such as symbols, maps, the grid, type and colour specifications. Having established these, the designer puts together finished visuals of some double page spreads to show the design in its final form.

Finished visuals. A typical spread of hotel information is essential, as is a page of introduction to a resort or region. If there are to be pages dividing sections for each country then a sample of these will be prepared. It is a good idea to now look at the introductory pages to the brochure and develop a style for these in keeping with that already established for the main body of the brochure.

The cover is a vital part of the brochure design as it is the impact of the cover which will entice customers to pick the brochure off the travel agent's shelf. Ideas may already have presented themselves during the course of the work so far, and the designer may have made preliminary sketches to develop at this stage.

The cover image, whether it is photographic or illustrative, has to convey the type of holiday on offer: beach resorts, mountains, skiing, etc. It must also convey the country or area of the world which is included and the type of holiday-maker being aimed at, e.g. families, singles, senior citizens, etc. The designer needs to make use of type to complete the parts of the story which cannot be communicated in the image. It is likely that the client will also require certain sales messages to be prominently featured on the cover.

When the visuals are complete the next stage is full presentation of the designs to the client company. If the initial discussions were well founded, this next presentation stage should be a matter of routine with no major upsets. At this stage the client may wish to submit the visuals to formal or informal market research, to test the design before committing funds to production.

Layouts. At this stage the routine work begins. A typical travel brochure might have some dozen pages of 'intro and extro' (the pages introducing the company and its products at the start of the brochure, and the pages giving booking conditions, flight details, and booking forms at the back). By contrast there might be anything from 30 to 300 pages of holiday information, every page carrying almost the same information as the one before.

Work is delegated to a layout artist or junior designer who can produce layouts following the established design guidelines incorporated in the approved visuals. The designer supervises this work and ensures that standards are maintained, and is also required to solve any new design problems which arise during preparation of the layouts.

The layouts are working documents and not made up to a presentation standard. They may be prepared on a printed grid, with the various elements attached with low tack tape so that they can be easily repositioned. Headlines, text areas, photographs, symbols and areas for P&Ds are shown. The position of photographs is indicated by simple keyline boxes, with keyline traces to indicate their content or screened PMTs of each transparency, trimmed to fit the keyline box. The latter is ideal from the client's point of view, as it enables checking that the correct transparency has been selected, that it is the right way round and that the cropping is acceptable. It is much cheaper to make changes at this stage than it is when the colour proofs arrive.

It is likely that several stages of proofs will be required; for example, typesetting galleys, initial layouts, and revised layouts.

The last of the layouts to be completed will be the intro and extro pages, as these contain a great deal of information which has to be finalized at the last minute.

Stages in the production of a brochure for Crown Suppliers

1 Initial roughs following picture selection.

2 Illustrator's pencil rough — i.e. his first response to the brief. As can be seen in **9** the Basic Concept was approved.

3 Marked-up manuscript

4 Uncorrected galleys marked up for revision

5 Final galleys

6 Prints of selected photos — later enlarged or reduced to correct size for accurate position guides on artwork

7 Artwork (note position guides for pics) marked up for colour

8 Corrected colour proof

9 Final product

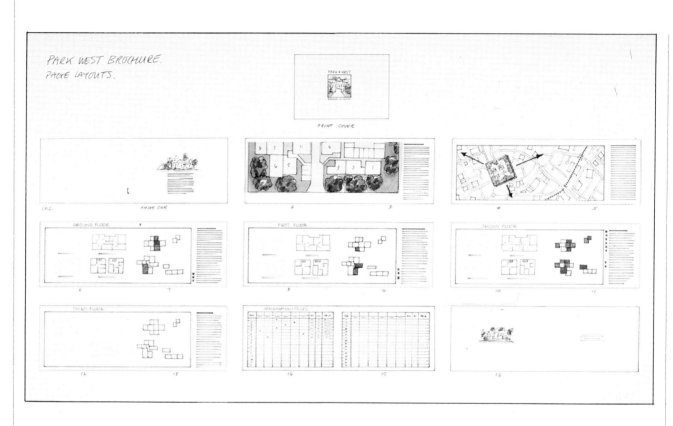

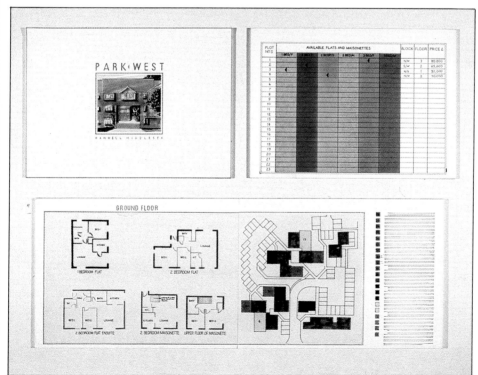

Designed specifically for the prospective purchaser by John and Jones, this brochure had to present a great deal of information in a simple and understandable format. The client wanted to sell the apartments prior to their completion. The use of colour-coding and logical layout enabled the purchaser to see the exact location and ground plan, as well as elevations and other details. Shown (above) we see the flat plan devised for the arrangement and number of pages, a dummy page layout (left) and the brochure cover (far right).

These require considerably more design input than the other layouts.

Supervision of production. The designer is normally responsible for ensuring that all necessary instructions have been given to the repro house, and liaison over technical matters.

If electronic page makeup is to be used, the revised layouts go to the repro house together with the transparencies and artwork for any items which are to appear in colour. From this material the repro house will produce full colour proofs for client approval and only after that stage is the black text added. Alternatively, if conventional reproduction is to be used, complete camera-ready artwork is produced with text in position, from which the repro house produces a colour proof complete with black text.

In both cases it is unlikely that the P&Ds will be available at this stage. Inevitably they are subject to last-minute changes due to commercial factors and are likely to be typeset only at the very last minute. They are usually supplied on film to the printer, to be combined with existing film when making plates.

SUPPORT LITERATURE

This area of promotional literature has to function in support of the sales effort being made by the marketing literature. The emphasis is quite different because the purpose is not to sell, but to provide backup information, to inform, even to educate.

As an example of the design processes involved, we shall look at a visitors' guide to a site of interest. Such publications promote their subjects in a much less direct way than do travel brochures. The reader may have received a promotional leaflet as an encouragement to visit the site, but it is this main explanatory brochure which is fulfilling the central role. A visitor who is assisted to understand the site, to appreciate its qualities and to enjoy the visit will be the best possible ambassador to attract further visitors.

The distinct phases to be worked through for this type of publication are:
- Briefing and site visit
- Design concepts
- Illustrations and diagrams
- Detailed layouts
- Supervision of production

This area of promotional literature is provided for a

different type of client. Of course, they are concerned with marketing their sites to the public, but educational and recreational aims are equally important. The major demands placed upon the designer are for accuracy, quality and a design which captures the mood or the historical connotations of the site.

Briefing and site visit. The first task for the designer is to read the text of the proposed document and acquire an understanding of what the site is about, what features are important, what are its unique qualities. Much of this may be contained in the brief received from the client and the designer's skill is to present the detailed, factual information provided by the author in a way which the layperson will find attractive and easy to assimilate.

A visit to the site is the next vital step. A relaxed day out is required, not a hurried whistle-stop tour. The designer must take time to absorb the atmosphere and get in tune with the subject. There must be time for strolling around, looking and thinking. The public will be doing exactly the same, and every thought and question which enters your mind is likely to be what will enter theirs.

The author is concerned with providing the facts to answer those questions, but the designer can contribute considerably by ensuring that the information is presented in a logical sequence, with the correct subdivisions and flow. The author may have distinct ideas about the relative interest of different aspects of the site, yet the layperson may have a very different view. It is important for the designer to establish a balance and ensure that the brochure captures the reader's interest.

The problem here was to produce an interesting brochure dealing with a dry subject — finance for business — with a predominance of text. It was designed by QDOS, whose solution was to commission witty illustrations, use coloured tints inside and foil-blocking for the cover.

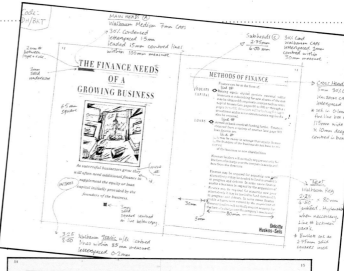

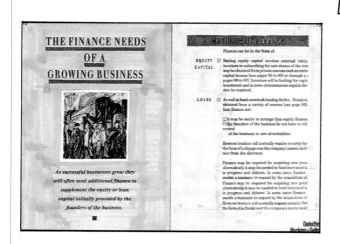

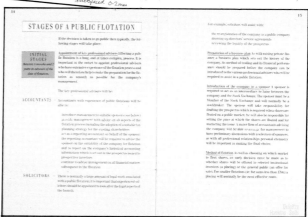

SPECIALIST FINISHING TECHNIQUES

Adding something extra with specialist finishing techniques:

FOLDING
Many specialist folds can now be achieved even on Web presses — 'throw-out' pages and 'short' pages are possible.

DIE CUTTING
Shapes can be cut die-stamped into pages and covers to produce pockets or cut-out shapes, or create a unique shape of brochure.

PERFORATING
Perforating of tear-off coupons can be achieved when finishing or even on press. Gummed strips, attached envelopes, reply stamps — all are possible from specialist presses.

BLIND EMBOSSING
A raised image of a logo or type without an ink impression. Or, if something less subtle is required, emboss behind a printed image.

BLOCKING
Matt, gloss and metallic foils in many colours can be used when blocking a logo or other simple shapes.

VARNISHING
Varnish can be applied on press or as a separate operation. Gloss or matt finishes are available. This is useful on covers to avoid finger marking. If printed on to the sheet the varnish can be applied just to certain areas, ie over photographs.

LAMINATING
Film laminating gives a very high-quality feel to covers and provides good protection from wear. It is available as gloss or matt finish.

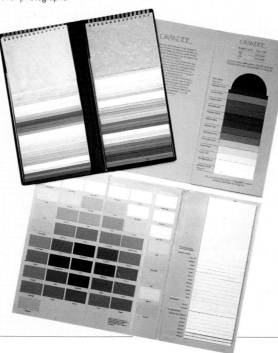

COLOURED PAPERS
Wide range of colours available in a variety fo qualities.

QUALITY STOCKS
Laid papers, watermarks (even of your own design) and specialist high-quality stocks are available.

STIPPLE EFFECTS
Stipple effects and patterns can be embossed onto your paper after printing.

TRANSPARENT MATERIALS
Tracing paper and film can be used as interleaves or overlays to impose additional printed information over backgrounds.

METALLIC BOARDS
Metallic-finish boards can be used for covers, folders etc.

LEFT Coloured papers are now made in such quantities and in such a wide range of colours that manufacturers will supply potential clients with expensively produced sample books such as this.

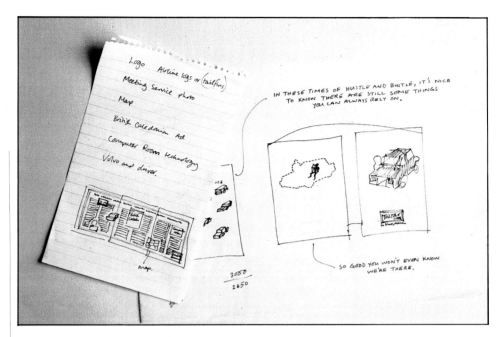

Grey marbled paper, heavily leaded text, specially commissioned photography, illustrations and diagrams all combine to give this brochure designed by QDOS for a chauffeur-driven car company the sophisticated executive look which was felt would open new market areas for the company. The brief contained three key elements for inclusion: a nationwide computer network, existing services at airports and the cars themselves, one make and one colour.

LEFT AND BELOW This company has a US-based and a UK-based operation, necessitating two different brochure headlines. The American version (left) is considerably more explicit.

While looking around the site, the designer can also keep an eye open for interesting visual aspects which may be of use in the design.

The warden or custodian of the site is likely to be a mine of information on how the public react to their visits. What aspects of the site do they find most interesting? What areas do they have difficulty in understanding? Do they find their way round easily? Do certain objects or areas attract repeated questions? Are there criticisms of the existing literature or guide book? All these questions are best answered on the spot, by the people who deal with the visitors every day.

The author or editor will have prepared a selection or relevant illustrations and photographs for inclusion in the brochure. However, as a result of the visit and consideration of conditions on site, the designer may have further suggestions to make, in particular to meet a specific need which the author has not so far had to consider. For instance, the designer may want a device to act as an end marker for text, or an interesting viewpoint to be photographed for a frontispiece.

Design concepts. By now the designer has developed an idea of how to tackle the structure of the document. After discussion with the author, a page plan can be drawn up. Decisions are made about how to group information, about the order and the level of illustration in each section.

A guide may best be divided into 'tour information', which is to be read as the visitor walks around the site, and 'background information' which can be read at leisure after returning home. The two sections need quite different design treatment. The former requires a size of type and a measure which can be read easily while walking along. The illustrations need to be co-ordinated with what the visitor will see on the tour, and a map will be required to explain the route in a way that relates to the order of information in the text. The layout ideally contains a complete section within one double page spread – so that all the relevant information is accessible at one time, making it easy for the visitor to glance away and return again to the text when ready.

The section of background information could use a smaller type size and a wider measure, the illustrations might be wider ranging and the layout can flow continuously over several pages.

The visual style can now be considered. Both this and the chosen typeface need to be sympathetic to the subject. When devising a grid the designer must take into account the extent and type of illustration which will be required. This type of publication is likely to be heavily illustrated and the sizes of illustration and the method of detailing captions need to be carefully considered.

Visuals should be prepared to demonstrate the overall style of the publication: a cover, the first double page spread and perhaps an example of each different section in the publication, showing how each might be treated visually. Sample settings are needed to show the typefaces, sizes and measures.

Illustrations and diagrams. Photographs, illustrations and diagrams play a vital role in this type of publication as they are a means of conveying information quickly and easily. The client usually supplies photographs with the manuscripts, as these are often taken for other purposes and can be made available when a brochure is to be produced. Further photographs may be needed to convey certain aspects or to meet design needs.

When objects need to be photographed for use in the publication the designer needs to decide on a treatment. Should they be seen on a background, or as cut-outs? Should there be shadow to give depth? How is scale best indicated? The designer should be capable of selecting a suitable photographer and art-directing the work.

Some aspects of the subject may not lend themselves to photography but instead require illustration: for example, illustration might be used to recreate mediaeval scenes inside a castle; a cutaway drawing to show the workings of a steam engine in a railway museum; or a line illustration showing the planting of marram grass to reclaim sand dunes. The commissioning of such illustration is dealt with elsewhere in this book.

A specialist area is the research of illustrations from archives, picture libraries and other sources. The designer may call in such an expert to seek out illustrations which are required to cover specific points in the brief, or just to provide a selection of relevant material to assist in the layout.

Diagrams, plans, maps and charts are another way of conveying information in a visual form. How much easier it is to understand density of population when presented with a chart relating population to land area than to face two pages of figures. The designer must be able to identify from the text and from the site visit, what information would benefit by this type of presentation, and then create a diagram which communicates the information clearly and with style.

Detailed layouts. After the visuals have been approved by the client, work can commence on typesetting to the agreed style. It is likely that the full text will be available, but captions may be dealt with at a second stage. They are often written only when the context of the illustration is finalized.

With this type of publication almost every element should be available at the time of preparing layouts. Using PMTs of photographs, illustrations and diagrams the designer is able to prepare working layouts complete in every detail.

Care will be taken to maintain a balance between text and illustrations, with each section having its own style and 'pace'. Decisions are needed in regard to the sizing of illustrations and the positioning of captions, but almost all other aspects will have been established through the initial creative work.

At this stage the author checks the whole document, not just for typesetting accuracy but also to see that all illustrations have been correctly related to the text. There will probably be debate between the designer and the client about the relative importance of items within the layout, about the clarity of diagrams, about the size of photographs, etc. This is an important part of the process of achieving the best result and the points must be resolved to the satisfaction of both parties. Revised layouts are prepared to show the changes.

There may be committees or boards of governors to satisfy but due to the unchanging nature of the subject there should be very little to alter at this stage.

Supervision of production. As with any job, the designer supervises the production through artwork and reproduction to the printing of copies. Paste-up artwork presents no difficulties but the preparation of complex colour-separated artwork for diagrams needs careful attention to detail and a good knowledge of reproduction methods.

The mixture of original material to be reproduced – from transparencies to line illustrations, from finely detailed maps to bold colours on bar charts, and from delicate watercolours to dark etchings – will be a challenge to the reproduction house. The designer needs to pay special attention to the colour proofs.

It is worthwhile having full machine proofs for this type of publication, preferably backed up so that an exact dummy copy can be made up by hand. When all is in order the proofs can be passed for press.

MARKET RESEARCH

Market research can play a vital role in the preparation of a product or service for the marketplace. This includes the design of promotional literature in support of those products or services. Of course, many client companies may feel that the expense of market research is beyond their means and may prefer to build up their own view of the marketplace.

There are many research companies which offer an independent service to test designs and to compare them against competitors' literature. These services may be used prior to preparing the designer's brief and/or at the presentation visual stage. Techniques do vary, but one standard method is to bring together and consult with small groups of people representative of the target market. Discussions are lead by a researcher and a report is prepared for the client.

DESIGN SKILLS

This field of graphics is very broad, unlike specialist areas such as publishing, advertising, packaging or newspaper design. The designer working in this field needs to possess a wide range of skills to cope with the variety of demands.

Communication skills are needed, to be able to relate to a broad range of clients and to quickly get to understand their needs. Analytical skills get to the root of design problems and visualizing skills create the designs and styles suited to the various markets the product is addressing. An understanding of market matters is required, and the designer must be able to art-direct illustrators and photographers. Typographic skills are useful in order to be able to handle detailed and complex information, and a good understanding of reproduction and printing processes is also essential. Of course, it may be that some of these skills are beyond the individual and then it is important to bring in the services of a specialist where necessary.

The reward for the designer working in this field is to have a broad range of clients and industries and to have to deal with an ever changing set of design problems. This can be a stimulating area of graphic design.

Presentation visual for a sample spread in a winter holiday brochure. The marked-up layout (above) and the printed result (right) show how important it is to present a large body of information in a persuasive way. The designers were Thumb Design Associates.

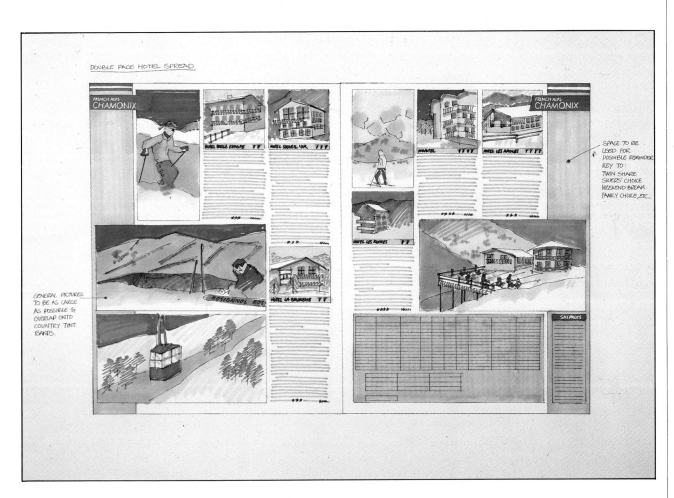

Here we see a colour visual (above) for the same brochure, together with the rough for the cover and the final printed cover (right).

12/MAGAZINES

The development of inexpensive methods of colour printing in the 1940s and 1950s gave rise to the magazine explosion of recent decades. Somewhere between a book and a newspaper, the magazine has evolved with aspects of both these long-established products into a specialized form of its own. The range of magazine formats extends from the original classified papers advertising articles for sale, printed on cheap newsprint, saddlestitched and sold weekly (now threatened by local free sheets), to the highly sophisticated glossies, designed with beautiful images and printed on coated paper, perfect bound with laminated covers. Within this range are magazines to cater for all tastes and specializations: sports and special interests, automobiles, rock, media, fashion, architecture, news, and sex. If there is a market interest, a magazine will exist to cater for it

TOOLS OF THE TRADE

The most important factors governing the look of a magazine are the paper surface, the method of printing, and the art direction.

The two main methods of printing are gravure and web offset lithography. Gravure is an intaglio process worked on large, copper-surfaced cylinders which give 8-16 pages to view. It puts a photomechanical screen over everything, including type. Although it may not pick up fine rules and fine serif type, the advantages of gravure are that the reproduction detail in the mid tones is very rich, and it is good for long runs. For this reason it is used for magazines with a large print run, such as colour supplements distributed with Sunday newspapers; women's monthlies, for example, do not require long runs.

Web offset lithography which has recently become more economical for short runs, is very popular because of the vastly improved paper stock available for this process. It gives from 8-64 pages to view in multiples of eight, and is more flexible on machine sizes, and therefore the format of the magazine, and in output. Most of the glossy monthlies are printed by this method.

Letterpress, once common, is rarely used now; but it can create a great sense of urgency due to the impact of the type on the paper surface, and the associations with newsprint. With sensitive typography printed on coated paper, it can look very exclusive.

TYPOGRAPHY

As fashions change in magazines, so they do in typography, but many stylistic characteristics of previous decades have been incorporated into new magazines and into the typography of the eighties. In magazine layout, it is important that the typography reflects, in mood and colour, the content and style of the magazine. The range of available typefaces is enormous: from Bodoni in *FMR*, to News Gothic in *The Sunday Times*, to Futura in *Elle*; Franklin Gothic, Plantin and Baskerville. The choice lies with the designer, the deciding factors being size, weight, leading, letter space and line lengths. Now, photosetting enables designers to distort typefaces, or to extend or condense them (not always with success).

Text setting is now generally photoset on digitized phototypesetting machines. Headlines are produced by headline photosetters. This system can condense or distort typefaces and vary letter spacing to the designer's instructions, and is important for quality control, as ordinary text setting deteriorates in quality over 18-point size.

New technology. Magazines are moving slowly to direct input of typesetting and direct keying of type matter, producing galleys which can be arranged and laid out

In this newsagent's shop, magazines can be bought to meet all needs — women's fashion, style in the home, DIY, hobbies, fishing, automobiles and so on. The range is vast, from glamour and high design to small-circulation professional magazines such as *Pig Farmer's Monthly.*

directly on screen. This is giving rise to some interesting new typographic treatments. The equipment allows the designer control in changing sizes of type and running around shapes, while still being able to see the working layout, and makes it unnecessary to mark up type and wait for galleys to be returned from the typesetter.

STYLE

The style of a magazine is its particular blend of editorial content, pictures, typography, and use of white space. The way in which all these aspects are combined is what gives the magazine its identity.

Given a set of pictures, headlines and captions, a good designer could produce a number of pages suitable for *Vogue, The Sunday Times* magazine, *Paris Match* or *Stern,* just by the different techniques used to tell the story: the cropping of the pictures, the display and choice of headline and captions, and the use of white space create the internal rhythm of the magazine. It is important to maintain the image of the magazine, with its layout presentation, typography and photography, in order to retain the product identity. One magazine differs from another in the same way

that a Ford car differs from a Mercedes: underneath the structure conforms roughly to the same basic principle, but the exterior style is easily identifiable.

The different magazine styles are easily recognized: colour supplements have a restricted use of white space due to editorial limitations, and may be printed gravure on less glossy paper stock. Glossy magazines have superior reproduction quality, printed by web offset or sheet feed on coated paper, and may have a more adventurous approach to editorial and design style. In weekly reviews the text is on cheap paper, closer in appearance and texture to newspapers.

NEW MAGAZINES

A new magazine must first of all identify the market in which it hopes to achieve its sales, and the profile of the readership. An identifiable audience attracts advertising, and the advertising will finance the magazine, provide its operating profit, and recoup the start-up cost, which, with initial promotion campaigns, could reach over a million depending on the softness of the market and the type of magazine. Most magazine profits are provided by the advertiser, with a smaller percentage coming from the cover price. An increase in advertising means bigger issues, more editorial space, a better product, increased circulation, leading to more advertising, and so on.

But this is the ideal profile, and there are many factors which can affect it, such as limited readership interested in the subject, limited source of advertisers, competition with other magazines for both advertising and circulation.

In identifying the market, the design concept should address the reader in a style which reflects the content of the magazine. There is no point in a weekly magazine which relies on late pictures and copy looking like a magazine with long lead times. Wide column setting for example, is associated with a more leisurely absorption of editorial content on the part of the reader. We all carry a subconscious style of news presentation, and a news review styled like a monthly does not indicate the appropriate sense of journalistic urgency.

The UK launch of *Sportsweek* in 1986 was a good example of very good intentions put into the wrong visual language. The body copy (text) was too open and slow in appearance, the column width too wide, and the relationship of pictures and headline had no sense of the late lead times and special qualities of the magazine.

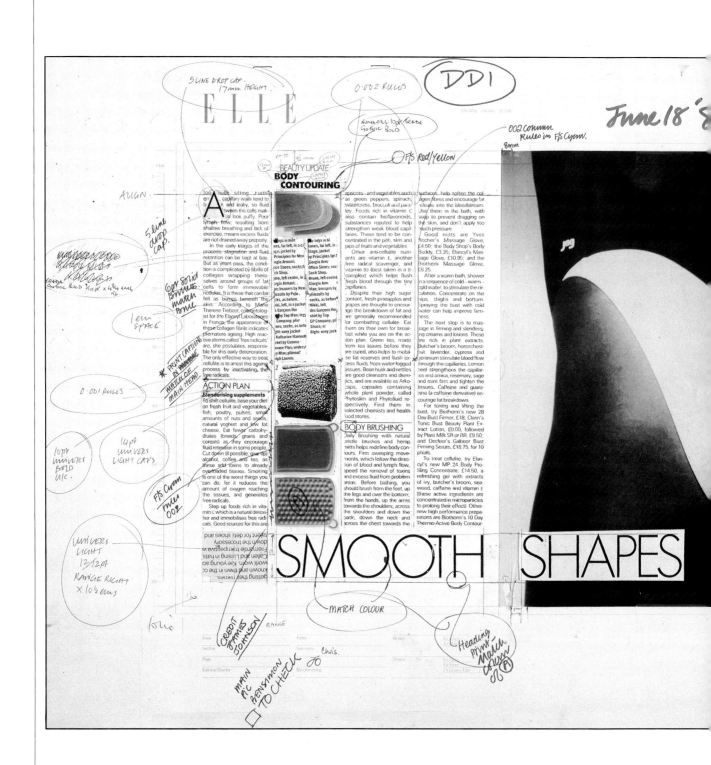

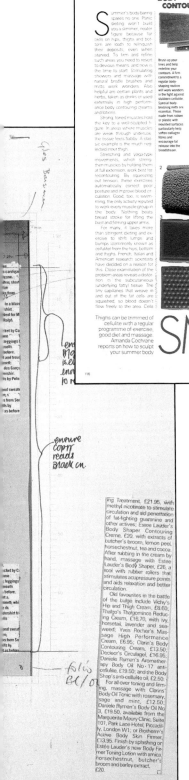

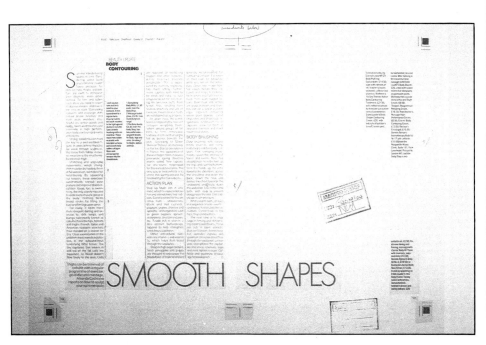

Marked-up layout (left), chromalin (top) and ozalid (above) for a spread in an issue of *Elle* magazine. It is interesting to note the amount of information for printer which is contained in the layout. The rough is marked up for typesetting, position of type and pictures, and colour for type and pictures.

PRODUCTION STAGES

The first element needed is the advertising list, which contains the names of advertisers and the positions guaranteed to them in the current issue. The different positions are: pages facing editorial matter (FM), page of colour, double-page spread (DPS) pages colour, or mono. Facing matter commands more money on the rate card, as do early positions in the magazine, and the outside back cover, because advertisers believe that these get better exposure and increased reader traffic. Response to the advertisements is monitored by the agencies which designed and placed them. In some cases, coupon returns indicate the success of an advertisement in selling the product.

The editor, features editor and art director meet to discuss the presentation and length of features. The art director then produces a flat plan, mapping out the space needed for editorial features and fashion pages. The advertising has to be fitted around these pages, as far as possible fulfilling the guarantees made by the advertising sales department; otherwise the advertiser may be entitled to a partial refund. There is generally a balance of advertising space within magazines from 50 to 75 per cent but this may vary, depending on the size of the issue, or the type of magazine.

Domination by the advertising can kill the editorial product, and will, in turn, diminish the attraction of the magazine to advertisers. In the UK this was demonstrated when a major colour supplement newspaper, *The Sunday Times,* closed down for a year: its direct rival, the *Observer* magazine, became crowded with advertising without a proportional increase in editorial space. This finally resulted in complaints in the media press from the advertisers.

Technical preparation. Text copy is sent for typesetting, and when returned in galley, print and pictures are laid out on grid sheets. Ideally black-and-white photoprints should be used, scaled to the size and position they will appear when printed. This avoids unfortunate juxtapositions, ensures that the printer can see the exact crop of the picture, and produces better layouts and typography. It is always a better solution than tracing outlines on a copy scanner and using these for the visual guide. The PMT machine with tonal paper is ideal for this, and black-and-white prints can be made from colour transparencies or prints.

The grid is the means by which type matter can be structured and related to the pictures thoughout current and subsequent issues. The grids are printed in

Photography is the dominant feature in this spread from the *Observer Magazine*. Clever juxtaposition and careful positioning of three images of model Jerry Hall ensure a successful fashion feature, as do the precise instructions for the printer seen on the rough (left).

Left: sleeveless rayon tunic, £230; organza frill skirt, £276. Shoes by Manolo Blahnik for Ozbek from Manolo Blahnik, 49 Old Church Street, London SW3 Below: black organza blouse, £115; black rayon skirt with gold frogging, £310 Right: rayon frill dress, £460 Previous page: ruffle front taffeta shirt, £276; rayon frill dress, £460 Cover: fuchsia singlet, £80; ottoman ribbed cardigan, £147; Venetian wool skirt, £184. All clothes are by Rifat Ozbek and will be available from August from Harvey Nichols, Knightsbridge, London SW1; Browns, 27 South Molton Street, London W1; The Beauchamp Place Shop, 55 Beauchamp Place, London SW3; Hoopers, The Strand, Torquay, Devon; Matches, 34 High Street, Wimbledon Village, London SW19. Gloves, £30 by Cornelia James for Ozbek (stockists as above). Tights from a selection at Fogal, 36 New Bond Street, London W1

Hems are always just above the knee. Necks and backs plunge, evening wear is liberally embroidered with chains, tassels and bows

blue on white stock and can take layouts, galleys and photoprints. They can be simple or complicated, depending on the variation of presentation within an issue. *Newsweek* and *Time*, for example, are highly structured to accommodate the various international sections which have to fit into the main magazine and still look part of the whole, but some magazines use the grid only as a basic structure, to provide a framework in which the typography is related to the pictures.

Once the layouts are complete, headlines are written, together with intros. Captions are written to the layouts when the pictures have been chosen and positioned on the page.

Mark-up and proof-checking Clear instructions should be marked on the layout for the engraver as to the kind of result required from the originals. When producing black-and-white originals on colour pages, a stronger result can be achieved by printing on 4-colour black. Tints such as gunmetal, red, black, duotones or sepia, can also be used. Background tints can be used behind the pictures to improve page layout, and the reproduction quality of the original.

Chromalins, match proofs or 'wet' proofs are produced from the separations, and checked for colour and position. At this stage, colour corrections can be made in conjunction with the engraver, to correct or try to improve the final printed result. Once the job is on machine, minor modifications can be made. But with four pages in track on each cylinder, and up to 32 pages to view, correcting one picture can distort the colour balance of another. It is usually better in practice to go for a compromise at this point, in order to achieve an overall balance to the sheet.

Binding. Magazines can be saddlestitched (mostly weeklies) or perfect bound – the square-backed effect seen mostly in monthly magazines. Perfect binding allows for more flexibility in adding different sections within the issue, including regional sections which enable advertisers to target certain areas of distribution.

When printed separately, all sections can be either 4-colour, or 4-colour backed by mono, or mono. These can be distributed through the magazine as required, or as determined by the budget.

Lead Times. This refers to the time it takes from typesetting the galley to the appearance on the newsstands of an issue. It may vary from a few days, as with news magazines like *Time* and *Newsweek*, to 12 weeks, as in

1

2

3

4

5

6

the USA where printing and distribution centres are widely dispersed, so that transportation becomes an important factor in the schedule. To avoid this problem *Time* and *Newsweek* are printed in various centres, with regional sections of the magazine inserted. The pages are transmitted by satellite to the centres, which reduces the final distribution time to the subscriber or retailer. Short lead times can in any situation prove more expensive, due to extra demands on the printer, and increased staff levels needed to maintain production to meet the schedule.

THE ART DEPARTMENT

Overall responsibility for visual presentation of a magazine belongs to the art director. The role requires continual liaison with the editor, features editor and specialist editorial staff to ensure that pictures are being generated for forthcoming issues. If there is no picture editor, as on most monthly magazines, the art director covers this role with the help of an assistant, seeing photographers' books (portfolios), commissioning photography and artwork. If the magazine has a picture editor, the art director is involved in discussing the pictures for specific features: it is the picture editor who contacts and briefs photographers and co-

ordinates the shoot, though the art director may attend.

The art director is kept in touch with the schedule for reproduction and printing by the production department. He or she may be present at proofing, and also on press when an issue is printed, or this job may be assigned to a deputy. Passing on press is not possible, however, on weekly magazines, as the schedule is too demanding; in this case the production department assumes the responsibility, checking back to the art director on the progress of the work.

Picture editing is done by the art director, deputy art director or picture editor. After full discussion, the deputy or the art editor, who looks after the illustration requirements of the magazine, processes the layouts through the art department before they are passed to the sub-editors for headlines and captions. Depending upon the size of the magazine, there may be two or more assistants in the art department, sometimes employed on a freelance basis.

Freelance services and contributors. Art department staff may need to call on the services of professional stylists to arrange hair and makeup for portraits, fashion and beauty shots, and to research and organize locations, transport and props. Home economists deal with food

7

8

9

10

The team working on the launch of *The Artist's and Illustrator's Magazine* had found that they had differing opinions as to what kind of cover they should work towards. Concepts were refined down to three main options. A traditional all over bleed design (**1, 5, 6**); an up-market image cover with lots of space around a smaller picture (**3, 4, 7**), and a busy, 'grab you' cover with lots of images and cover lines fighting for attention (**8, 9, 10**). Various different combinations of type and wording were tried plus a commissioned photograph of an artist at work in an idyllic setting. The designer also introduced a white 'frame' (**2**) as an alternative. A number of practising artists were invited to offer their opinions, and the team finally plumped for the busy 'selling' jacket, partly because it was very different from all the competing magazines and partly because it presented an opportunity to put over the 'fresh' editorial approach. This was followed through with a number of roughs which resulted in the advertising issue (**9**), which is used to show potential advertisers. This cover was felt in retrospect to be too dull and the final launch issue (**10**) was redesigned with a white background.

preparation prior to photography for cookery features. These people usually work freelance and are briefed by the art director in conjunction with the editor, or by the features editor responsible for the particular piece.

The contribution from photographers and illustrators is part of the life-blood of a lively magazine. They generally work freelance and are commissioned for a specific story. Editorial work can allow the photographer or artist more creative input than may be encountered in advertising work; this stimulation in some part compensates for the smaller fees affordable from editorial budgets. They can use the creative platform of editorial work in their portfolios, and the more prestigious the magazine, the better the effect.

It is essential for anyone on a magazine design team to keep a good contact book with details of photographers and their specialist fields of work. You should take the opportunity to see artists' and photographers' work to find out who is producing the kind of images required by your magazine. Pictures may be hired in from picture agencies, and these may also provide international links if pictures are to be commissioned abroad. Reference directories such as *The Creative Handbook* in the UK and *The Black Book* in the USA list services and contact numbers, a useful resource. For illustration work, artists' agencies represent a range of artists, many of whom have specialized talents.

Using illustrative material. It is important to respect the work of photographers and illustrators. If cropping is necessary, for example, this should be done in an intelligent and sensitive way, always working from the original transparency or artwork. A few basic rules should be observed: ensure that verticals are vertical; cut off tops of heads rather than chins; remove extraneous matter unrelated to the subject, make sure horizons form horizontal eyelines across a spread.

Watch out for the intended relationship of pictures where more than one is used on a page or spread. Colour combinations should be checked on a light-box. The scale of pictures is important, one to another; small variations in the scale of figures, for example, can make a picture spread look unresolved, whereas a marked contrast in scale will give a dynamic look.

When an issue is complete, agency pictures should be returned immediately, to avoid unnecessary holding fees. Original material commissioned by the magazine is filed as stock, and may be re-used as appropriate, or sold to other magazines, especially abroad, as an additional source of income; this is called syndication.

13/BOOK DESIGN

For five hundred years books have monopolized the transmission and storage of information, a role that is now seriously threatened by the new technology of video, microfilm retrieval systems, computers and audio-visual information media. But a book has an intrinsic tactile quality: with its own unique smell of fresh ink, impressed upon a block of firm white paper, skilfully stitched and encased, it is an object to cherish. Can this be replaced by a flickering cathode ray tube or an oscillating monitor screen?

The field of book publishing is still healthy and immense: every industrialized country has some form of publishing industry for home and export markets and many thousands of new titles come into circulation every year. (In the UK alone in 1986, for example, 52,500 new titles were published and 444 million books printed.) All these books have to be designed – in one way or another – which means that someone has to decide what they should look like, and take on the awesome responsibility for their visual and physical wellbeing.

THE HISTORY OF THE BOOK

The development of the book into the form in which we know it was a long and complicated process. The earliest known portable written records were clay tablets used in Mesopotamia (Iraq) and papyrus rolls in ancient Egypt dating from about 3000 BC. Books began to take on something of their modern format in the first or second century AD, with the appearance of the codex – sheets of papyrus or parchment folded vertically to make leaves, or pages. Despite this more portable and accessible form, books remained precious and carefully conserved objects, maintained in libraries annexed to palaces and places of worship. The Book of Kells, once called 'the most beautiful book in the world', represents the fine early tradition of the decorated book; the work of monkish scribes from the community of Iona off the Irish coast, it is handwritten in precise lines of Insular Majuscule script and intricately illuminated.

The earliest printed book to survive was produced in China in AD 868, roughly contemporary with the Book of Kells. Known as the Diamond Sutra, or Wang-Chieh's book, this was printed from wood blocks onto a scroll. The first evidence we have of printing from moveable type is also attributable to a Chinese printer, Pi Sheng, in the thirteenth century, but the most significant development in printed matter came with the invention of moveable type in Europe, in the fifteenth century, credited to

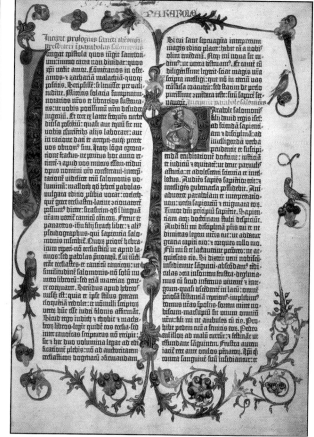

LEFT AND BELOW The private presses did much to heighten design awareness. William Morris's Kelmscott Press looked back to an earlier age, while Francis Meynell's Nonesuch press utilized modern means.

BROKEN-BROW

A TRAGEDY BY
ERNST TOLLER
TRANSLATED BY
VERA MENDEL
WITH DRAWINGS
BY GEORG GROSZ

PUBLISHED IN LONDON
AT 16 GREAT JAMES STREET BY THE
NONESUCH PRESS

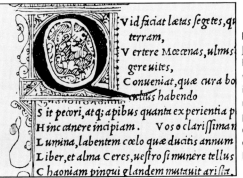

FAR LEFT AND LEFT Nicholas Jensen's Roman typeface of 1470 and Franco Griffo's Aldine italic of 1501 were marvellously simple innovations which addressed the new problems of machine production in Renaissance book design. But note that in both examples the decorative initials were hand drawn.

Johann Gutenberg of Mainz, in Germany.

Moveable type was the real key to book publishing and the wider availability of printed matter; type which could be set in page form, printed, dismantled and used again. This introduced the economics of mass production to the distribution of the written word. Gutenberg referred to his printing techniques as 'the secret art', and offered to sell his knowledge to those who could pay the price. Although a printer by trade, even in those early days he demonstrated the spirit of the publishing entrepreneur.

In Renaissance Europe the printing craft developed to become the industry we know today. The alphabet of European languages clearly influenced this development; its 26 characters are extremely versatile and economical, whereas printing of the Chinese language in the time of Pi Sheng would have required multiples of some 80,000 symbols and ideograms in the type case.

THE ADVENT OF PUBLISHING

Publishing is the industry which supports book design, and the meaning of the word publishing is 'to declare ideas publicly and openly and make them generally known'. Before the impact of typography, the number of books in Europe could be counted in thousands: within 50 years of the invention of moveable type, there were nine million books in circulation.

In these early days the printer was the dominant force in the book trade, controlling nearly all the means to publish: metal foundry, typecasting, typesetting, printing, editing and bookselling. Only papermaking and bookbinding were traditionally outside the printer's domain. Nowadays the publisher is the dominant element, with the ultimate responsibility for text, design and the very existence of a book. However, the traditional association between printer and publisher is still evident in many publishing houses today.

THE FOUNDATIONS OF MODERN BOOK DESIGN

The centre of printing gradually moved from Gutenberg's Germany to Italy. In 1500 there were 150 presses operating in Venice alone, which had become the printing capital of the civilized world, and two printers then working in Venice had a decisive influence on the form of the modern book.

Nicholas Jensen, a Frenchman, in 1470 perfected the Roman typeface which superseded the decorative and not universally legible Gothic blackletter forms of northern Europe. Jensen gave us the forerunner of the serif roman typefaces which are familiar in their various forms today.

Aldus Manutius began printing with a series of classical Greek authors in 1490. Some ten years later, he conceived the idea of publishing cheap pocket editions, printing 1,000 copies at a time instead of the more usual 200 or so, to keep costs low. To fill the pages economically, he commissioned a new type style, which was designed for him by Franco Griffo and became known as 'italic' type.

These marvellously simple innovations of clearly legible type and elegantly designed pocket editions laid the foundations for modern book publishing. The significant influences on modern publishing occurred in the nineteenth century and were concerned with the means of mass-production. With the industrial revolution came mechanical methods of papermaking, typesetting and printing which finally set in place the publishing industry we know today.

STANDARDS OF BOOK DESIGN

One of the less welcome results of mass production techniques was a general decline in publishing standards. To some extent, we still today have to suffer the shoddy, inept or ugly among published materials, and perhaps there is always an element of this. But determined efforts have been made at various times to reintroduce care and craftsmanship in the production of books. In England towards the end of the nineteenth century, William Morris set up the Kelmscott Press with the express intention of promoting better standards of typography and book design. He hoped to improve public tastes and heighten awareness of design. The Kelmscott usually produced limited editions printed on handmade paper, which ironically soon became elitist items for private collectors only.

Another private press which influenced the quality of book design was the Nonesuch Press, founded in England by Francis Meynell in 1923. Meynell believed that mechanical means could be made to serve fine ends, and although the Nonesuch's books utilized mass production methods, great attention was paid to the quality of editing and design, typography and illustration. An important objective for Meynell was 'to have fun with our business and to make experiments within the limits of appropriate book design'.

Design opportunities in book publishing are broad and varied — from the mass-market paperback to the specialized work of reference. Because of the variety, they present many different design problems and solutions.

Other discerning publishers were aware of the importance of a well-made product, and by the mid-1920s companies such as Chatto & Windus and Jonathan Cape in London, and Alfred A. Knopf in New York, were acknowledged as being forward-looking in standards of design and production. It became more commonplace for publishers to employ the services of artists and typographers, and even to appoint art editors to make informed and conscious choices about typefaces, layouts and illustrations. Book design had emerged in its own right as a branch of the commercial arts.

CATEGORIES OF BOOKS

There are hundreds of categories of books and many branches of publishing, all with different design requirements but reliant upon the same fundamental design skills. The spectrum covers the mass market paperback through the general interest non-fiction book to the specialist text or reference book, and includes limited edition art books and the work of small private presses. Any listing of books in print demonstrates the scope of the publishing field and the breadth of the market, and of the opportunities for designers.

Whichever kind of book you find yourself involved with, they all require the same fundamental design skills and disciplines and a creative approach to solving the problems in hand. The target is to produce legible, attractive and appropriate visual solutions within the parameters of budget and production limitations.

BOOK PACKAGING

This is a relatively new aspect of book publishing, but its influence on book design today has to be acknowledged, with many packaging groups producing fine books for the commercial market. Book packaging is an activity in which every aspect of a book – editorial, design and the very concept, including targeting the appropriate market – is in the control of a company or creative group who are not the publishers.

The function of the packager is to create the product, in this case books for the market. A simple analogy would be with the traditional role of the author. Just as an author approaches a publisher with the text (manuscript) of a book in hand, with the hope that the publisher will accept the work and eventually produce it as a finished book, so the book packager approaches the publisher with the total creative and production package. The text, the format, the idea and the means to realize it

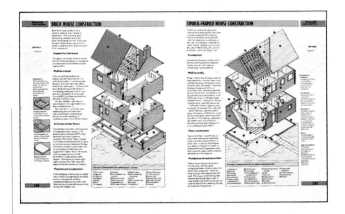

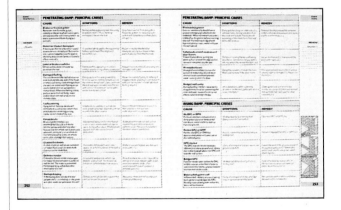

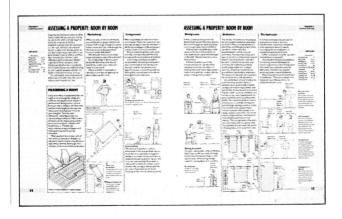

The four double-page spreads from a DIY manual demonstrate a variety of visual techniques used to convey information. In order to make the daunting technical aspects of the subject accessible to the reader the designer has utilized clear typography, simple tabular matter, photography, diagrams and illustration artwork to create an informative and visually interesting design.

are sold to the publisher. The packager is, therefore, the creator responsible for the very being of the book. The packager's idea is then taken on by the publisher (subject, often, to complex contractual and royalty-interest arrangements) and the publisher finances the work of the packager and promotes and distributes the finished product. A book packaging company may offer its products for sale to a publisher as camera-ready copy or lithographic film from which the publisher can make plates and print, or as totally finished bound and jacketed books which the publisher can market.

Many satisfactory books are being produced by this arrangement. There are many design-led packaging companies and book packaging is an ideal environment for the book designer since it presents excellent design opportunities.

THE INTEGRATED BOOK

The economic climate, technical developments, raised outputs, lower costs, photocomposition and high-resolution colour printing (particularly photolithography) have created the fertile environment for the growth of the integrated book. This is a book that, no matter what the area of interest, employs the techniques of typography, photography, illustration and precise editorial skills to present integrated, legible and visually interesting and stimulating information to the reader. The integrated book is a challenge to the designer and supplies greater visual opportunities than the straightforward book of text.

The graphic skills required to solve the problems presented by the integrated book are not exclusive to the design of books. Good typography, well-judged picture cropping, good colour sense and creative art direction can be applied equally to any graphic design problem, and therefore much of the information in other chapters of this book is applicable to the book designer. Book design is not an isolated activity, but it does have its own unique and specialized problems.

The physical book. You are in a fortunate position in having the category of design under discussion right here in your hands. You are holding and looking at an integrated book on the subject of illustration and design. Take a good look at it, firstly as a physical object. You have to understand the fundamental physical nature of a book in order to design it properly. What does a book do? What it doesn't do is hang on the wall, like a poster or a print:

THE PUBLISHING PROCESS

It is very difficult to formalize the process of creating a printed book, both because the various roles and areas of activity overlap and inter-relate a good deal and because procedures vary from company to company. However, the flow chart below attempts to explain the areas of activity and the personnel involved, from the initial concept of a book to its appearance in a bookshop.

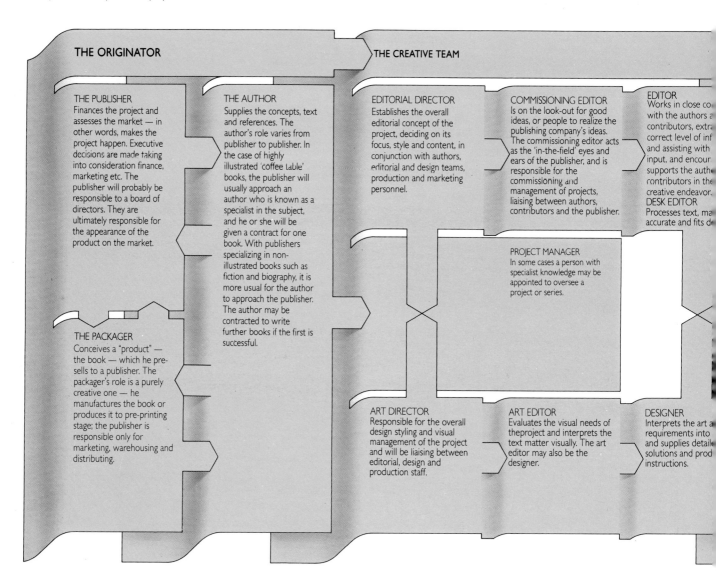

THE ORIGINATOR

THE PUBLISHER
Finances the project and assesses the market — in other words, makes the project happen. Executive decisions are made taking into consideration finance, marketing etc. The publisher will probably be responsible to a board of directors. They are ultimately responsible for the appearance of the product on the market.

THE PACKAGER
Conceives a "product" — the book — which he pre-sells to a publisher. The packager's role is a purely creative one — he manufactures the book or produces it to pre-printing stage; the publisher is responsible only for marketing, warehousing and distributing.

THE AUTHOR
Supplies the concepts, text and references. The author's role varies from publisher to publisher. In the case of highly illustrated 'coffee table' books, the publisher will usually approach an author who is known as a specialist in the subject, and he or she will be given a contract for one book. With publishers specializing in non-illustrated books such as fiction and biography, it is more usual for the author to approach the publisher. The author may be contracted to write further books if the first is successful.

THE CREATIVE TEAM

EDITORIAL DIRECTOR
Establishes the overall editorial concept of the project, deciding on its focus, style and content, in conjunction with authors, editorial and design teams, production and marketing personnel.

COMMISSIONING EDITOR
Is on the look-out for good ideas, or people to realize the publishing company's ideas. The commissioning editor acts as the 'in-the-field' eyes and ears of the publisher, and is responsible for the commissioning and management of projects, liaising between authors, contributors and the publisher.

EDITOR
Works in close co with the authors a contributors, extra correct level of inf and assisting with input, and encour supports the auth contributors in the creative endeavor.

DESK EDITOR
Processes text, ma accurate and fits de

PROJECT MANAGER
In some cases a person with specialist knowledge may be appointed to oversee a project or series.

ART DIRECTOR
Responsible for the overall design styling and visual management of the project and will be liaising between editorial, design and production staff.

ART EDITOR
Evaluates the visual needs of the project and interprets the text matter visually. The art editor may also be the designer.

DESIGNER
Interprets the art a requirements into and supplies detaile solutions and prod instructions.

but it does have to be seen from a distance – the spine on a library shelf, for example, or the jacket in a bookshop where it is competing with other titles for your attention. While it doesn't have to package contents, like cornflakes or soap powder, it is still a three-dimensional, tangible object. The jacket or cover protects it, and gives the first impression and a summary of the contents.

So take this book in hand, look at it and flick through the pages. A book is a physical object, a machine which acts as an information retrieval system. It has to be read, therefore it has to be legible, and the information within has to be accessible.

Like any manufactured mass-produced object, a book has parts and those parts have names. It helps if you know those names and what they mean. Words such as head, tail, facing, verso, leaf, spine, prelims, backmatter, bulk, extent, block. Everyone in the business uses this jargon and as when travelling abroad, it's much more fun if you know the language.

SYMPATHETIC TREATMENTS
The criteria of legibility, accessibility and attractive-

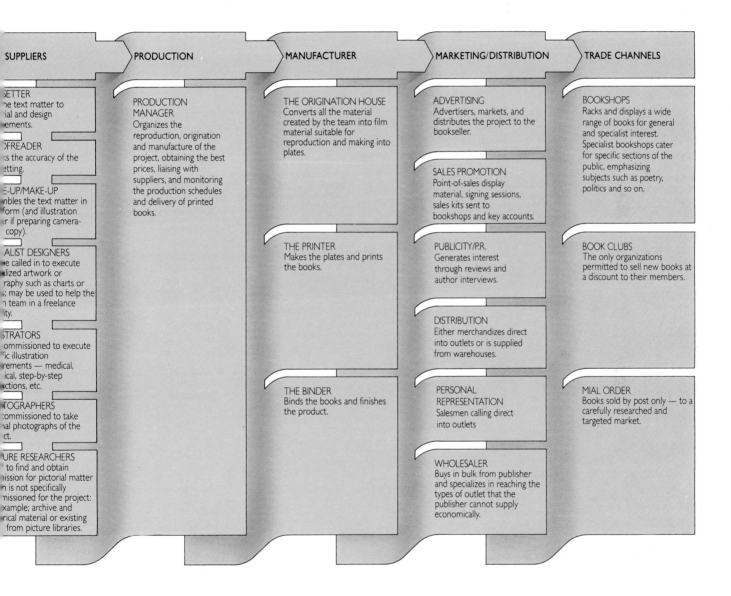

SUPPLIERS	PRODUCTION	MANUFACTURER	MARKETING/DISTRIBUTION	TRADE CHANNELS
SETTER ...he text matter to ...ial and design ...ements.	**PRODUCTION MANAGER** Organizes the reproduction, origination and manufacture of the project, obtaining the best prices, liaising with suppliers, and monitoring the production schedules and delivery of printed books.	**THE ORIGINATION HOUSE** Converts all the material created by the team into film material suitable for reproduction and making into plates.	**ADVERTISING** Advertisers, markets, and distributes the project to the bookseller.	**BOOKSHOPS** Racks and displays a wide range of books for general and specialist interest. Specialist bookshops cater for specific sections of the public, emphasizing subjects such as poetry, politics and so on.
...OFREADER ...s the accuracy of the ...etting.			**SALES PROMOTION** Point-of-sales display material, signing sessions, sales kits sent to bookshops and key accounts.	
...E-UP/MAKE-UP ...nbles the text matter in ...orm (and illustration ...r if preparing camera- ...copy).		**THE PRINTER** Makes the plates and prints the books.	**PUBLICITY/P.R.** Generates interest through reviews and author interviews.	**BOOK CLUBS** The only organizations permitted to sell new books at a discount to their members.
...ALIST DESIGNERS ...e called in to execute ...lized artwork or ...raphy such as charts or ...; may be used to help the ...n team in a freelance ...ity.			**DISTRIBUTION** Either merchandizes direct into outlets or is supplied from warehouses.	
...STRATORS ...ommissioned to execute ...ic illustration ...rements — medical, ...ical, step-by-step ...ctions, etc.		**THE BINDER** Binds the books and finishes the product.	**PERSONAL REPRESENTATION** Salesmen calling direct into outlets	**MIAL ORDER** Books sold by post only — to a carefully researched and targeted market.
...TOGRAPHERS ...commissioned to take ...nal photographs of the ...ct.				
...URE RESEARCHERS ... to find and obtain ...nission for pictorial matter ...n is not specifically ...nissioned for the project: ...xample; archive and ...rical material or existing ... from picture libraries.			**WHOLESALER** Buys in bulk from publisher and specializes in reaching the types of outlet that the publisher cannot supply economically.	

ness are primary concerns of the book designer. Fundamental to these design considerations are the qualities of appropriateness, relevance and sympathy. Your design solution must complement the subject in hand. For example, you wouldn't consider using a highly decorative typeface, with embellished capitals, set within decorative frames and borders, for a book on step-by-step first aid. You would obviously want a sympathetic treatment of a subject in which rapid access to information in an emergency might be required – a straightforward, communicative typeface, a clear and logical system of headings and sub-headings, illustrations which are unambiguously descriptive and simply understood. Whereas a book on embroidery or other needlecrafts could well lend itself to a more decorative graphic solution.

THE DESIGN BRIEF

The best way to go about designing a book is to start with the complete text (manuscript) in hand, in a beautifully clean, typewritten and finally edited form, with all the intended picture reference clearly indi-

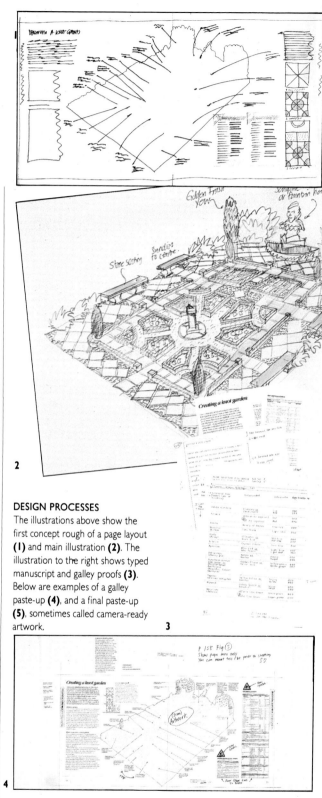

cated. Experience shows that this is rarely the case: even if you obtain the full text in one batch, commonly the manuscript is dog-eared, the text underscored with revisions, amendments and late inclusions. But in whatever form it comes to you, the manuscript is the basic material from which you must work.

You can assume that you will be working with an editor from the publishing house who commissions you and (possibly together with the author) briefs you. Remember that you have been hired as the designer because you can offer a skill and a service that they cannot contribute. Listen to their information and ideas, take notes, read between the lines and ask questions in order to extract a brief which establishes the direction for a sympathetic treatment.

Bear in mind that the editor is very busy, probably in charge of several other books going through at the same time, and may also be visually inarticulate. In some publishing houses you may be dealing with an art editor who probably has strong opinions on the visual style of the book, based on market research or previous experience: but you cannot count on this degree of direction.

Marketing and production information. Collect as much information as possible from the author and editor. This should include marketing and production information, a category essential to any brief you extract from the publisher. Marketing information should tell you who the book is aimed at, the socio-economic aspects and so on. Marketing considerations almost certainly also have some contribution to make on the jacket design: styling of a jacket may be quite precisely tailored to the intended market and the format and retail price of the book.

Production details are equally essential and fundamental to your brief. You should know the binding style (hardback or paperback), number of pages and also the printing method, how many colours are to be used, the colour fall (distribution of colour) and how many transparencies and/or commissioned illustrations the budget allows.

The first aspect of your job is to come away from the briefing session armed with all the information relevant to the design process. Some possibilities for the approach to the design should have suggested themselves already during the meeting.

The budget and the schedule. The budget must be discussed and understood at this stage in order to prevent

DESIGN PROCESSES
The illustrations above show the first concept rough of a page layout **(1)** and main illustration **(2)**. The illustration to the right shows typed manuscript and galley proofs **(3)**. Below are examples of a galley paste-up **(4)**, and a final paste-up **(5)**, sometimes called camera-ready artwork.

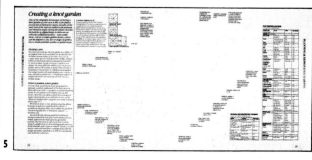

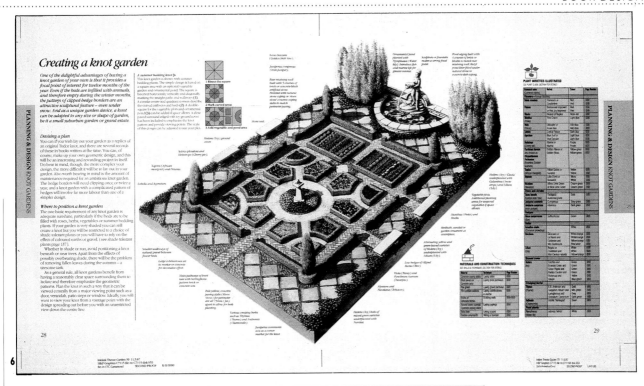

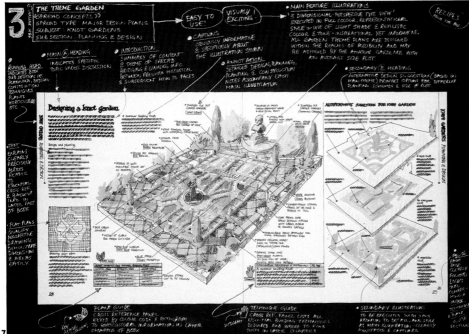

THE INTEGRATED BOOK

The type of double-page spread for the gardening book (**1, 6**) can be seen in many non-fiction works of reference. The design is composed of the elements of typography for text, display and tabular matter, diagrams, graphic symbols and a main full-colour illustration.

The double-page spread (**6**) will start life as a concept sketch (**1**) sometimes drawn as a thumbnail sketch, sometimes drawn full-size to a pre-designed grid. It is often necessary to produce a more developed rough layout (**7**), in this case with design notes to explain to the client the function of the visual and editorial elements. The typographic elements begin life as typed manuscripts which are marked up by the designer and converted to typeset galley (**3**). The galley is then pasted in position in double-page spread form, and at this stage the final position and proportion of the illustrative and tabular matter can be determined.

The final typesetting is pasted in position (**5**) to register with the artwork illustration and other colour work. Similarly the main colour illustration starts life as a rough layout (**2**), which is detailed and referenced before handing over to a specialist illustrator for final artwork. The other drawn images on the spread follow the same process. The designs for the key symbols for cultivation and construction start life as sketch concepts (**8**) before becoming finished artwork (**9**).

any misunderstandings or later acrimony. Budget information – how much money is available for the job – is also crucial to your design solution. Will you have a budget for photography and illustration? Will you be paying for typesetting and presentation materials? Does the budget cover your design fee and time adequately? All this must be clearly understood and put in writing from the outset. You'll probably have to write to the publisher confirming and itemizing the financial position, possibly providing a quotation for the overall design fee for the book.

As with the budget, the schedule must be established and committed to writing from the outset. Timing is crucial in publishing, with the publishing date (i.e. delivery to the bookshop and availability to the public), printing dates, delivery to warehouse, and so forth, legally enshrined in contracts which have probably been agreed months before design work begins. Make sure you meet the dates set, since failure to deliver your work is not only professionally unsound, but

can create a knock-on effect of dramatic proportions.

DESIGN FEES IN PUBLISHING

Publishing is a risk business. It is the publisher's business to take the financial risks and the designer's business to design the book and get paid for it. In order to minimize the risk, a publisher may want to buy cheaply to keep costs low, to avoid being badly out of pocket in the event of a publishing failure and to maximize profits if the book does sell. Do not subsidize the publisher: insist on a proper design fee for the work. If you are expected to share the risks, ask for a royalty agreement.

Fees depend on several factors, such as the age, experience and reputation of the designer, the attitude of the publishing house towards design, and even the courage of the designer in holding out for a good fee. Word of mouth is the best way to find out about the average going rate for a job. Publishers rarely pay by the hourly-rate method: this is quite understandable with an

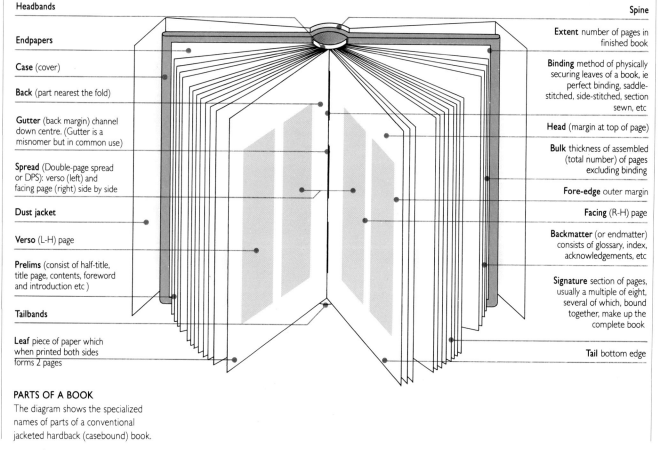

Headbands

Endpapers

Case (cover)

Back (part nearest the fold)

Gutter (back margin) channel down centre. (Gutter is a misnomer but in common use)

Spread (Double-page spread or DPS): verso (left) and facing page (right) side by side

Dust jacket

Verso (L-H) page

Prelims (consist of half-title, title page, contents, foreword and introduction etc)

Tailbands

Leaf piece of paper which when printed both sides forms 2 pages

Spine

Extent number of pages in finished book

Binding method of physically securing leaves of a book, ie perfect binding, saddle-stitched, side-stitched, section sewn, etc

Head (margin at top of page)

Bulk thickness of assembled (total number) of pages excluding binding

Fore-edge outer margin

Facing (R-H) page

Backmatter (or endmatter) consists of glossary, index, acknowledgements, etc

Signature section of pages, usually a multiple of eight, several of which, bound together, make up the complete book

Tail bottom edge

PARTS OF A BOOK
The diagram shows the specialized names of parts of a conventional jacketed hardback (casebound) book.

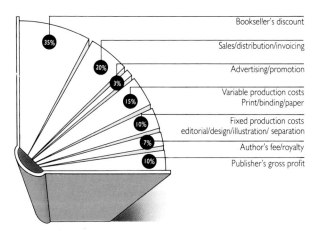

Bookseller's discount
35%

Sales/distribution/invoicing
20%

Advertising/promotion
3%

Variable production costs
Print/binding/paper
15%

Fixed production costs
editorial/design/illustration/ separation
10%

Author's fee/royalty
7%

Publisher's gross profit
10%

LEFT Like all manufacture'd items the retail price of a printed book, marked on the jacket, is determined by carefully calculated economic factors.

BELOW The first visual thinking in book design usually takes the form of a 'storyboard' visual flat plan and small thumbnail sketches.

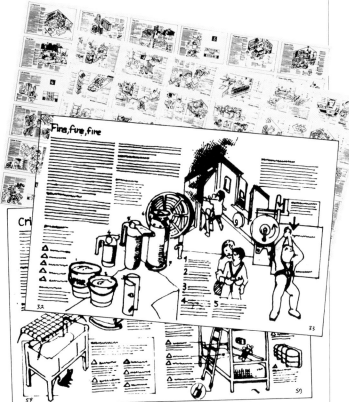

integrated book, for example, which may be so complicated and time-consuming that the clock runs away with the budget. More often than not, page rates are suggested (so much per page) or a lump-sum fee is offered, and it is up to the designer to make that viable in terms of time-against-money. A fee may be based on your own estimate, if you have been asked to submit a budget.

The more experienced you become as a designer in publishing, the easier it is to assess fees for the work. Ensure your time is paid for, giving you the equivalent of the professional salary for the job, and make sure any out of pocket expenses are covered; for example, if you have to pay for typesetting, photography, illustration, etc. If you work on your own premises, make sure a proportion of overheads is covered in addition to fees and outgoings.

It is easier for in-house designers to assess their own value, as any position carries a salary with it, and it is possible to find out the going rate by studying job vacancies in the trade and design press. Some publishing houses have a scale of rates agreed with a trade union, but more often it's a free-for-all situation and open to some negotiation. Remember to take into account the value of paid holidays, insurance and non-contributory pension schemes when considering a staff position.

THUMBNAIL SKETCHES AND INITIAL LAYOUTS

With the brief in mind and the initial design direction and parameters of production agreed with the client, the first physical evidence of visual thinking will probably be in the form of a 'thumbnail' sketch, or small storyboard layout or visual flatplan. You mould the book into shape, getting a fix on the extent and the density and tempo of the work. It is at this stage that you begin to get a feel for the weight of type and illustrative matter, and the range of possible visual solutions comes to mind. A good term for this aspect of the job is the 'overview': as with film

and television storyboards, a page-by-page miniature plan emerges with editorial and design styles noted as they occur. These are used for future reference.

STYLING AND PAGE LAYOUTS

An approach towards styling probably emerges as a result of your briefing with editor or publisher and the next phase may be to produce three or four typical but contrasting double-page spreads: for example, one pictorial, one text spread, one using diagrammatic conventions. These should be a good cross-section to demonstrate the variety and visual tempo of the book. By this time, you should have a grid system in mind, with ideas for photographic treatments developed from the thumbnail design phase.

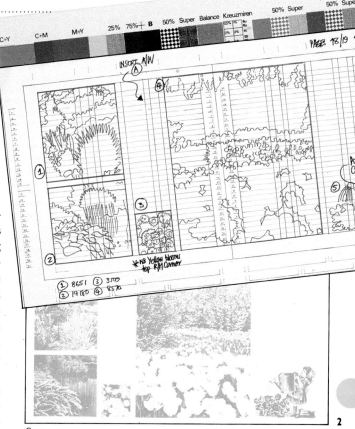

The styling and first layout stage should be considered as experimental and conceptual – an ideas phase – but be prepared to reject a lot of your thinking and ideas, even changing type styles and grid arrangement. It is at this stage that the client possibly wishes to get involved, and it is quite normal to have to show tight layouts to demonstrate your methods and proposed design solution, in order to move to the next phase. This is a good time to get feedback and input of fresh ideas from the reader's point of view, the reader being represented by the client.

Some clients are quite able to visualize the direction of the design from rough layouts, but in some circumstances mocked-up presentation spreads will be required with actual live copy or dummy type in position, with indications of artwork and photographic styles.

THE GRID

It is practical and sensible to utilize a grid system for book design. The grid is a typographic and pictorial framework used in many aspects of design, but particularly in the editorial area. The grid should be flexible, yet functional: flexible enough to accommodate a variety of layout permutations and type measures, functional enough to allow adequate margins for trimming and binding. The format or trimmed page size is usually suggested by the client to fit in with a production plan, a series format or house style, or specific marketing considerations. But it is well within the domain of the designer to suggest formats from the point of view of both elegance and function as a significant design consideration.

TYPOGRAPHY AND TYPE FITTING

Type sizes and line feeds, and type measures, are selected for elegance, appropriateness and legibility, but the text matter must physically fit the book. There is some degree of flexibility when fitting type or casting off manuscript for the integrated book. Type can be adjusted to fit a layout by skilful editing, but it is important to cast off the text matter to gain an accurate evaluation of the ratio of type to page. An expedient method of casting off text is to work from typewritten manuscript that has been typed or word-processed to a fixed measure, or number of characters per line, which closely matches the measure you have chosen for your layout. It certainly makes life easier and can speed up the design process, enabling the designer to make accu-

Cyan

Cyan and yellow

Cyan and yellow and magenta

Cyan and yellow and magenta and 'black

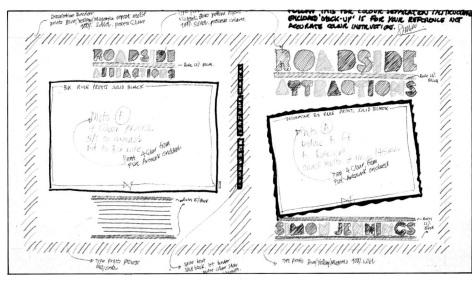

Clean accurate artwork **(7)** and clean unambiguous instructions marked on an overlay **(8)** are essential for the successful reproduction of the design ideas. The small image **(6)** shows the designer's initial rough, and **(9)** is the first proof, again clearly marked, for colour correction and modification. The central photographic images on the design are reproduced from full colour flat artwork, and the lettering and borders are reproduced from black line artwork which the designer has specified to be printed from a combination of the four process ink colours.

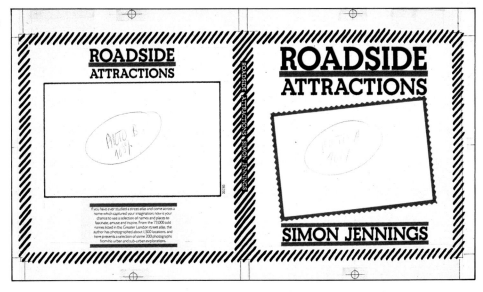

LEFT Most mass-market books are reproduced by the process of offset lithography. Photographic images are usually reproduced from transparencies whose size and position on the page are indicated on the gridded layout sheet with drawn keylines **(1)**. These are then separated **(2, 3, 4)** by scanners and reproduced on a four-colour press resulting in the four-colour proof **(5)**

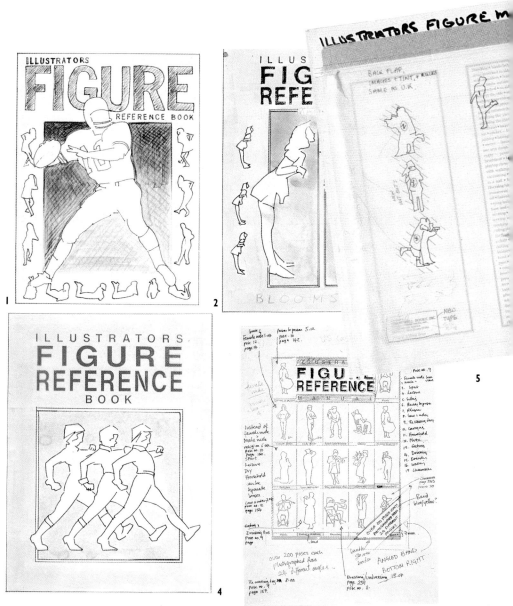

The jacket design will go through many stages of design concept and rough presentation **(1-3)** before a solution is arrived at **(4)**. Photography may have to be commissioned and artwork mechanicals produced **(5)** before the design finally becomes ink on paper **(6)**. The final printed jacket **(7)** is often laminated with a transparent varnish to render the printed surface more hardwearing.

rate page layouts quickly. With the advent of desktop publishing, it is possible to produce finished set text matter quickly from word-processor discs.

VISUAL TREATMENTS

Assume that the overall style, the grid, the typeface and the fundamentals of your design solution are now established. This is the stage where the designer has to show virtuoso skills as designer, visualizer, stylist and art director. It's not just a matter of making a fixed amount of type and given number of pictures fit the space. If you go for a solution because it is quick and convenient, this will show in the finished product. You have to analyse a large amount of text and suggest ways of making it more stimulating through the use of diagrams, charts and so on.

Your design ideas are now to be converted to working layouts, and it is here that you come into contact with fellow professionals. You have to commission illustrations, artwork and photographs, and be able to articulate your requirements through clear layouts and verbal and written instructions. You also have to coordinate various suppliers, particularly typesetters.

INTO PRODUCTION

Making your layouts a reality and preparing your designs for the press can be achieved by various means – often depending on the approach and preferred method of the publishing house. Your work will almost certainly become ink-on-paper via the process of photolithography. The elements of typography, photography and illustration can be presented for reproduction in various forms. Camera-ready copy is probably the best way to ensure that your designs get into print exactly as you intended them, but whatever the method, clear, precise instructions, clean artwork and sharp photographic

transparencies are essential for good end results.

THE BOOK JACKET

Jacket design is an integral part of the editorial design process, but it is an area that is becoming increasingly specialized and in the case of a novel or work of text, is often the only opportunity to visualize the contents of the book and compete visually for the reader's attention.

A jacket should communicate honestly the contents of the book, be attractive in itself and have functionally clear typography on the spine for easy selection from the library or bookshop shelf. But it has to be remembered that the jacket is a marketing tool which advertises the book and competes with other titles. When you are considering design solutions for a jacket, your brief will almost certainly contain some marketing information. This may not always be well informed, or scientifically or demographically based, but you should be aware that it is influencing your client's opinion.

This aspect of the work often involves a lot of subjective opinion and there may be much heated discussion and capriciousness before the solution sees the light of day. As with other aspects of editorial design, take on board as much information as possible to establish the direction, and apply the criteria of creativity and good design.

SUMMARY

Late nights, deadlines, and a million things to do all at once are all in the game, but book design is a satisfying branch of the design profession. It creates a product for its own sake, and one of lasting value not almost immediately destined (one hopes) for the rubbish bin, or to be seen blowing down the high street on a wet afternoon like so many designed by-products of the marketing, packaging and media industries.

14/SIGNS

Everyone has had the experience of standing before a maze of different signs, desperately trying to find a particular piece of information. Lack of signing can be equally frustrating, especially for anyone trying to travel in an unfamiliar place by means of a poorly signed motorway or underground rail system, for example.

A glance at the illustrations presented here, however, underlines the fact that there is no simple formula for producing a good sign. There are many sign types, as there are sign requirements, and there is often more than one solution to a particular problem.

Reflect a moment on the scale and function of a major rail or air terminal compared with a high-street boutique, or an inner-city office block against a small suburban house, and the corresponding diversity of appropriate signing is immediately apparent. A good sign is perhaps best exemplified by one that isn't: a handwritten direction sign on a busy road would quite obviously not be seen by passing vehicles; an animated neon fascia would be inappropriate on a rural hotel; gold-leaf letters for a unit on an industrial estate would invite vandalism and be a gross expense. Although such signs might be visually stunning and perfectly made in themselves, if they do not serve their purpose they have failed.

In addition to the specific location and function of the sign, design must take into account the geographical location and conditions. A sign that works well in a cold, rainy climate could be disastrous in tropical conditions, and vice versa. Broad considerations for extremes must also be taken into account, for example, exposure to high winds, excessive heat or cold, sea air, bright sunlight, pollution from factory chimneys or motorways, and so on.

WORKING IN CONTEXT

As with any successful design solution, good signing results from first identifying and then correctly responding to a particular requirement. The basis for achieving this lies in a threefold collaboration: the client defines specific needs, the designer creates a visual image to suit, and the sign-maker takes the theory from the drawing board up on to the wall.

Above all, a sign must communicate, and can only do so effectively by a judicious selection of legible and appropriate elements. Arriving at a workable solution involves a systematic process of elimination, from the most fundamental considerations through to the more

ABOVE The glazed-relief tiles and decorative detailing of this Edwardian hospital sign have now given way to a modular sign system which ensures consistently clear presentation of information.

LEFT A confusion of signs is nowhere more dangerous or frustrating than on the roads; simplicity and legibility should always be the watchwords for successful road signing.

These illustrations (below) show sign scheduling for complex sites. The locations for signs are marked on an outline plan of the area showing main access/exit points and key traffic flow (pedestrian and vehicle). Each sign type and position is indicated by reference number and colour coding. The bottom illustration is a sign schedule summarizing details for each sign, which can be listed by sign type and/or location. Shown on the left is a typical signing brief, setting out all the relevant information.

1 SIGN BRIEF

1.1 Visual
Basic design concept
Integration of corporate identity elements
Typeface/weight/size
Legibility
Incorporation of more than one language
Spacing and layout
Colour and colour coding; matching to BS and Pantone
Pictograms, logos and symbols; official approvals for use, copyright

1.2 Construction
General fabrication type or method: eg built-up letter, fascia, box and panel, integral architectural detailing
Materials: eg metal (aluminium/LCSS/stainless steel etc), acrylic timber, resin, neon
Finish: eg anodized, stove-enamelled, vitreous, gold leaf, ceramic
Size
Fixing: eg secret-fixed wall mounting, suspended, projecting
Specialist skills: eg sign-writing, etching, glass engraving
Lighting: eg integration with existing or new
Maintenance and repair: any sign will at sometime in its life require maintenance or repair and this consideration should be reflected in the construction.

1.3 Timing and budget targets
Preliminary timetable
Ball park costings

2 PREPARATION

2.1 Site Survey
All necessary measures of existing building(s) or space: drawing check for proposed new building
Building materials and colours
Photographic references
Sight lines, long views, positioning levels
Footings: eg tarmac, earth, special paving etc.
Record of removals of existing signs and making good
Associated lighting, ambient and local
Access plant or special equipment

requirements, power supply

2.2 User questionnaire
Building or space usage for staff/visitors/public
Traffic flow patterns: pedestrian and vehicle
Peak times: daily and seasonal

2.3 Planning considerations
(particularly with illuminated signs)
Local planning authority restrictions
Listed buildings: conservation and preservation
Regard for the environment

2.4 Geography and weather
Temperature
Climate
Exposure, to wind, sunlight etc
Special conditions, eg industrial pollution, salt spray in coastal location, etc.

3 SIGN PROPOSAL AND DEVELOPMENT

3.1 Presentation and approvals
Based on the sign brief and survey findings and to include:
Preliminary sign schedule keyed to location plan
Pedestrian or vehicle flow charts where applicable
Sign summary for multi-site or sign programme projects
Related quotations for supply and installation

3.2 Prototypes and pilot sites

3.3 Finalization of design and construction specification and the sign schedule

4 PRODUCTION AND INSTALLATION

4.1 Applications for necessary planning permissions

4.2 Timetable for production and installation of the agreed sign schedule

4.3 Co-ordination with other manufacturing specialists and sub-contractors

4.4 Liaison with site(s) to agree precise installation dates and access

4.5 Liaison with other sub-contractors on site during installation

4.6 Photographic references of completed installation

4.7 Agreement of maintenance requirement and timing.

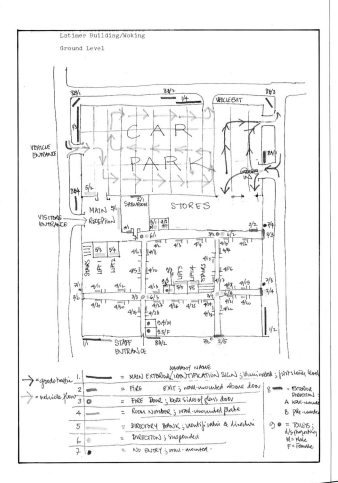

particular. For example, the proposed sign may be interior or exterior, illuminated or non-illuminated, a modular system or custom-made, hand-crafted or mass-produced, pedestrian or vehicle, and so on. In addition to the vast range of traditional sign-making skills and materials that can be employed, the new technologies are now further expanding the possibilities of sign origination and construction into exciting and often dramatic new areas: current examples include digital displays and holograms.

A typical signage project, whether one-off or system, will run through six main stages from outset to completion: brief/survey/proposal/development/production/installation. The more detailed expansion of this standard sequence given opposite can therefore serve as checklist or memory-jogger for any signing exercise, although the mix of detail elements involved will of course vary from case to case.

We'd be lost without them, but signs do more than simply direct or identify. They can promote, inform, warn, decorate, prohibit, inspire confidence, encourage, impress. Regrettably they can also, and all too often do, bewilder, infuriate, confuse, exasperate and disfigure. Whatever their nature though, and however seemingly mundane their function, anyone connected with their origination should remember that a successful sign will not only ease the pressures of the day for those who use it, but can also enrich our lives and the environment in the process.

The Olympic symbol, interlocking rings symbolizing the friendship of nations, is internationally recognizable.

7

Sign Category: Hanging sign 1200 X 300

Material: 12 swg AL. regular spec

Construction: Two aluminium sections. Curved top and bottom edges, with flat aluminium sheet sandwiched between.

Dimension: 1200 X 300 X 43

Size of letter/number: 200

Information: 'Exit'

Colour/finish, sign: Outer surface: Pantone Warm Red, Pantone Reflex Blue, Pantone 354 Green, Pantone 116 Yellow. Centre sheet: aluminium Satin Silver

Colour/finish, letters: Cut out

Fixing: Suspended from existing M8 bushes pre-cast into concrete

Location: Above Exit doors from main building to towers

Quantity: 13 - Red
13 - Green
10 - Blue
33 - Yellow

Notes: Sign is suspended from centre sheet of aluminium. Aluminium front and back panels should 'hook' into position allowing removal for cleaning.

Edge of aluminium is visible at top, bottom and sides of sign, and should fit flush with aluminium sections.

EXIT
ABCDEFGHIJ
KLMNOPQRS
TUVWXYZ12
34567890

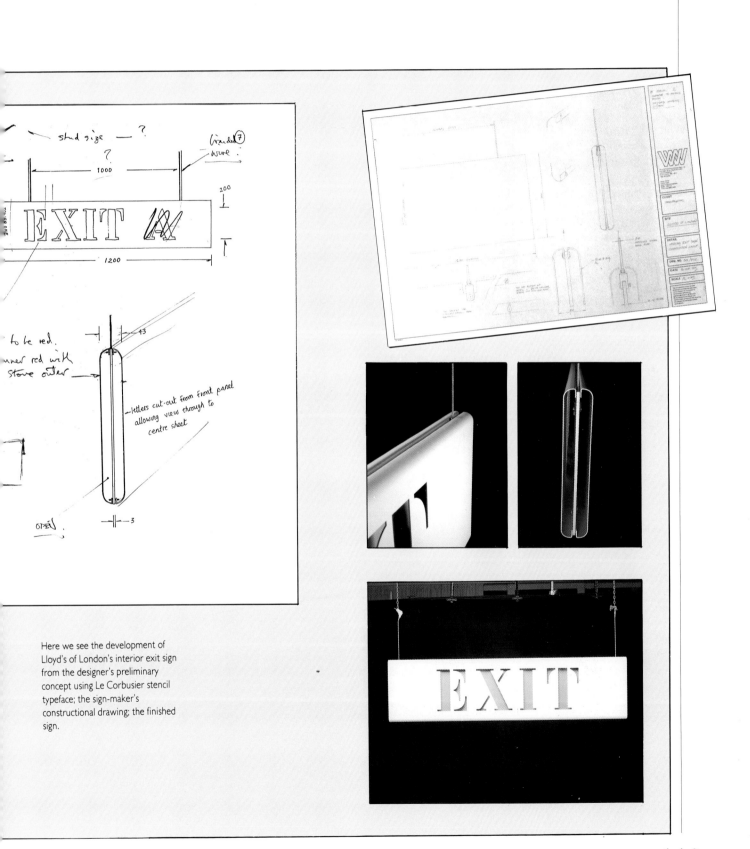

Here we see the development of Lloyd's of London's interior exit sign from the designer's preliminary concept using Le Corbusier stencil typeface; the sign-maker's constructional drawing; the finished sign.

15/COMPUTER GRAPHICS

The last twenty-five years have witnessed the beginnings of a profound revolution in visual communications. This revolution is the product of the convergence of several new technologies – television, video, microelectronics, satellites, fibre-optics, lasers, remote scanning, digital-optical storage, and the digital computer – and has resulted in the vast new range of image creation and manipulation tools now available to the graphic designer. The increasing variety and sophistication of these tools, and the inexorable effect of mass production in steadily reducing the unit costs of hardware, suggest that computer graphics technology will soon be cheaply accessible to most designers.

Even the most complex images can be stored in digital form, as a sequence of binary numbers. In this state they can be subjected to a wide variety of manipulations, and can then be relayed via satellite and finally displayed or printed out as an exact duplication of the original. This suggests the eventual global nature of the effects of the new technology.

COMPUTER GRAPHICS AND THE GRAPHIC DESIGNER

Contemporary graphic design students will mature in a world where instant digital communication of images (and sound) are a commonplace; where the market for images and image-makers will be global (and omnivorous); where the new interactive technologies will create wholly new concepts of aesthetics and of communication design; where artificial intelligence techniques will provide 'expert' design systems for designers; and where the continuing convergence of hitherto disparate technologies will produce hybrid entertainments and educational tools of enormous subtlety.

Within relatively few years of its introduction, the new technology has significantly affected the way graphic designers work. Computer typesetters and laser-scanners for colour separations are now the norm. Word processors with automatic character counts are increasingly being used for the preparation of copy for books, magazines and newspapers. Many designers are now using desktop publishing and computer 'paint' systems.

The main areas where computers are being used to assist the graphic designer are:

word processing – the preparation of copy for print;

copyfitting – software that calculates column depths, type sizes and settings required to fill a column, and the number of words needed to fill an area;

grid design – software that controls a plotter, enabling the designer to prepare layout grids and have them printed immediately;

computer typesetting – systems that provide an enormous range of typefaces and type sizes, and the most minute control of kerning, slanting, leading, columns, tabulations and typeface distortions;

desktop publishing – systems that allow medium-high resolution on-screen page makeup, including limited grid design, typesetting, digital illustration and photo-scaling capability, with output to laser printers;

computer 'paints' – paintbox-type systems and software that provide a very sophisticated set of image generation and manipulation tools, including a vast number of colours, distortion and scaling, unlimited types of 'brushes', geometrical tools, input of video images, etc.;

The Aesthedes graphics workstation ergonomically designed to be 'user friendly'. Systems like this combine an extensive range of 'soft' design tools, including image manipulation in 2-D and 3-D, a wide range of type fonts, and very high-resolution output to mask cutters or colour-separated printing plates.

3-dimensional modelling and animation – systems and software that allow the construction of 3-D objects in 'computer space', and the design of sophisticated animations from these;
image-scanning and very high resolution page makeup and production – at the top end of the computer-graphics-for-print market, completely integrated systems that combine typesetting and type design, page makeup, image manipulation and retouching, and direct output to colour-separated plates, ready to print.

DESIGNER-FRIENDLY SYSTEMS
There are two main factors responsible for the widespread impact of computer-graphic technology – rapidly decreasing hardware costs, due to mass production, and the development of 'designer-friendly' systems. These are computer graphics systems that can be operated by designers who have no knowledge of computer programming. Containing suites of programs that are accessible to the user simply by selecting from a menu of choices, they require only a few hours of training time. Image processing has become as accessible as word processing.

There are three main types of designer-friendly software available for computer graphics systems:
3-D solid modelling software – allowing the construction, manipulation and animation of quasi three-dimensional objects;
'paint' and graphics software – offering a wide range of two-dimensional image and text creation and manipulation devices;
page makeup software – desktop publishing packages allowing the on-screen integration of text, graphics, photographs and illustrations, for output to medium-high resolution laserprinter.

3-D SOLID MODELLING SOFTWARE
Because of its now widespread use on television, this aspect of computer graphics is the most familiar to the public. It is also the main area in which the traditional notion of graphic design – as design in two dimensions for reproduction in print – is changing most radically. The increasing use of computer-generated title sequences, identification symbols (idents), captions, graphs, maps and diagrams – and advertisements – for television has created the new definition of 'time-based' graphics, in which graphic imagery and letterforms are displayed in three dimensions and animated through time. This is the most significant change in typography since Gutenberg invented the moveable typeface.

Most 3-D systems are menu-driven and controlled either from VDU prompts or from overwrites on the colour monitor. The designer inputs specific choices through the keyboard and/or through the digit pad.

Object construction. All systems involve the creation of two-dimensional sections and then either the extrusion or rotation of the section through space to create a three-dimensional object. Initially this object will be a 'wireframe' construction, and in this condition can be scaled, moved or rotated around three axes (x, y and z axes) singly or together. A colour for the final solid-modelled image must also be specified at this stage.

Object manipulation. When the designer is satisfied with the disposition and colour of the constructed object, the data is stored on magnetic disc and a sub-program chosen from the menu which allows the creation of a solid-modelled object.

This sub-program requires the input of at least three bits of information. On menu prompts, the designer must specify the position from which the object is viewed (the eye position); the area to be viewed (the object position – where it is in xyz space); and the position of the light source (the light position) from where the object is to be illuminated.

The solid, shaded model is then computed and rendered on screen.

Animation. Animations can be plotted using another sub-program. There are generally two options available. Firstly, the animation can be plotted, and then viewed in wireframe as the computer plots the object's movements through space. The resulting wireframe images are drawn quickly in sequence, one frame at a time, and then superimposed one over the other. This allows the designer to check the 'choreography' of the animation quickly, without having to wait several minutes (or hours, if the model is very complex) for the full solid-modelled object to be plotted and rendered.

Secondly, when the designer is satisfied with the choreography, the final animation can be called up automatically, frame by frame, and downloaded on to videotape.

A wide range of parameters is available in plotting the animation. The object position, eye position and light position may be manipulated to give the desired effect. The object may be rotated through space around the x, y and z axes, and moved through xyz space in relation to the eye position. The eye position and light position may also be moved through space, so that tracking, panning and tilting 'camera' movements may be simulated.

Systems vary in detail, but generally the designer can expect a basic software system (as outlined above), plus a range of optional refinements such as smooth-shading, transparency/translucency, texture mapping (applying 2-D surfaces to 3-D objects), cushioning (differential frame speeds for more realistic animations), multiple light sources.

Storing animations. To create a smooth animation from a series of still-frames, the images must be projected in sequence at a speed greater than about 15 frames per second (fps). At lower speeds, the eye perceives each frame as a still image and the animation becomes jerky. Traditional high-quality animation is loaded to video-tape at 25 fps. Lower quality animations can be loaded at 12 fps, which each frame being shot twice, or at a variety of speeds to provide pace and rhythm.

There are several available videotape formats ranging from VHS (video home system) up to 2-inch (5 cm) broadcast. The most popular format in the 'industrial' or 'corporate' non-broadcast video sphere is low-band U-matic, which offers a good cost/quality ratio.

Essential tools for offloading frames to videotape include a TV converter, a digital-to-analogue converter which converts RGB (red-green-blue) data to video signal; a VTR, and single-frame edit controller.

Most animation software packages include programs for the automatic control of animation offloading. For long animations, or for sequences involving complex solid models, some form of animation control software is essential, as it allows overnight or 'downtime' offloading, and obviates tedious manual operation.

PAINT AND GRAPHICS SOFTWARE

These systems are used for a variety of graphics applications, including illustration, digital-image retouching, preparation or artwork for audio-visual slides, and live computer presentation.

Paint (or paintbox) systems are designed to provide the user with a close digital approximation of a wide range of image-creating media. Great efforts have been made to present these media options in ways that relate to the traditional working methods of artists and designers. Some systems have the digit pad overprinted with a set of labelled boxes, each box representing a particular program function. These functions can be accessed by the user simply pressing a stylus into the required box. The layout of the box resembles, in diagrammatic form, the layout of a studio table, with its drawing-board, paints and drawing materials, brushes, scalpels, adhesives, rulers and compasses, etc. The following are the main functions available on such systems.

Colour. Generally, there is a choice of 256 on-screen colours, from a potential theoretical maximum of 16.7 million. This enormously high figure is a product of the mechanics of high-definition monitors, which contain three electron guns – one each for the red, blue and green phosphors available on the monitor screen. Each gun can output at 256 different levels of brightness, and by multiplying these factors ($256 \times 256 \times 256 = 16.7$ million) the full range of colours is achieved. This wide range allows considerable subtlety in the mixing of specific hues and tints.

Other colour options include facilities for flood-filling areas; defining a particular colour to be 'invisible', to enable complex montage effects, or to function as a transparent wash; creating smoothly graded areas of colour; and most importantly, to rotate colour automatically or manually through all or part of the palette, allowing 'colour animations'.

Image creation. The digit pad is an electronic drawingboard. Attached to it is a stylus, which has a microswitch inside it such that when pressed down on to the pad, a start signal is sent to the computer. So, for instance, when the stylus is pressed into the colour box on the pad, a 256-colour palette appears on screen, allowing the designer to select a particular colour. Basic programs for drawing with the stylus include colour, various widths of line, and an almost infinite range of 'brushes' – areas of the screen defined as shape, texture or colour – for painting. Digital versions of traditional drawing tools, like the ruler and compass, are available, along with other effects like airbrush, watercolour, and special 'merge' programs which allow areas of different colours to be smoothly merged.

Pictures may be created using the digit pad, with its attendant stylus, or by digitizing an image though a video camera. This process, known as 'frame-grabbing', converts the analogue video image to digital RGB data, in effect allowing any flat or relief composition to be input to the computer. Such frame-grabbed images can then be treated as if they had been entered through the digit pad.

Various 'fonts' of digital type are also available, and can be 'set' on screen. The designer has a limited range of options – ranging the type left, right or centred, adding drop shadows, setting each letter or word in a different colour, etc. Other type styles (or logotypes) can be input through the video frame-grab and then retouched and scaled on screen.

Image manipulation. Mid-price-range systems provide a wide variety of image manipulation functions. The simplest of these is a program allowing enlargement and reduction, either in a fixed-aspect ratio or in the free distortion of a defined image by compressing or expanding it horizontally or vertically. Further unlimited freeform distortions can be produced using programs that allow the definition of any shape on screen, with the facility for distorting any image into that shape: for example, the rectangular screen image can be distorted into a circle.

Images or parts may be moved around the screen or montaged together using the brush program. Freeform shapes can be vignetted, allowing complex overlays of images and mixes of drawn, painted and photographic material.

Most systems have a zoom facility, allowing various ratios of temporary image enlargement. This function can be used to examine and re-colour individual pixels (picture elements), permitting precise image retouching, or the addition of fine detail.

Colour rotation animation. This operation allows for the disposition of colours and shapes on screeen in such a way that when the palette (or part of the palette) is rotated sequentially, various parts of the screen image will change colour. If this is carefully designed and organized, realtime animation effects can be achieved. This relies on the phenomenon of retention of vision, the colours being rotated at speeds fast enough to provide a powerful illusion of movement.

Various applications for colour rotation animation in video production include wipe-on/wipe-off titles or captions, rolling credits, bar or pie charts that 'grow', schematics and cutaway diagrams that have animated parts, effects of colour and texture such as shiny metallic highlights, rippling colours over typography, etc.

Colour rotation can also be used to try out quickly thousands of possible colourways in an image, for example, in textile or graphic design.

Hardcopy and softcopy. One of the first questions asked by artists and designers upon being introduced to computer graphics is 'How do you get images out?' The answer is that there are several different methods and technologies used; but first of all, it is important to stress the difference between 'hard' and 'soft' copy.

Hardcopy is a reproduction or copy of an image created using the computer graphics system – printed, plotted or photographed on to film or paper.

Softcopy is an RGB- or TV-encoded copy of a computer-generated image, displayed on a monitor or stored on disc or tape as electromagnetic or digital-optical data.

Hardcopy options range from printers (dot-matrix or inkjet), to plotters (conventional drawing pens under computer control), and photographic techniques. A wide variety of electronic cameras is available, offering photographic images of up to 8,000 lines per inch (2.5cm) resolution, as used in top quality audio-visual presentations. These are an expensive option. If resolution is not a problem (some illustrators prefer screen resolutions), photographs may be taken directly off-screen. A tripod and a darkened room are essential, as slow shutter speeds (1 second at f5.6 with 100ASA film) are used to avoid frame-roll.

PAGE MAKEUP SYSTEMS

These are systems that allow the complete layout of magazine, book or newspaper pages to be designed 'soft', on screen, before being converted into hardcopy. All such systems include facilities for inputting text from a word-processing file; specifying columns, typefaces and type styles (bold, roman or italic, dropshadow, underlining, etc.); the input of graphic, illustrative and photographic images; and the scaling, proportioning, retouching and positioning of all these components.

The systems divide into two category areas:
● very high resolution output workstations, like the Quantel Graphics Paintbox and Aesthedes systems; and
● micro-computer-based page makeup software, such as the Aldus Pagemaker, running on computers such as the Mackintosh or RM Nimbus.

The main differences are in output resolution – 2,000 lines per inch (2.5cm) for the Quantel, 300 for the Mac; the range of options available; and the cost, counted in thousands but covering a wide price-range.

At the lower end of the page makeup market, the availability of micro-based systems – including output printers like the Laserwriter – is currently causing the mini-revolution of desktop publishing. In effect, these systems offer a complete design and print capability, allowing the in-house production of company reports, leaflets, brochures, newsletters and stationery. Such systems are of great interest to the student graphic designer, as at a very inexpensive level they model the operations of systems costing much, much more; and unlike the expensive systems, they can be operated with a minimum of training.

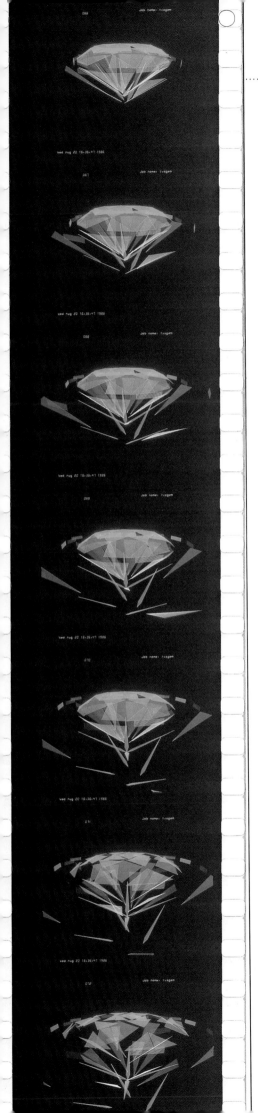

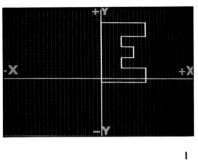

BELOW Stages in creating a 3-D solid model. A section is digitized **(1)**, and then either extruded **(2)** and solid-modelled **(3)**, or rotated **(4)** and solid-modelled **(5)**.

1

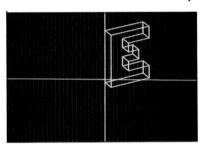

2

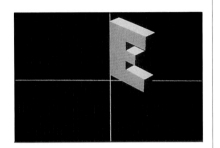

3

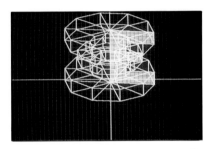

4

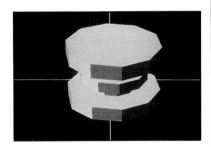

5

1. Video camera Used for 'frame-grabbing (digitizing) photos and other images so that they can be manipulated as if drawn in through a digit pad. **2. Video rostrum** Copying stand with lights. **3. Display monitor** High-resolution (about half a million pixels) RGB monitor. Displays for realtime manipulation, retouching, drawing etc. **4. Computer graphics system** A dedicated graphics device containing RAM memory storage and colour-controlled boards etc. **5. Visual display unit** A monochrome monitor to display program menus, cues and prompts. **6. Computer** The host computer, usually with a hard-disc memory, supervises the whole system using the graphics software (a suite of paint and programs). **7. Keyboard** For input of alpha-numeric data (eg file-names for saved images, angles of brushes, XYZ co-ordinates for 3-D models). **8. Digit-pad and stylus** The electronic drawing surface converts signals from the stylus with commands from the computer — either to draw in a particular style, or perform special programs such as typesetting — and displays the results on the display monitor and VDU. **9. VTR and TV monitor** Video tape recorder usually with a single-frame animation controller, for recording animations from the display monitor and the computer. The TV monitor shows the results as PAL, SECAM or NTSC encoded pictures.

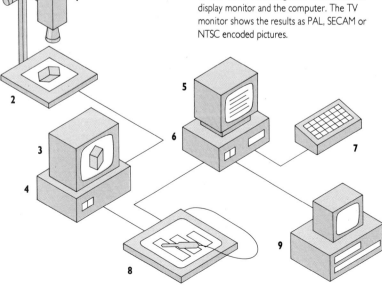

16/GRAPHIC DESIGN IN FILM AND TELEVISION

The first examples of graphic design related to filming can be seen in the early black-and-white movies. Titles, credits and dialogue captions for silent films and early talkies were of hand-styled lettering superimposed on backgrounds, usually unremarkable. Typography was rarely used, and the lettering and backgrounds were not always well matched. However, this tradition continued as a device for film, and subsequently television titles, over a long period, and can sometimes even be seen today.

Design for film and TV began to change radically in the 1950s, particularly due to the influence of the American designer Saul Bass. He made a tremendous impact, bringing a totally new way of looking at this area of graphic design. He employed a variety of film techniques and graphic effects in his work; for example, simple collage shapes, typographic devices, sophisticated animation and live-action cinematography. In 1962 he produced a milestone in title sequences for the film *Walk on the Wild Side:* live-action film of two cats, edited to focus them separately and then produce the effect of a cat-fight, was superbly coordinated with the theme music. This title sequence acted as a prologue quite different from the main film yet strongly related to it, setting a mood for the audience and bringing them in to the opening scene.

THE DEVELOPMENT OF FILM AND TV GRAPHICS

Graphic designers moving into film and television came from a print background and the initial main function of the title sequence was to give information – about the director, producers, technicians and artists. The size of credits for artists appearing in the film were extremely important, often specified in the contracts of the actors.

Graphic titles on television were originally based, like movie captions, in the signwriting and hand-lettering tradition. Skilful signwriters produced captions and credit rollers transmitted at the end of a broadcast. Considerable design breakthroughs occurred in British television design in the 1950s and 1960s when art-school trained designers were taken into the BBC to work on the graphics sequences. During the sixties the field broadened to take in designers with an interest in animation and film techniques. Rather than just showing static images on screen to convey the necessary information, these designers began to experiment with animated sequences and rostrum camera work, tracking and panning on stills to give movement to the design. Robert Brownjohn was influential in producing exciting feature film titles; he also worked on commercials but is well known as the designer of the original title sequences for the James Bond films.

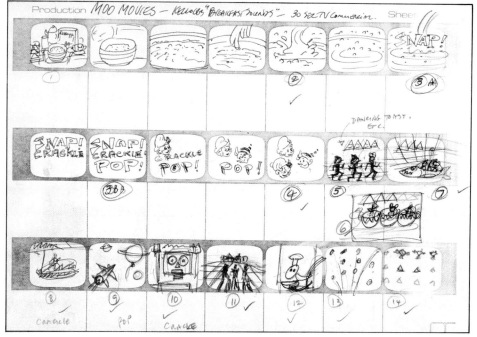

The original storyboard for a TV commercial (left). The designer's sketches (above) act as reference for style and treatment by animators and background artists.

TECHNOLOGICAL DEVELOPMENTS

Early films were black-and-white and the film stock material and equipment were unsophisticated. The increasing use of colour photography and wider variety of film formats, together with new equipment, offered greater challenges and visual opportunities to designers. The regular 35mm film format (roughly 3:4 ratio) gave way to wide screen formats with less depth in relation to width. In television the 3:4 ratio was standard, with screen dimensions the main control factor.

Early black-and-white TV cameras had problems of definition and it was necessary to use a strong, bold typeface. In the sixties, the advancement of colour technology offered new opportunities to use colour as a means of expression and to set a mood. However, to begin with, designs still had to be capable of being adequately and legibly transmitted in black-and-white, and great emphasis was put on this.

On the typographic side, captions were no longer entirely drawn by hand: lead types and hot-press coloured foil systems were being employed, but these were adapted to rather basic technology, such as roller captions, in which the caption would be printed on to a roll of paper about 12 in (30 cm) wide or photographically made into 35 mm slides. The paper roll was loaded into a machine which was placed in front of a studio camera, and on cue the credits would roll from bottom to the top of the screen. Slides, on the other hand, offered the studio director a facility to cut or mix between sets of credits. Nowadays, these are nearly always produced electronically by a caption generator.

THE ROSTRUM CAMERA

An essential tool of the graphic designer working in film or television, the rostrum camera is used for shooting single frames in a sequence. The camera is mounted on a stand which allows it to travel up and down, and on a base which can turn in any direction, so all the camera movements are variable. Images can be enlarged or reduced by tracking in or out, or moved across the screen by panning.

The camera usually works on a single frame. The most normal and satisfactory method is to shoot a single frame, move the artwork, take a single frame, move the artwork, and so on. It is also possible to have a running sequence where the camera is left running and the artwork is panned under the camera. In television the rostrum camera is used for animation or shooting stills, and it is the most suitable method for shooting stills for a documentary production, or reference material for either television or movie film. By rewinding the film in the camera magazine, further exposures can be added; normally white lettering is burnt-in using this method.

USE OF COMPUTERS

A big development in rostrum cameras came with the addition of computers to control the movement sequence. With the artwork under the camera, the first position is selected, and the next position, and so on, and the computer stores the coordinates at each stage. The camera can then be allowed to run through the whole sequence of movement under the computer's control.

More recently in all areas of this field of design, computer systems have become more highly developed in the complexity of the work they can produce and the speed at which they can produce it. The latest development is texture mapping, which allows the designer to put different textures on the surfaces in an animated or object-designed sequence. The generation of designers coming into this field will accept the computer as a standard tool. The design can be developed on screen, and a lot of the basic artwork stages of the job are cut out. This does not mean that ideas are not prepared and set down in some tangible from to begin with, but it does mean that the slow process of producing artwork, with painting and airbrush work, for example, will gradually become less of a necessity. There has been considerable growth in television graphics since the introduction of increasingly versatile video and computer systems. Graphic images are an effective way of explaining information relating to news and current affairs, for example, with maps, charts and graphs.

VIDEO EDITING

Video technology is a major area of advance in television graphics. In the early stages, video editing was very difficult, with the tape being cut for editing in the same way as audio tape, but the equipment is now much more sophisticated. The great advantage of video is that it gives an instant playback of what has been produced. The problem with film was of waiting for the film to be processed before seeing whether it had achieved what was expected, or whether there were any mistakes created on the camera side. With video, you have immediate replay which allows designers to see the results of their work and if necessary make adjustments.

AREAS OF WORK

Major broadcast television companies employ the large majority of graphic designers and design assistants. There are also animation companies that take on trainee animators, and facilities companies that have developed more recently to supply independent programme makers with equipment and operators. Another category is that of independent design groups. It is usual to start work in any of these companies as a design assistant, and gradually work up to being a designer with control over the work on a particular project. The structure in television companies tends to be broader: groups of specialist designers work in specialized areas, with perhaps a senior designer in charge who is the main point of reference for the production.

In addition to traditional graphic design skills, the designer has to be interested in analysing and creating movement. This is always very much related to a soundtrack, which is most often a music track, and it is essential that a graphic designer in this medium understands how to break down the musical episodes in a track and use these to advantage to emphasize certain points in any moving graphic sequence.

Photography is an important element, and it is necessary to know how to set up a shot. A professional photographer is there to see to the technicalities, but the designer has to communicate with the photographer and understand what is required for studio work or location shooting and how, if the photographs form a sequence, they actually relate to each other in the sequence. The designer must compose the shots and give a very clear briefing to the photographer.

The main sources of typography are photosetting and electronic character generators. The designer is usually required to produce typography that will work when superimposed on a background. Type styles have to be bold and there are technical constraints, especially in television where the system of transmission breaks up the images into hundreds of lines: fine serif typefaces, for example, are not suited to this medium. In certain circumstances, computer functions are used to create typography by means of electronic character generation, and this can be put up on the screen almost immediately, for example, in sports or current affairs broadcasting.

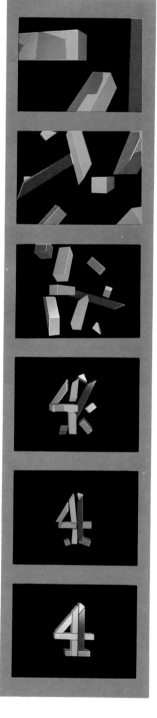

RIGHT Opening title sequence for a TV documentary series. The animation was created using a free-style drawn treatment with the action taken from various live-action film sequences using a rotascope technique (making simple drawings from each frame of live-action film).

LEFT Designed as part of a corporate image. The logo was produced completely by computer animation in 1982, and was the first 'station ident' to be created in the UK using this technique.

SOLDIERS
A HISTORY OF MEN IN BATTLE

PRESENTED BY
FREDERICK FORSYTH

BELOW Opening title sequence using original live-action material shot on video which was edited electronically and combined with electronic graphics techniques.

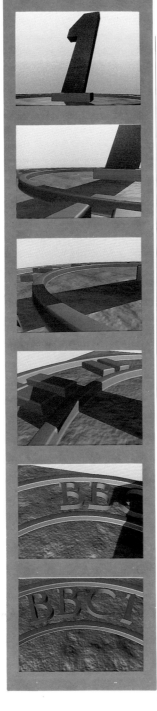

ABOVE TV seasonal promotion spot to advertise forthcoming programmes. The sequence was produced by computer using fully shaded graphic images.

WORKING PROCEDURES

In a production for television, the first stage is to discuss the requirements with the director, and these vary very much according to the type of production. In drama, the designer's task normally includes an opening title sequence and end credits. In addition to understanding what the director intends, it is necessary to read the script and get to know the mood and period of the production. From there a storyboard is prepared, which should take into consideration any musical background which the director intends to add. This is shown to the director and when the treatment is agreed, the designer's next objective is to cost the sequences and start to book the necessary facilities. Sometimes the costing is written in already, so the storyboard and the facilities required to realize the sequence must be geared to the budget allowed.

When working in television graphics, you may have to brief a photographer, modelmaker or animator, and arrange typesetting. If the sequence is to be filmed, camera facility must be booked and the type of camera specified. All the information is assembled and broken down to frame numbers.

There are 25 frames to every second of television time, though this does not mean that you necessarily have 25 pieces of artwork for each second, as some may be held for a continuous period: however, every frame has to be accounted for.

WORKING WITH CLIENTS

As with every design activity, it is important that you identify your client's needs and establish a useful working relationship. The storyboard is the most important feature of this interchange, because it is here that the director, or other person commissioning, must fully understand what you are trying to contribute to the production.

You are also in the position of providing the link between the director and the facilities companies who will be carrying out your ideas, so it is important to be able to present your briefing clearly on both sides. You have the responsibility of using the budget wisely and meeting the time requirements set by the production. To meet the deadlines, you may be working concentratedly for long periods and must be able to justify decisions taken quickly and under pressure, and effect any compromises which may become necessary as work progresses.

17/PRESENTING YOUR WORK

The method by which designers and illustrators present their work is as important as the work itself, but slick presentation is no substitute for poor design or sloppy craftsmanship. The experienced client or art director quickly sees through the superficial gloss and surface confidence. By the same token, excellent work that has been thought through and superbly executed, representing hours of thought and skilled labour, should never be undermined by scruffy presentation.

PERSONAL PRESENTATION

Assuming that you are not represented by an agent, you are the one to deal with the client. To get quickly to the business in hand – which is to sell your ideas and gain acceptance of your work – avoid any unnecessary resistance or prejudice by arriving at presentations punctually and smartly dressed. This is not to say that you should adopt a particular uniform or dress code, or submerge your own personality and natural style: just apply a bit of common sense to presenting yourself well. Even if you have been working all night, this is not something that a prospective client needs to know just by looking at you.

Some people do not suffer anxiety about giving a presentation, while others can be alarmingly self-conscious. If you are one of the latter, some careful forethought about how you present yourself will be of use. There is no panacea for nervousness, but there are ways of coping with it, although experience is the only real cure.

Remember that the focal point of any presentation is the work. You are supplying a skill and a service which the client needs, and is prepared to accept from you: that is why you are there. In other words, the presentee wishes to have confidence in you, and if you take the right mental attitude and combine this with good self-presentation which encourages you to feel confident in yourself, you are on the right track.

The problem with a nervous presentation is that it can be contagious. An anxious presenter can embarrass the audience and make it uneasy. Like some kind of 'bad magic', this can lead to events which aggravate the problem, such as the zip jamming on your portfolio, transparencies becoming irretrievably lodged in the projector, or the all-too-frequent occurrence of coffee being spilled over artwork.

Your presentation of work must be prepared and in order. If you are showing a series of related work or the development of a concept, make sure everything is in sequence and easily accessible. There is nothing worse than seeing a dishevelled person rummaging through bags and folios pulling out work in the wrong sequence while extraneous personal effects are tumbling out on to the floor. The same goes for a presentation of transparencies which are upside down and the wrong way round, or covered with specks and smudges that loom even larger in projection. Aim to let your work speak for itself, and you can supply an informed narrative.

Clients like and expect to be talked through a presentation. Deliver your explanation clearly and unhurriedly, but don't speak as if assuming that the client is familiar with your thought processes. Provide all the necessary links and details, with a little additional anecdote and insight if this seems appropriate. This aspect of your presentation may require a dress rehearsal, but don't go over the top.

It's a tall order having to combine being a salesperson and a graphic designer or illustrator, but the need to sell yourself is a fact of commercial life. The more you do it, the easier it gets. If you really can't handle standing in front of an audience and articulating your ideas, then get an agent or partner who can, but take into account that you will miss out on a lot of useful feedback and first-hand knowledge.

ENVIRONMENTAL RECONNAISSANCE

The following information is probably more applicable to presentation of a large-scale design job than a one-off illustration. But depending on the type of job and your relationship with the client, a bit of environmental reconnaissance, another type of forward planning, may be well worthwhile and can assist you in making a good presentation.

Office space is notoriously tight and in order to get the best surroundings in which to present your work, ask your client to book a meeting room for the date and time of your presentation; most companies have this amenity, but even if they don't, it shows that you are serious and professional and may prompt the client to provide a suitable venue. It is a confidence-building measure for both of you, and much better than trying to show and explain your work over a cluttered desk while other office business goes on around you.

If you are showing slides or videos, the right facilities are essential – power points, a projector and screen, blackout curtains, a video machine and monitor. To ensure that what you need is available, alert the client well in advance to the kind of presentation you will be making.

THE PORTFOLIO

The simplest and most efficient 'walk-in' presentation is a portfolio of your work up-to-date, in order and well mounted. Mount the work on even tone or matching materials, in clear plastic sheets ring-bound into a folio with a protective all-round zip fastening. There are several types of portfolio available in this style, in various sizes. The transparent plastic sheets protect the work and the ring-binding allows you to take out or change the order of individual pieces. The outer cover is usually of a sturdy vinyl. This is not only a good means of presenting your work, but also efficient for storing and transporting it.

Consider the sheet size when building a presentation system of this type. If it is too big, you will soon have had enough of hauling it around during a day of interviews. Most art directors prefer a compact, small-format presentation for ease of handling and viewing.

An alternative and very efficient way of showing samples is to have the work laminated between plastic sheets – this is especially good for photographs and printed specimens. You can have the laminated sheets hole-punched to fit a ring-binder, but more commonly they are carried loose in a case or portfolio. One advantage is that your samples can be handed around for close scrutiny without fear of damage or finger-marking. The main disadvantage is that this system is relatively expensive, as it utilizes a special heat-sealing process, and when your work becomes outdated or you no longer wish to show a particular piece, all you can do is throw it away, as the laminated sheets are not re-usable.

SLIDE PRESENTATIONS

The only effective way to show slides is to project them. An on-screen slide presentation can be a dramatic and attention-focusing method of presentation and it is an especially good way of presenting your work to a large audience.

If convenient and practicable, it is probably better to take your own projector to the presentation. The advantage of this is that you know how it works and understand its foibles, and you can use prearranged slide magazines. This may not always be possible or necessary, but it avoids the anxiety of using strange apparatus.

If you wish to use a client's equipment, give advance warning that you will need a projector and make sure that your slide magazines are compatible. It's useful if you can arrange to have a few minutes on your own to set up and have a run-through. This allows you a last-minute check that all the material is in the correct order, the right way up and the right way round, and clean and sharp when projected.

A desktop slide projector, with its own screen similar in appearance to a portable television, works in the same way as an on-screen projector, and the same rules apply to a presentation by this method. Some desktop systems have integrated cassettes and you can include a co-ordinated soundtrack.

Of course, slides can be shown just as they are, although it's not the best way to present them. Much design and illustration work is recorded on 35mm format and it is difficult to appreciate images at this small size. Nevertheless, it is sometimes the only way to present the work, particularly when you are asked to send in material or leave samples behind for consideration. Pre-cut mounting systems are available in international standard A sizes, usually made of black card with a protective transparent plastic sleeve, or you could easily make your own. These mounts are very useful for showing groups of 35mm transparencies, as they provide an immediate overview of the work and can easily be held up to the light or viewed on a light-box. This system is more efficient than presentation of individual slides, and more stylish than plastic storage wallets.

TABLETOP PRESENTATIONS

Sometimes it is necessary to make a simple yet logical presentation of a sequence of ideas or related materials at the sketch or layout stage, and this may require turning pages or proceeding through a series of boards. If you are presenting to a group in a fairly formal situation, it may be worth investing in a tabletop easel or lectern. Many of these come with size-compatible layout pads and can be folded down for easy transportation. There are several types and sizes of easel available and these can be found in stores and catalogues selling office supplies and graphic art materials. It is probably more desirable to make a presentation in this way than to improvise with supports found on the spot.

1,2,3 A presentation for a series of stamps designed by Tricket & Webb. The roughs are both drawn in magic marker, that on the far right being done in dots which simulate a printed screen and the other drawn quite freely. In **(1)** the designers have used a base photograph with an acetate overlay so that they could put in new material as required.

4 This presentation for a specialist farming magazine, showing a cover and one spread, gives the client a feel for the illustrative style and the typography.

5 This type of portfolio is particularly suitable for presentations as it can be opened out and stood on a table or desk top. The printed specimens here are stationery, menus and a brochure designed for a catering service.

6 A storyboard by Lambie Nairn for an animated TV commercial.

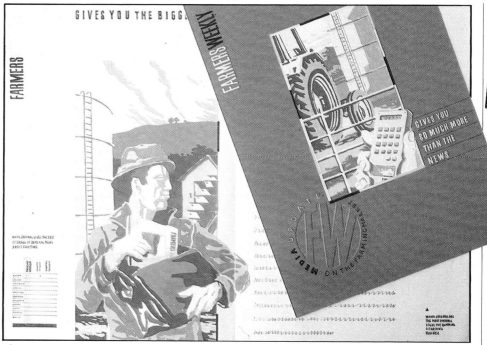

VIDEO PRESENTATION

It is now possible for anyone who can operate a camera, and has a little understanding of photography and composition, to make a videotape presentation. This creates many visual opportunities: for example, you can show on-screen straight examples of work, three-dimensional models and mock-ups, or live-action sequences accompanied by voice-over sound and music.

It is feasible to present your work with the dimensions of sound and time, by utilizing simple film-making techniques such as panning, tracking and dissolving in order to emphasize details or particular points. A small video cassette enables you to present succinctly the case history of a job, including some background research if appropriate; this would be impossible by presentation of all the physical material.

You can make a video yourself using the increasingly simple 'cam-corder' systems which are now available, most of which have facilities for shooting slides and including titles. This means avoiding the need to edit material, so it should be shot to a strict storyboard on a 1:1 basis. It's probably best to avoid using professional video-making services, as this could turn out to be very expensive.

MODELS AND MOCK-UPS

Many design disciplines require presentation of three-dimensional models and mock-ups: for example, architectural models for retail or exhibition schemes, physicals for packaging concepts, book jackets fitted to bulking dummies. Clients like to see these tangible items, and they can make the presentation particularly successful and memorable. More than that, models or mock-ups are often the only way to demonstrate how a design really works, and therefore these have to be presented.

Take into account the problems of transporting the materials and setting them up in place. Place them well if they are fragile, and allow plenty of time before the presentation to construct or check the object after unpacking. Some samples involve special problems for delivery, such as designs for beer bottle labels which are best shown on the bottles: it has happened that such a presentation has simply been mailed to a client, with the foreseeable result that what arrived was a mess of broken glass and wet paper.

Obviously three-dimensional design solutions can be shown as drawings, slides or photographs, but it's well worth making the extra effort to show the three-dimensional application in a realized form.

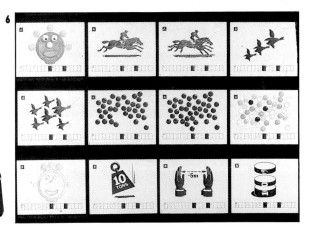

7 A packaging presentation: two coloured pencil roughs stuck down on box lids, together with the printed results. The client has asked for some changes, notably the reversed-out type and the inclusion of the Statue of Liberty instead of the rather weaker images on the rough.

8 Presentation boards for the American Festivals Café at New York's Rockefeller Center, showing a glass, serviettes, matchbooks and a plate.

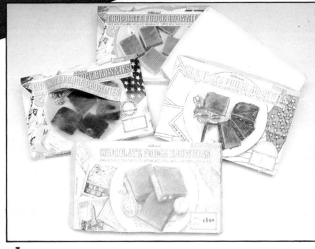

7

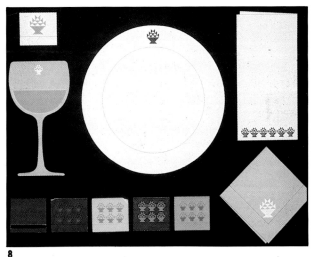

8

GAUGING YOUR PRESENTATION

There are broadly two types of presentation: one is the self-promotional sampling exercise that shows what you can do; the other is the specific presentation where you present to the client the results of a commissioned assignment. The techniques and equipment discussed above should be of value in either case, but it is important that you pitch the presentation correctly.

In the first category – that of self-presentation – the work should be selected as appropriate to the particular client area or to demonstrate the range and quality of your skills, so be selective. Do not overload the presentation, and be ruthless in discarding irrelevant or superfluous material. The client, whether a business manager or art director, wants to get immediately to the point of what you are selling.

Success in the second category of presentation – showing roughs and finished artwork for a commission – depends upon a thorough understanding of the client and the specific requirements of the job. The technique of presentation – using boards, slides, tabletop easel or video cassette – you must judge for yourself as suited to the work stages and the end product.

This also applies to the studio and art techniques you use and the degree of finish in the presentation materials. These again are geared to the client's expectations and the way the brief is stated, and also to certain economic considerations. For example, a client may well be able to see what you plan to do via a tightly worked rough, scamp or layout; on the other hand, high investment in a prestigious job may call for design proposals to be presented as printed samples.

Whatever the case, the true purpose of the presentation must not be lost: this is to present good work in the most appropriate form and in a professional manner, in order to clinch a deal or move on to the next stage of development.

Part of a corporate identity slide presentation, showing a proposed logo and its application on various items.

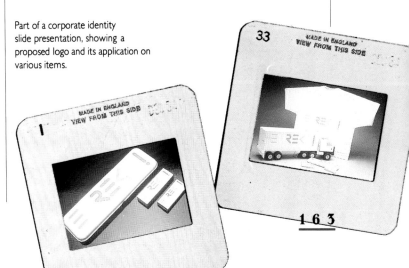

18/PROFESSIONAL PRACTICE

By the time you reach this chapter you will have come to an important decision that affects your entire creative outlook. You are working as an illustrator or designer, not as a fine artist: a deliberate choice has been made. Working as an illustrator or graphic designer means working with clients. It does not mean that painters cannot be illustrators, or illustrators painters, at the same time. It means that you have chosen to make your living in a client-related manner, commonly known as commercially, rather than by selling original works. There is a good reason for this. Traditionally there is more likelihood of making a living as a client-related designer than as a fine artist.

Another major reason for choosing client-related work is the desire to work with people, to contribute to a total project, to be part of a team. Painters and sculptors usually paint or sculpt on their own: designers, on the other hand, work sometimes on their own and sometimes in groups with other designers as well as with their clients.

This chapter is about the relationship between designers and their clients, and is concerned with two main themes: how to relate to clients, and how to manage your own design business. Both themes are related to profitability. This is significant because the client's business should be more profitable because of your work, and your work will be more profitable because of the professional way you manage it. Profitable not only in the financial sense but in job satisfaction also.

PREPARATION FOR PROFESSIONAL PRACTICE

The following headings constitute a checklist for a student, graphic designer or illustrator beginning a career:
• Ways of working • Economics of work • Conditions of work • Types of freelance work • Methods of work • Working with clients • Work titles and definitions.
Many big books have been written on the subject of professional practice. Where a topic is not covered in detail here, and advice is required, there are relevant professional bodies and appropriate books which should be able to help.

While still at college, and especially before the final exhibition of your work, begin a 'start-up pack' which includes a diary, an address book, a card index, a filing system, a calendar of events important to your work, designed letterhead for stationery and business card, curriculum vitae, and a telephone contact number. With this kit you can start sending applications for jobs or getting clients. This will lead you into employment or self-employment and these basic business requirements are necessary for both in-house and freelance designers. If you work freelance you will eventually need an accountant, a business bank account, and perhaps a microcomputer.

WAYS OF WORKING

Graphic designers and illustrators usually work in one of two ways and it is important to understand, when planning a career path, what both these ways involve.

The first is as a salaried graphic designer or illustrator. The work is usually in-house, that is to say, as part of a business or industrial company. You may be working, for example, as a technical illustrator in the automotive industry, an illustrator in medical, botanical or archaeological services, or as a graphic designer with responsibility for packaging in the retail industry. A salaried graphic designer or illustrator may also work on the staff of a design consultancy.

The second way of working is as a freelance designer or illustrator. The majority of illustrators work in a freelance capacity; graphic designers choose this or salaried work almost equally. This chapter will describe what both salaried and freelance designers or illustrators can expect to find in their chosen working pattern.

ECONOMICS OF WORK

It is sometimes very difficult for any artist, in fine art or commercial, to relate their work to the payment of fees or money. There is often a conflict between idealism and harsh reality. There are ways of dealing with reality, however, that can put the work into a much more professional framework. This enables not only the client or employer, but the designer as well, to see the work for what it is worth. Don't think that design doesn't mean money: equally don't think that it only means money – that's dangerous.

Salaried. In either an industrial company or a design consultancy, the personnel structures for graphic designers or illustrators will be very much the same. The usual pattern is to start as a junior designer, then be promoted to senior design status. In some cases designers are promoted even further, to directorship within the company, taking on a much broader role that involves supervision of many if not all of the company's design activities. Design supervision in this case embraces not only graphic considerations but also environmental and product development aspects. The role is broadly what is known as design management. The designer in this case is not designing at all but dealing with major design decisions or managing the design process.

Information on prevailing salary levels for junior and senior designers and principals of design consultancies is published by the Chartered Society of Designers.

It is well worth obtaining up-to-date information on salary scales. A designer's time is billed in a special way when working through a company. It is quite useful to understand that the way the time is billed out is totally different from the way the designer is paid.

In order to understand that, one has to be able to calculate realistically the selling cost of time. The next section describes how a freelance designer calculates scales of charges or fees. For in-house work the considerations are the same. To the basic cost of billable/worked time (salary) must be added non-billable time and real overheads. This figure very often is arrived at by a standard of two-and-a-half times the salary. It is essential for freelance designers to know what all the ingredients are, and important for salaried designers to understand the ramifications.

There may be a greater differential of salary scales between senior designers and principals than applies to other categories. Perks such as lunches, travel allowances or company cars can amount to a considerable value. In larger offices company shares, health insurance, pension schemes and office outings supplement wage packets.

Freelance. When starting out in business and beginning to work for fees, it is important to remember that there has to be a basis for working out these fees in the first place. They do not just come into the mind haphazardly, or because a friend has recommended them. To be meaningful and business-like, they must be prepared in a structured way. First of all, the basic desired 'salary' is established, which is what you need to maintain the standard of living that you require. On top of the basic hourly rate must be added the cost of non-billable time, i.e. holidays, sick leave, public holidays, office administration, client search. Then there are the studio overheads, cost of materials and equipment, and business administration costs. For a self-employed designer working alone, the following expenditure has to be considered: Rent and rates, heat/light/power, telephone, maintenance, consumables (non-chargeable), postage/stationery, professional materials, insurance, accountancy/legal fees, travelling (non-chargeable) and equipment deterioration.

Supposing one week's costs are being analysed, then the overhead rate would be the total of all these expenses in that period: this can be sub-divided by 5 for a daily rate, and by 35 or 40 for an hourly rate.

When you are devising a fee for a particular project, the basic cost is the sale of professional time. The information that you are gathering can be used continually, updated when necessary, so the ingredients for a contract are as follows:

materials used + subcontractors paid + labour by the hour + overheads

Together these equal the price of commission, to which a service tax if applicable, is added.

The materials are as used or bought. Broadly speaking, designers' time is charged out at two rates:

Labour at professional rate: • selling time • client contact • research • designing • presentation
Labour at junior rate: • making models • fetching and carrying • working drawings • office-keeping.

The contract total costing therefore will include materials, labour, and overheads. If you want to suggest that there will be a 10 per cent discount on payment within 14 days, add the discount to the total and this final amount constitutes the stated fee.

If a handling fee percentage is going to be charged, the client should be advised of its inclusion in advance.

CONDITIONS OF WORK

As with any other design discipline, the fields of graphic design and illustration bring with them specific work traditions and legalities. Many of these traditions and customary practices will become apparent even during training years. They should become a natural part of your consciousness of how the work is carried out. But traditions evolve and laws change, so the graphic designer and illustrator must be aware of the changes and how to safeguard their own rights. There are recognized professionals and established professional organizations who offer just this sort of advice; these are listed later in this section. Experience is a great teacher. But you cannot expect to start out knowing all that you need to know. Ask questions, research, read and when necessary pay for the professional advice that you need, i.e. from lawyers and accountants.

Salaried. Both in industry and design groups, contracts of employment should include details of trial period, if any, holiday entitlement, sickness arrangements, wages and overtime, and a notice period for either side. Common sense should dictate the clarification required as to the extent to which, and in what circumstances, work may be taken on a freelance basis while in salaried employment. Where the job specification is vague, the standard questions to ask are: How is the company set up? How is the studio set up? What is the organization within it? Who am I responsible to? What am I going to be doing? How might the job develop in the future?

To give you an example of a job specification in industry, here are two samples of advertisements for jobs in the illustration studio of a large national telecommunications service. The studio deals with many types of graphic design (excluding packaging) including visual aids, audio-visual presentation, exhibitions, computer graphics, design for print.

One advertisement is for Visual-aids Designers and asks for:

Commercially experienced and imaginative visual aids designers who are used to working to very tight deadlines. The successful candidate will join a team of dedicated designers whose tasks include the production of illustrations, diagrams, cartoons and graphics for both OHP and 35mm slides, using conventional artwork and computer graphics. A knowledge of the Dicomed computer graphics system would be an advantage but not essential.

The second asks for an Artworker/Designer to join an existing team:

The successful candidate will have a broad knowledge of design, typography and print techniques, and be capable of working on his or her own initiative. He or she will have the ability to see projects through concept to completed product, producing finished artwork where necessary. All candidates must have at least two years commercial experience and have a City & Guilds Certificate in Design for Print or in Technical Graphics, or an equivalent or higher academic qualification.

Here is another example of an advertisement for a Graphic Designer for a large department store chain. They ask for a graphic designer who will be a member of the creative team attached to a buying group:

Your task will be to design and to commission design for packaging, promotional and photographic material in response to marketing requirements. This will involve close liaison with the buying department to establish a brief and to commission outside designers, visualizers and photographers. It's a demanding role which combines tight deadlines with a considerable diversity and volume of projects, which you will have the satisfaction of controlling from concept through to completion. Such responsible and wide-ranging duties demand that you should be adaptable and commercially aware, a graduate with 3–4 years' experience of retail graphic design. This will have been gained with a major store or design consultancy. Besides the ability to follow and interpret briefs professionally and creatively, you will need to be an effective communicator, in discussing projects with both the Senior Designer and Merchandise Promotions Manager.

The advertisement then continues with the salary and a description of a range of benefits including pension scheme, life assurance and a profit sharing scheme.

Freelance. There are two areas involving legal aspects that are of major concern to both illustrators and graphic designers. One has to do with copyright, the other with contracts. (The way a contract can actually be drawn up is described under 'Working with clients'.)

First a word about ownership of artwork. No matter what arrangement is made about copyright, original artwork should generally belong to the designer or illustrator. It is important to establish, before undertaking a commission, who will own the eventual artwork. If at all possible, a designer or illustrator should insist on retaining ownership and on having the artwork returned once it has been reproduced for the purposes of the commission.

Copyright law is an extremely important aspect of the work of graphic designers and illustrators. It is important to know what to do to protect your interests. Copyright is the right to copy something. It exists as soon as a drawing takes shape and continues until 50 years after the death of the designer (unless the drawing is reproduced in 3-D form, in which case it may only last for 15 years). Copyright of any commissioned work, or even a sketch on a paper napkin, belongs to the creator except in special cases (photographs, the painting or drawing of a portrait, the making of an engraving) when it belongs to the commissioner. Like any other piece of property, you can sell it or otherwise dispose of it in any way you please. You can also divide it up and sell it in a number of different ways. Illustrators should never assign full copyright of their works to anyone without making firm conditions as to the use of the work. Remember, though, that copyright law is in the process of changing and it is therefore important to ascertain from the professional bodies what the up-to-date position is.

Contract law is common law: that means that it is not government legislation but has evolved over time into what is known as customary trade practice. Whenever one person agrees to provide goods or services in exchange for money or some other consideration, a contract is created. The agreement is sometimes written, sometimes verbal and sometimes implied with no exchange of words at all, or it can be a mixture of all three. It is more difficult to test the validity of verbal and implied contracts as compared to written ones, but they are nonetheless binding. Illustration is a profession that is full of implied contracts, just by the nature of the work itself, so you should never think that because there is no written document, there is no contract. It is obviously a good idea, however, to have a written contract whenever possible.

For example, illustration for newspapers or magazines may be commissioned at a moment's notice with no time at all for an exchange of contract, let alone an order. The fee and deadline will probably be agreed on the telephone. This is the verbal part of the contract. The implied part concerns ownership of artwork and copyright, both of which belong to the illustrator. Customary trade practice (or the Copyright Act itself, for example, in the case of employed illustrators) allows the magazine to use the illustration for the purpose for which it was commissioned only, and not for any other copyright purposes.

Illustration for advertising, on the other hand, is so well paid that guidelines on ownership of artwork and copyright are less clear. This has much to do with the fact that a large proportion of the work is commissioned through artists' agents, who tend to be less concerned with ownership rights of illustrators. By some quirk of law, engravers and portraitists are even less protected than others, and even customary trade practice cannot help here. The best advice is to make sure your agent retrieves your artwork and watches out for the copyright.

Book publishing is the one area where a formal contract is bound to be written. This is because the publisher, the client, needs to have access to almost all the copyright in your work. In this way the publisher can license foreign editions, film or TV rights, merchandising, and any other projects based on the book. According to the Association of Illustrators (AOI) in the UK, the main provisions of a publishing contract are:

1 To give the publisher an exclusive world licence for the period of copyright – the practical equivalent of copyright itself.
2 To lay down what payments the publisher will pay to the author, usually in the form of royalties and percentages of rights fees.
3 To stipulate a reversion clause which says that if the publisher goes bankrupt, or if the book goes out of print for a certain period, the rights will revert back to the author and sometimes the illustrator.
So the main headings that you are likely to encounter in a book publishing contract are as follows:
● Rights granted ● Delivery of artwork ● Permissions ● Production ● Royalty terms (percentages on copies sold in the country of origin and overseas, hardbound and paperbound editions) ● Advance payments ● Translation and other subsidiary rights (including rights for serialization, newspaper, broadcasting and television, dramatic and film, book digest condensation, strip cartoon and merchandising) ● Accounting ● Presentation copies ● Author's and illustrator's copies ● Conflicting editions ● Failure of the author to complete ● Cancellation of agreement ● Single copy reprints and microform editions ● Author's or illustrator's warranty ● Proceedings for infringement
Book packagers are a relatively new type of book publisher who operate without large capital and in a much speedier way than traditional publishers. A standard contract between a book packager and an illustrator may differ from the terms of a publishing contract.

It is important to get advice before signing a book publishing contract.

Professional bodies. It is not essential, but it is well worth considering joining a professional organization. The design field is developing rapidly and the easiest way to keep up with the changes, and meet to discuss common problems, is by belonging to a professional society or association. Certain organizations and employers also expect trade union membership, and these conditions should be made clear to you when you accept a staff position or long-term contract.

Accountants. Professional bodies and consultant designers agree unanimously that of all the professional help required by a freelance designer, the accountancy service is essential. Inland Revenue legislation changes continually and it is necessary to seek professional advice, not only for making tax returns and fulfilling tax obligations, but also in setting up a system within the office or studio that can relate directly to the accountant's requirements. This makes the whole procedure of accounting and record-keeping less of a headache and more of a pleasure.

Insurance. Insurance cover is required for the studio or workplace, especially including a portfolio of work. Some professional associations also advise insurance for hands and fingers.

TYPES OF FREELANCE WORK
The following is a modified extract from 'Study of Professional Practice in Graphic and Industrial Design', SIAD 1974, defining types of assignment a designer may expect to come across.
A single assignment is usually completed in two stages: a rough sketch, and a finished drawing.
A multiple or period assignment (a package) is when a number of designs are to be supplied either in a single batch or over a certain period of time. It might be convenient to regard the whole job as a single assignment instead of negotiating a separate fee for each design.
Advisory services. An independent designer may be retained in a purely advisory capacity. The scope of the advice should be defined in advance. It may be defined as attendance at a number of meetings, or services may be called upon as and when required. In either case, advisory services may be combined with the preparation of designs as outlined in the two previous paragraphs. Advisory services are normally engaged on an annual basis subject to agreed conditions of renewal.
While design commissions vary considerably in both scope and complexity, the following procedure occurs in

almost all cases as the normal sequence of events:

- At the first meeting the client outlines the requirements. A full discussion should ensure that these are thoroughly understood and agreed on both sides. Alterations and revisions during the course of a job, involving loss of time and money, can usually be avoided by an adequate briefing at the outset. (Briefing is covered under 'Working with Clients'.)

- When a comprehensive brief has been established, the designer calculates how long (in hours) the work is likely to take and states the fee in writing (not off the cuff). He or she also undertakes to complete the work or carry out the first stage by a given date. If the client agrees to the terms the designer is instructed to proceed with the work. This instruction, which may be given verbally, should always be confirmed in writing, either by an order issued by the client, or by a letter from the designer confirming the terms.

- Any conditions which the designer may wish to impose must be stated at this stage. The designer is entitled to propose any conditions and the client is, of course, equally free to accept or reject them. A client cannot be held to any conditions unless he or she has been told of them and has agreed to them. Disputes arising from such questions as the designer's right to sign work, or the client's right to alter a design without the designer's consent, should always be settled in advance; otherwise, in the event of any subsequent disagreement, the designer will have no redress.

- Within the agreed period, design proposals are submitted to the client in the form of a rough sketch, dummy or model. In some cases a written report may precede the preparation of designs. In submitting designs or proposals, the designer should discuss them with the client; in fields of practice where it is customary for the designer to employ an agent, the agent should, of course, be kept fully informed about the talks that have taken place. If the designer's work or proposals are approved there and then, he or she can proceed at once to the next stage, which is the preparation of 'finished art'.

- In designing for certain industries, immediate approval of first stage recommendations is unusual. The client will probably wish to consult sales and technical staff. In the course of such discussions, at which the designer should always be present, modifications to the original design may be suggested. It is important for the designer to know not merely what changes are suggested but also why they are suggested; hence the importance of being present when they are discussed.

- Such modifications as have been agreed are incorporated into revised design proposals which are resubmitted for approval or further discussion. (Since the extent of revisions during the development stage can

rarely be foreseen, it is customary to charge for them according to the time entailed. A fixed fee should not be negotiated in advance when the probable extent of the work cannot be accurately assessed.)

- On receiving the client's final approval, design proposals are returned to the designer for the preparation of 'finished art' together with any requisite production specifications. On completion, these are delivered to the client and approved (after amendment, should any be required). The designer's responsibility may end at this point, when it is customary to render the account. On the other hand, the designer may be required to advise on production problems which may arise in connection with the carrying out of the designs. In such cases, interim payments at specified stages of the work may be negotiated.

Methods of payment. *Lump sum or fixed fees.* This applies to work being done for projects in advertising, editorial (magazines or newspapers, special projects in publishing), graphic design generally (corporate identity, packaging, book jackets, record album covers, calendars, videos, and most work that is done through design consultancies). The rates are established normally by market forces. Rejection fees are based on a percentage of stated fee. If the client's requirements change, the illustrator or designer should be paid the full fee. If the rejection takes place at the rough sketch stage, the designer should receive 50 per cent of the fee, if it takes place at the artwork stage, 75 per cent of the fee. All this assumes that the client is at fault, not the illustrator or graphic designer. Adjustment will have to be made if the graphic designer or illustrator admits having not understood the brief and accepts blame.

Hourly rate. This is used when the project time span is unknown. It would be accepted by a client if the quantity of work is unknown at the outset. If the brief given is vague, this method is of advantage to the designer. It can also be used for presenting a first stage rough.

Royalties. These are mostly used in publishing of books, greetings cards, posters, and calendars. Payment can also be a combination of a lump sum and royalties.

Retainer. This is paid when a designer's or illustrator's clients want to retain his or her service exclusively for a period of time, or to procure services so that other companies in similar industrial areas cannot use the designer or illustrator at the same time, or for competitive reasons. This area must be negotiated and monitored carefully. A typical fee structure sequence occurs in three stages. 1 The initial concept – rough sketch, 2 The detailed design, 3 Production artwork.

Letters of contract: A typical letter of contract for a project will include the following paragraphs (modified and updated from *The Professional Practice of Design* by Dorothy Goslett).

Introduction: relating to courtesy acceptance of relationship with client for a particular project.

Summary of the brief: relating to meetings and conversations regarding the nature of the work to be undertaken, and the envisaged cost and deadlines involved.

Services provided:

- Stage One: Discussions with client's departments, printers, advertising and publicity agents, etc. in agreed number of visits, preparation and submission of preliminary design proposals.
- Stage Two: Development work.
- Stage Three: Finished artwork, layouts, printers' specifications etc., adaptations for size and for department uses (stationery); foreign language adaptations.
- Stage Four: Advising on production, checking proofs and first runs.

Deadlines: Envisaged completion dates for each stage.

Fees: A fixed proportion of the fee may be payable at the completion of each stage.

Special clauses: Ownership and conveyance of copyright; breaking clauses and fees payable for abandoned work; permitted modifications; free specimens, signed work and design credits.

Additional fees: For extra visits, extra work, changes to brief, expansion of brief, travelling time.

Special costs and expenses chargeable.

Request for written acceptance of letter and *Conclusion*

Footnote: A contract or agreement must include the question of expenses and what they are and how far they go. Clients often assume either honestly or dishonestly that all expenses are included in the fee, unless they're told to the contrary. Designers tend to assume that expenses are extra. Designers must have the confidence to be able to spell this out right from the word go. Don't just accept a proposed payment: have an idea of what you're worth and base that idea on what your costs and expenses are. Sometimes you might want to do a job for a low fee to get other jobs, but make sure you know that you're doing it for that reason. By the way, the contract should include the brief, not the other way round.

The AOI advise that it is sometimes extremely difficult, because of the timespan allotted to various projects, for a letter of contract to be written. They suggest that illustrators ask for an order form from the client and if that is not possible, then they write an order or a confirming letter themselves. In that document, a reference should be made to the following:

- The order form should have a number which is to be quoted on your invoice ● The stated fee + service tax if applicable ● Agreed expenses such as research (picture library fees), model fees, travel, postage, messengers, special materials ● Deadline ● Rejection fee percentage (a

good knowledge of the client will dictate whether to include or omit this clause) ● The ownership of artwork (this belongs to the illustrator or designer unless otherwise agreed, which is standard trade practice) ● Copyright (under the terms of current copyright legislation) ● Any further usage rights, i.e. merchandising ● Terms of business should be stated (e.g. discount for early payment, percentage added for late payment).

Clients' delay in payment is a perennial problem to watch out for. Regular billing and invoicing and regular statements are necessary. A business-like, no-nonsense approach is worth cultivating when dealing with fees and the payment of fees.

Professionalism in presentation. If you take your portfolio to a client for the first time, leave a good card or brochure with an impressive image; it doesn't matter how small. The objective is to make sure that the client remembers you and your work. Organize your portfolio correctly and for this seek advice from professionals or tutors. Find out about the client before you present your portfolio for the first time. Clients welcome questions about their companies, so ask questions and do not be afraid. Pick up the telephone and ask for company reports.

If you're dealing with a large commercial company, do some library research to find out what the company is all about. Read the financial journals for the company's current status and state of play regarding mergers or takeovers. Look at the commissioning style of the company especially as regards magazines and book publishing. Your portfolio should reflect the company's requirements and not be inappropriate to either the company or the project.

When you are presenting your work throughout the project, make sure you find out who in the company you are presenting the work to. Is it one person who you have dealt with already, or is it a number of people whom you don't know, or is it a committee? You are fully entitled to have that information in advance in order to prepare yourself adequately for the presentation. Do your homework.

Research about your client is tremendously important – it is no good just barging into a company full of confidence in your own work if you don't have any idea of what they are going to expect from you, and if they find out very quickly that you know nothing about what they do. You must be interested in the client, so respond to all phone calls and letters as soon as possible and sound interested.

When you send letters to clients, follow up with phone calls. The common courtesy involved in dealing with clients will bring rewards and will indicate to the client that it is not only your work that is professional but that you behave in a professional manner. Courtesy enhances reputation and it works the other way round too; for example, if you pay your bills promptly to your own suppliers. Working ethics implies a continuous commonsense approach to your work.

METHODS OF WORK

Most illustrators and many graphic designers set up an office where their work is carried out. Dorothy Goslett says, in her book *The Professional Practice of Design*: "There are three things which the trained designer should have in order to start a freelance career. The first is at least one client with a definite and fairly large commission. The second is some money in the bank with which to finance yourself until your client pays you. The third is somewhere to work."

You should find out what assistance is available from professional bodies and from government-funded projects when you set up on your own. Some organizations run seminars giving advice on legal and financial aspects and business administration. Grants may be available for special funding of small business enterprises.

Office organization. The following is a list of headings that will have to be considered when setting up an office.

Required office facilities

Professional advice (this has already been covered in 'Conditions of Work')

Accounts

Income tax

Registering for VAT or other service tax

Project organisation: ● Job documentation ● Office systems and procedures ● Invoices ● Timesheets ● Filing systems ● Order books ● Record cards (or software systems designed to cater for small businesses)

WORKING WITH CLIENTS

Design is a resource that industry and business require to be successful, just like marketing or financial considerations. Some clients understand and appreciate the added value that design gives to their businesses, others do not. Managers in most companies are not trained to understand how designers work and when confronted with this fact, the designer needs to take on the role of tactful teacher and add that additional skill to all the others that are continually being developed through experience.

Clients expect designers to create work which adds value to their product or project – book, annual report, packaging, or advertising campaign. They will gladly pay for that unique contribution to their business success. Designers expect clients to appreciate their unique contribution, to pay for it promptly, and to request further collaboration.

The difficulties that occur in designer/client relationships very often have to do with the inability of either side

to communicate these expectations successfully. A professional framework helps to clarify lines of communication, helps designers and illustrators to explain how they work, and helps clients to understand the important aspects of the intellectual design investment and the entire design process. It helps designers to price their work and their time correctly, and it helps clients to fit design resource costs into the overall business plan. A professional approach to a job creates an ideal climate for interface.

Agents. In the fields of graphic design and illustration, especially illustration, agents may deal with the clients on behalf of the designer or illustrator.

Agents are most commonly used when graphic designers or illustrators are quite well established. It is also helpful to use them if you are totally apprehensive about handling money or when there is an enormous amount of work. Most established professional designers or illustrators recommend that young graduate illustrators or designers should not use agents and should have direct contact with clients in order to gain the experience of receiving a brief, and helping to devise a brief, and to judge a client's reactions to not only their work but their business approach.

Briefing. When you start to obtain a brief from a client, you have to strike a balance between making sure that you understand what you're doing and, even more importantly, that the client understands what you're doing, so that there is agreement. It must be possible to formulate this agreement and write it down. And you have to balance that against the worry factor, your understanding of the work and the changes and revisions that may be imposed upon you. It's the responsibility of the designer to ask the right questions at the right time. It's sometimes very difficult.

These are some of the typical questions that should be asked and answered by both designer and client at briefing meetings, updated and modified from the 1974 SIAD study. Because obtaining a clear brief is of such vital importance to both designers and illustrators, the questions are separated under each discipline.

GRAPHIC DESIGN

1 What is the purpose of the design – e.g. to publicize consumer goods or services, or to enhance the company's prestige, etc.?

2 To whom is the message addressed – the general public, or a specialist audience (such as doctors, engineers, etc.)?

3 Is there a specific deadline or launch date?

4 Does the client have a budget or is the designer expected to state what the project will cost?

5 What quantities and printing costs are envisaged?

6 Will the client be responsible for production? Or will you be expected to put the work out to tender on the client's behalf?

7 Will the design be produced in more than one size, or will any features of it be adapted to other purposes? (If so, the question of full or restricted copyright arises.)

8 If the size or format is open to discussion, with what related literature or stationery should it conform?

9 Is any existing house style or design policy operated by the client? Is there a corporate identity manual in existence? Are there any special considerations involved, e.g. statutory requirements for labelling?

10 Does the projected design relate to any existing campaign or other material? If so, it should be inspected.

11 What is the client's general policy with regard to display, advertising and marketing?

12 What is the design policy of the client's principal competitors, and in what context will the new design be displayed? (The visual context of surroundings in which a design appears is relevant; e.g. the background in a supermarket differs from that of an exclusive store, and both from that of a hoarding.)

13 Are other designers being asked to quote for the job? Check the possibility of a limited competition.

ILLUSTRATION

1 What is the precise purpose of the commission – e.g. to illustrate a situation or an idea, to provide a personal commentary or to decorate?

2 What is the precise deadline for delivery of the work? With press work particularly, even the exact hour matters.

3 Does the client have a budget or is the illustrator expected to state a fee for the project?

4 How and where will the illustrations be used?

5 How many copies of the illustrations will be printed? If it is a very long run then the continuous good quality of the reproduction must be considered at the outset.

6 What are to be the exact reproduced sizes of the illustrations? If the use of the illustrations is not restricted to one size and purpose, then the extent of copyright sold should be discussed.

7 If the illustrations are for a book or any extended piece of text, what will be their relationship to each other in terms of positioning when finally reproduced?

8 What kind and weight of type or other visual matter will be used in conjunction with the illustrations?

9 What method of reproduction is to be used – e.g. screen, half-tone, letterpress, litho, photogravure? Will the original be scanned or photographed? (In the case of scanning your drawing will be on a flexible, not stiff, support.) If there is to be more than one colour, are the separations to be carried out by the artist?

10 On what kind and weight of paper is the work to be printed?

11 If some lettering or other textual matter is to be a part of the illustration, is this to be added by the client, drawn by the artist or to be a type specification by the artist?

For some kinds of illustration, particularly advertising, greetings cards, and jacket and cover design, reference should be made to Graphic Design (above) for additional guidance.

WORK TITLES AND DEFINITIONS

This is a list of definitions of various jobs and titles that graphic designers and illustrators might hold or come in contact with. It is extremely difficult to pin down exact definitions of jobs and job titles because they vary from designer to designer and from company to company. The following are broadly described because very often the jobs overlap according to the size of any organization. This also has much to do with the particular structure of management within any company or organization.

Editor – Directs the publication of a newspaper, periodical, brochure or book;

Creative director – Supervises creative output of an ad agency or design group. May also be called design director in design groups;

Art editor – Directs the selection, arrangement and cropping of images together with the overall layout of a book, brochure, magazine, etc.;

Art director (1) – Directs the layout (and sometimes production) of a magazine or the overall work produced by a publishing house;

Art director (2) – Conceives the visual content/layout on an advertisement;

Visualizer – Draws a clear picture not yet produced, usually for print (ads or brochures); draws pictures to be taken by photos or drawn by illustrator, and shows them incorporated into brochures, ads etc. for presentation purposes. Art directors sometimes do their own visualizing;

Illustrator – Nearest in a way to old-fashioned commercial artists; produces finished illustrations, drawn or painted, to be included in books, brochures, ads, posters, stamps, etc; varies from highly technical cutaway drawings to help explain how something works, to a sales promotion visual of a new product, to paintings, but always produced to a client's brief. Many illustrators go on to conceive, write and illustrate their own books, especially children's books and comics.

Graphic designer – Graphics is the medium of communication and projection of corporate image for companies, local authorities, etc. The graphic designer may be responsible for devising the layout and production of, for example, letterheads, posters, catalogues, record sleeves, book covers, technical literature, book typography, brochures, packaging, architectural signing, lettering, exhibitions, trade marks and symbols, magazines, calendars, stamps, design manuals and corporate identities.

INDEX